WHY READING BOOKS STILL MATTERS

"This is an important book that builds a strong case for the value of literature, literary reading, and book culture in the school curriculum. ... [It] stands as a wake-up call regarding our current screen-based culture and curricular focus on technology, science, and practical skills, arguing that they do not provide a sufficient basis for developing the full potential of children."

From the Foreword by Jack C. Richards, University of Sydney and University of Auckland

Bringing together strands of public discourse about valuing personal achievement at the expense of social values and the impacts of global capitalism, mass media, and digital culture on the lives of children, this book challenges the potential of science and business to solve the world's problems without a complementary emphasis on social values. The selection of literary works discussed illustrates the power of literature and human arts to instill such values and foster change. The book offers a valuable foundation for the field of literacy education by providing knowledge about the importance of language and literature that educators can use in their own teaching and advocacy work.

Martha C. Pennington is Professorial Research Associate in the Department of Linguistics, School for Oriental and African Studies, and Research Fellow in the Department of Applied Linguistics and Communication, Birkbeck College, University of London, UK.

Robert P. Waxler is Professor of English at the University of Massachusetts, Dartmouth, USA, and cofounder of Changing Lives Through Literature.

WHY READING BOOKS STILL MATTERS

The Power of Literature in Digital Times

Martha C. Pennington and Robert P. Waxler

Routledge
Taylor & Francis Group

NEW YORK AND LONDON

First published 2018
by Routledge
711 Third Avenue, New York, NY 10017

and by Routledge
2 Park Square, Milton Park, Abingdon, Oxon OX14 4RN

Routledge is an imprint of the Taylor & Francis Group, an informa business

Library of Congress Cataloging in Publication Data
A catalog record for this book has been requested

ISBN: 978-1-138-62973-8 (hbk)
ISBN: 978-1-138-62975-2 (pbk)
ISBN: 978-1-315-21024-7 (ebk)

Typeset in Bembo
by Taylor & Francis Books

CONTENTS

FOREWORD

This is an important book that builds a strong case for the value of literature, literary reading, and book culture in the school curriculum. It challenges people to consider the effects that our media-centered lifestyle is having on literacy and learning, and the beneficial countering effects that an enhanced focus on literature and what Pennington and Waxler call the "human arts" can have.

The book stands as a wake-up call regarding our current screen-based culture and curricular focus on technology, science, and practical skills, arguing that they do not provide a sufficient basis for developing the full potential of children. The authors offer evidence that a literature-infused curriculum builds advanced competencies in language and literacy while also promoting children's emotional and social development. They further describe how reading and discussing literature can foster empathy and social change, as demonstrated in studies with prisoners and with students in schools and universities.

The number and diversity of sources which Pennington, a linguist, teacher-educator, and creative writer, marshals in her collaboration with Waxler, a literary scholar who is also a teacher-educator and creative writer, is impressive, including a body of psychological research demonstrating the mind-expanding effects of reading literature. The authors also draw on a number of literary stories, novels, and poems to illustrate the power of literature to engage a reader's feelings and imagination, and how literature might be used in the classroom or a discussion group to raise important issues of human relationship.

Why Reading Books Still Matters: The Power of Literature in Digital Times will make readers think about the significance of literature as language-based artistic creation and why it might be more important than many people have realized. In effect, it asks educators and society as a whole not to bet everything on digital technology, science, and economics but to hedge our bets by placing an equal emphasis on literature within a larger arts and humanities curriculum. The book has an important educative purpose, and I hope it will have the impact on people's thinking and actions that it aims to have, shifting the focus in education more towards literature and the literacy of ideas rather than technical literacy, and ensuring that the next generation has the necessary foundation for addressing the problems they face with intelligence, imagination, passion, and compassion.

– Professor Jack C. Richards
Honorary Professor, University of Sydney and University of Auckland
Adjunct Professor, Victoria University of Wellington and Regional
Language Centre Singapore
Leading author for Cambridge University Press with over 50 million
books sold worldwide

PREFACE

Why Reading Books Still Matters: The Power of Literature in Digital Times makes the case that literature holds an invaluable place in human life which needs to be cherished and nurtured as a central aspect of our heritage and to be given a prominent place in society and the education of children. Literature stands at the intersection of art and language within a larger culture of what we call "human arts," giving a new twist to arts and humanities that stresses their contrast with business and STEM subjects. The book makes an original argument about the need for literature and human arts by:

1. challenging the potential of technology, science, and business to solve the world's problems without a complementary emphasis on social values;
2. demonstrating the power of literature and human arts to instill social values and foster change; and
3. bringing together a number of strands of public discourse which have largely been carried out as separate discussions, regarding the degradation of life by global capitalism, the emphasis on personal achievement at the expense of social values, the effects of mass media, and the impact of digital culture on the lives and education of children.

We argue that literature offers a needed corrective to our fast-lane, media-saturated, consumerist existence, in the way of the more meaningful and fulfilling life that can be promoted through a literate culture and that can get us back onto a healthier and more sustainable course for the future. Underpinning the book are the philosophy and educational initiatives of the Changing Lives Through Literature (CLTL) program, cofounded by Robert P. Waxler in the 1990s, which has repeatedly demonstrated the power of literature to change people in transformative ways.

The book has been written with an educator audience in mind that includes professors, graduate students, and teachers in Literacy Education and English and in other fields, in addition to university and school administrators and educational policymakers. It may be of interest also to parents and members of the reading public concerned about declines in literacy and the effects of digital media on education, language, and society. The book is organized in a problem–solution form in which approximately the first half focuses on what we see as the current culture and its problems, and the second half describes the culture we are proposing and how it can help solve those problems. It incorporates discussion of literary works selected to illustrate the captivating power of literature and of a wide range of scholarly and popular books and articles that address different facets of our argument, including scientific studies showing how readers are changed by literature. We discuss how technology is affecting literacy and language, education and society, and discuss the risks that media environments pose, especially for children. We review calls to limit technology in the lives of children and adults, and model the CLTL approach in a series of stories about brothers that can be used in a classroom or reading group, or in family reading.

Chapter 1 raises issues about reading and culture in digital times and introduces the arguments we will be making about the value of literature as a counterweight in education and in society more generally to the focus on screen media, technology, and consumer values and practices. Chapter 2 continues the discussion of Chapter 1 in describing what we see as the state of the world and problems that can be addressed by greater attention to literate culture. Chapters 3 and 4 offer a description and a critique of our fast-lane, self-obsessed, media- and machine-centric lives, which are problematized in relation to literacy and language, human values and culture, and education.

Chapters 5 and 6 describe literacy and language in the online screen culture and ways in which these differ from, and are in certain respects inferior to, literacy and language outside of that context. As we argue, our culture needs to maintain a basis in literary and human arts values and not be given over primarily to the values of technology, competition, and consumerism.

Chapter 7 takes a closer look at fiction and poetry, seeking to show by example the powerful effects they can have on a reader through artfully crafted language and story. Chapters 8 and 9 review research demonstrating the profound effects which reading and especially literary reading has on the brain and memory, emotional and social life, personality and empathy, and human experience and culture on the level of a whole society.

In Chapter 10, we review the effects of various initiatives in the Changing Lives Through Literature program and discuss specific readings that can be employed in schools and other contexts. In the final chapter, we paint recommendations in broad brushstrokes and then reinforce our message about the importance of keeping literary language and stories at the heart of our shared culture, from whence they came and where they should remain, as an essential part of what has made and will keep us human.

We wish to acknowledge a number of people who influenced and supported us during the writing of this book. Martha wishes to thank several writer-scholar friends for insightful critical input on the book's thesis and introductory material, including Pauline Burton, Colin Cavendish-Jones, Graham Lock, Dino Mahoney, and Simon Wu, and her friend Al Woodward for a scientist's perspective and invaluable assistance tracking down some original sources at the Library of Congress. Bob would like to thank Linda, his wonderful and patient wife, and Jeremy, his best reader always. In addition, we both thank the two Routledge reviewers for perceptive and detailed comments on our earlier draft. In their different ways, each of these individuals made a valuable contribution to this work, which we are grateful for and happy to acknowledge.

ACKNOWLEDGEMENTS

Permission to quote in Chapter 2 from the following source was given by Penguin Random House, 1745 Broadway, New York, NY 10019.

Díaz, Junot (1996/1995). How to date a browngirl (blackgirl, whitegirl, or halfie). In *Drown* (pp. 143–149). New York: Riverhead Books. Originally appeared in *The New Yorker*, December 25, 1995, pp. 83–85.

Permission to quote in Chapter 3 from the following source was given by ESADE Institute, Av. Pedralbes, 60–62, E-08034 Barcelona; and from IATEFL Special Interest Groups and Publications, 2–3 The Foundry, Seager Road, Faversham, Kent, ME13 7FD, U.K.

Pennington, Martha C. (2001). Writing minds and talking fingers: Doing literacy in an electronic age. In P. Brett (ed.), *CALL in the 21st century* (CD-ROM). Barcelona: ESADE Institute (Idiomas) and Hove, U.K.: IATEFL. Papers from a conference sponsored jointly by ESADE Institute (Idiomas), Barcelona, and IATEFL CALL SIG, June 30–July 2, 2000.

Permission to quote in Chapter 10 from the following source was given by Office of Correctional Education, Division of Adult Literacy and Education; Office of Career, Technical, and Adult Education, U.S. Department of Education, 550 12th Street, SW, Washington, D.C. 20202–7100.

Waxler, Robert P. (1997). Why literature? The power of stories. In Megan McLaughlin, Jean Trounstine, & Robert P. Waxler, *Success stories: Life skills through literature* (pp. 2–5). Washington, D.C.: Office of Correctional Education, U. S. Department of Education.

Permission to quote in Chapter 10 from the following source was given by The James Baldwin Estate, c/o Eileen Ahearn, 137 W. 71st Street, Apt. 4B, New York, NY 10023.

Excerpted from "Sonny's Blues" c 1957 by James Baldwin. Copyright renewed. Originally published in Partisan Review. Collected in GOING TO MEET THE MAN, published by Vintage Books (pp. 86–122). Used by arrangement with the James Baldwin Estate.

Permission to quote in Chapter 10 from the following source was given by ICM Partners, 65 E. 55th Street, New York, NY 10022.

Wolff, Tobias (1985). The rich brother. In *Back in the world* (pp. 197–221). Boston: Houghton Mifflin.

Permission to quote in Chapter 11 from the following source was given by the author.

Pennington, Martha C. (2011). Pool culture. *Southern Humanities Review*, *45*(3), 250–252.

1

THE VALUE OF A LITERATE CULTURE

In a very real sense, ... people who have read good literature have lived more than people who cannot or will not read. To read *Gulliver's Travels* is to have the experience, with Jonathan Swift, of turning sick at one's stomach at the conduct of the human race; to read *Huckleberry Finn* is to feel what it is like to drift down the Mississippi River on a raft; to read Byron is to suffer with him his rebellions and neuroses and to enjoy with him his nose-thumbing at society; to read *Native Son* is to know how it feels to be frustrated in the particular way in which many blacks in Chicago have been frustrated. This is the great task that affective communication performs: it enables us to feel how others felt about life, even if they lived thousands of miles away and centuries ago. It is not true that we have only one life to live; if we can read, we can live as many more lives and as many kinds of lives as we wish.

    – S. I. Hayakawa, Language in Thought and Action *(Hayakawa, 1990/1939,*
pp. 158–159)

Why We Wrote This Book

According to UNESCO (2006, 2011), the world literacy rate, which in the mid-19th century was around 10 percent, is now approaching 85 percent. Yet even though the vast majority of people have gone from illiterate to literate, knowing how to read is not a guarantee that people are in fact reading, or reading much – much less that they are reading anything good, or good for them.

    In the past century and a half, literacy, in the sense of being able to read, has risen greatly while the level of reading appears to have declined. The lowering of the level of reading is no doubt in part an inevitable statistical effect of reversion to the mean, as what was once a literate elite has turned into a literate public. There are however other factors causing a decline in the level of reading among the general population. One is the pull of other things pressuring people to spend their time not reading, especially visual media such as film, television, and all devices connected to the Internet. Another is the types of material available to be read.

Reading matter has been altered substantially since the mid-19th century, when, for example, a page in a newspaper was a large sheet of paper covered in dense print text with few, if any, pictures. In the era of the Internet and near-universal literacy, reading matter is changing rapidly, as both publishers and many writers cater to mainstream, media-generation tastes and to the types of media and formats in which reading matter is increasingly consumed. Aiming to fit popular taste and media formats, they use language that is familiar and informal, with smaller units at every level – shorter words, shorter sentences, shorter paragraphs, shorter articles and reports of all kinds, and shorter books – and they give written text less of a priority in relation to pictures, graphics, and other kinds of visual and audial representations such as video and film, animation, speech, and music.

Although the rise of the Internet may have aided in the spread of literacy, it may also be a cause of the lowering of the level of literacy, as media technologies and the culture which they promote are taking over from other forms of culture and infiltrating global literacy practices, both writing and reading – and indeed, all kinds of practices. The "hijacking" of culture by the Internet and media technologies can be seen especially in that part of culture which is least stable – what normally goes under the name of "popular culture," referring to the widespread preferences and practices of the global mainstream at a particular point in time, especially in entertainment and other leisure-time activities, fashion and other lifestyle trends, and current business and political affairs. A component of popular culture is also the new language that develops to express the novelty and innovations associated with each of these areas of rapidly changing human affairs. Rapid changes in popular culture are initiated by and spread through the mass media, in collaboration with other corporate giants whose reach is global, especially via the Internet. Popular culture can then be seen as made up, in general, of all topics and people that grab the attention of a mass audience and are in the news or trending on popular websites.

And it is not only what people think of as popular culture – defined by what is "in" at the moment, by fads and fashions that change year to year and even day to day – that has been infiltrated and shaped by the Internet and media technologies. So has the more stable part of culture – the beliefs, values, and practices that have developed over a long period and that are the background and backdrop to civilization and everyday life. In like manner, that part of culture often distinguished as "high culture," comprising literature and fine arts, has also been increasingly infiltrated and shaped by the Internet, mass media, and their attendant technologies, values, and practices (Pennington, 2013, 2017). We might even reflect that all of culture is becoming popular culture, through the influence of mass media and the Internet, and being pulled towards the values and agendas of the global business interests that control much of popular culture. These global business interests are increasingly using the Internet to advertise and sell their products, and to promote their ideas and agendas, as a way to grow their companies and enhance their power to influence consumers and world events.

As we will argue, some of the cultural changes wrought by media and online connectivity, often married to the interests of global business, have not been positive: some represent cultural shrinkage or loss, while others represent diversions or even perversions of culture to the purposes of consumerism and self-centeredness, or "Me-ness," and to a focus on the momentary excitement gained from things that are shiny or showy – that, in current parlance, exhibit "bling" and "pop" (as in a burst of sound or light, or a "pop" of color). These kinds of focus embody what might be dubbed a "pop-and-bling" lifestyle, which we maintain is a shallow way of living bought at a high cost: at the expense of depth and meaningfulness, and through abandonment of other values and pursuits that are important for sustaining human life and indeed the life of the planet.

The cultural effects of media and online connectivity are especially visible in the current generation of children and young adults, who were born into a world already saturated with the pop culture practices and values of television and other mass media. These young people grew up in a digital world which, having absorbed the values and practices of their parents' and grandparents' generation, is now rapidly developing its own new practices and characteristics, based especially on the wireless technology of the smartphone and other portable devices. The current generation is one that is always *on* – always doing something on mobile devices and always connected to the Internet. The absorption of culture, and people's time, by media, especially digital media and the Internet, concerns us, as does the upbringing and education of children in an era when "literacy" is as likely to refer to digital literacy as to reading and writing in the traditional sense.

In this book, we will be expanding on these points to make a case for the importance of reading something good and good for you, in the form of literature. We argue that such reading – most especially in the form of literary fiction and poetry – offers an important corrective to the increasing emphasis in today's world on nonprint digital media and the culture of global capitalism, as it helps build knowledge of language and general knowledge as well as empathy, open-mindedness, and social skills. Reading about the adventures of Gulliver and Huckleberry Finn, of Ulysses and Robinson Crusoe, we travel out of ourselves, journeying in our imagination by their sides, seeing what they see, and learning what they learn. Journeying with them, we grow close to these characters; and seeing things through their eyes, we share their point of view, developing new perspectives that incorporate their ways of thinking and being. Thus do the memorable characters of literature catch and hold our attention, and draw us into the worlds that great writers are able to depict through words on the page. And walking along with those authors, through the characters and worlds they draw us into, our minds and our sympathies are expanded, and we are changed by the experience.

Beyond the literal journeys of a Gulliver, a Huck Finn, or a Ulysses, great literature offers opportunities for us to journey for a time in the minds and hearts of people whom we can imagine as ourselves or as people we know. We can enter for a while into the mind and heart of a Jay Gatsby and feel for the man doomed by obsession for a woman out of his reach, just as we can journey into the emotions and perceptions of an Elizabeth Bennett or a Caleb Trask and be reminded of the confusions and passions of youth, and the human capacity for love and forgiveness. So can we take a narrative journey into the worlds of Anne Shirley on Prince Edward Island, of John Grimes in Harlem, and of Bigger Thomas on Chicago's South Side, and, by walking in the shoes of those characters, gain an insider's view of the lives of people in those communities. Great poetry provides for such narrative journeys, too, in characters like Don Juan and Richard Cory, and for journeys of another kind, deep into language and into the poet's – and our own – emotions: into the feelings inspired by John Keats' contemplation of his own life through the vision of a Grecian urn or by Lord Byron's vision of she who "walks in beauty." These are all journeys of an affective kind, engaging mind and body through the emotions, as triggered in finely crafted narrative and poetic language. They are the kinds of profound, eye-opening and mind-expanding experiences offered in the merger of art and language that can be found in literature.

Yet the perspective-widening, life-changing experiences that come from engaging with art-in-words are, we maintain, at risk in the era of the Internet and screen media. Some would argue that similar and equally valuable expansive experiences are available through screen media and the Internet. The American Academy of Pediatrics (2016b), for example, notes in its policy statement on "Media Use in School-Aged Children and Adolescents" that there are benefits from media use in the way of "exposure to new ideas and knowledge acquisition, increased opportunities for social contact and support, and new opportunities to access … information" (p. 1). Clearly, film, television, and digital media offer important imaginative and artistic works and educative experiences for children as well as adults. We remain concerned, however, about the great pull of the younger generation towards an outer life of appearance and style defined by mass media and consumerist culture at the expense of an inner life defined by literate culture, independent thought, and social values reflecting attention to not just their own but also others' needs and well-being. We share the concern of the American Academy of Pediatrics (2016b) about "risks of media use for the health of children and teenagers … [including] negative health effects on weight and sleep; exposure to inaccurate, inappropriate, or unsafe content and contacts; and compromised privacy and confidentiality" (p. 1).

We are concerned, too, about the education of our youth and the over-emphasis on STEM – science, technology, engineering, and mathematics – at the expense of the other side of the curriculum – variously labeled "arts" (as contrasted with "sciences"), "liberal arts," or "humanities" – which we will label *human arts.* We intend this as a memorable conceptual amalgam or hybrid that captures our emphasis on both the human and the artistic features of language and literature and that does not have the (unfortunately) negative connotations which many attach these days to "humanities" and "liberal arts." We are alarmed by both the vision and the reality of a world that pursues achievement within the STEM fields unconnected to, and unbalanced and untempered by, the human arts and that is increasingly run by machines and also modeled on them, as they set the pace and the focus for people's lives to be lived with speed and efficiency. We maintain, as Carl Honoré stresses in his book, *In Praise of Slowness: How a Worldwide Movement Is Challenging the Cult of Speed*, that "some things cannot, should not, be sped up. They take time; they need slowness" (Honoré, 2004, p. 4). We agree that "[i]nevitably, a life of hurry can become superficial. When we rush, we skim the surface, and fail to make real connections with the world or other people" (p. 9). We are alarmed by the extent to which the gigantic forces of mass media allied with global business have permeated our culture and are setting the agenda for the current age. We believe that it is time – past time, in fact – for a correction of the superficial lifestyle which so many are pursuing nowadays towards pursuit of a deeper kind of life.

In a very real sense, our higher species is losing ground. At this point in history, we humans find ourselves on a slippery slope and are starting to slide backwards from the highest point to which we have evolved in our knowledge and our humanity. We are in danger of degrading language and literacy to the point where our knowledge and our brain structure, even our intelligence, are affected; and there are already signs that we are losing many of our most valuable human qualities and suffering the consequences of such loss, including serious effects of social and environmental degradation on our own health and the health of the planet. As we will seek to convince you, literature and the human arts offer ways to boost our individual and collective knowledge and humanity, and our immunity to all that, in the current age, threatens our accumulated human advantages.

How Much and What People Are Reading

It is undeniable that the culture which has been created by mass media and digital technologies has attracted the current generation away from the literate culture of the past. This fact seems to be of less concern to the educational establishment – which has been rushing with the large commercial interests of Google, Microsoft, Apple, and the many other companies capitalizing on the electronic revolution to digitize the whole educational experience – than to the arts establishment, which seems to have more of a concern to preserve traditional cultural values and practices. Two controversial reports by the National Endowment for the Arts (NEA) – *Reading at Risk: A Survey of Literary Reading in America* (National Endowment for the Arts, 2004) and *To Read or Not to Read: A Question of National Consequence* (National Endowment for the Arts, 2007) – raised alarms about a decline in the quantity and the quality of reading by Americans – particularly by children and adolescents and particularly as regards the reading of literature. These reports connected Americans' declining reading life to declines in civic life and education, shared culture, and the strength of our national economy.

The NEA reports acknowledged what has become a fact of 21st-century life: that our reading activity has moved away from the reading of literature and a focus on the kinds of activities that have traditionally surrounded the reading of literature. Today a great deal of people's reading takes place on the Internet and by means of digital screens and e-reading devices such as the Kindle, which, it can be noted, was introduced, with some initial hope that it might help reverse the decline in reading, on the very day that the NEA's 2007 report was released. A follow-up study (National Endowment for the Arts, 2009) found an increase in adult literary readers from 47 percent in 2002 to 50 percent in 2008, but this appears to have been a statistical blip, or short-lived improvement, as another NEA study carried out in late 2012 matched the figure of 47 percent reported in the 2002 study (National Endowment for the Arts, 2013). The NEA Survey of Public Participation in the Arts taken in July 2012 discovered that while 71 percent of American adults consumed arts through electronic media (including television and radio) and 59 percent went to the movies at least once in the preceding 12 months, only 58 percent did voluntary reading (as contrasted with reading required for work or school) at least once in the preceding one-year period (National Endowment for the Arts, 2013, p. 8). Of the 47 percent of Americans who reported doing any literary reading in the preceding year, 45 percent said they read novels or short stories, 7 percent read poetry, and 3 percent read plays (p. 24).

There does not seem much reason to cheer a population in which almost everyone is literate but less than half read literature – a smaller proportion than did so in 1982 (56.4%), when the NEA survey was first carried out. It can be considered especially alarming that, according to the 2013 report, "Since 2002, the share of poetry-readers has contracted by 45 percent—resulting in the steepest decline in participation in any literary genre" (National Endowment for the Arts, 2013, p. 24). The story is not as bad for fiction, which remains a popular genre among the books that people are reading and buying,[1] perhaps because, as one blogger writing on the *Psychology Today* website suggests, it provides an escape from the concerns of life in today's world (Bergland, 2014).

The declines seen in the NEA figures for the reading of literature and offline arts activities can be considered in the light of figures for 2013 published by the Pew Research Center (Zickuhr & Rainie, 2014a, 2014b, 2014c) that include not only voluntary reading but also reading at work and at school, and that break down the media that people are using for reading. The Pew survey paints a more positive picture of Americans' book-reading activity. It indicates that the number of books that Americans read on average in the previous year (including books related to school and work) remained stable at 12, which is an encouraging average of a book a month. However, this average masks considerable variation in the amount of reading that Americans do, as the 2013 survey records a decline since their 2011 survey in the number of adult Americans reading at least one book in the previous year, down from 79 percent in 2010 to 76 percent in 2013 (Zickuhr & Rainie, 2014a). Examining the Pew statistics in terms of reading media, we note that 69 percent of American adults said they read at least one print book in the previous year, while 28 percent said they read an e-book (ibid.), with a higher percentage of e-book readers among young adults and those in their 30s and 40s (Zickuhr & Rainie, 2014b). The results of the 2013 Pew study, when taken together with those of the 2012 NEA study, suggest that the decline in the reading of literature, and books in general, by Americans is tempered by those who still read multiple print books and by the reading of e-books on the part of some.

A potentially encouraging sign from the 2013 Pew study is that the Millennial Generation – those under 30, who have also been referred to as Generation Y or the Net Generation – while being big users of the Internet, especially social media, were somewhat more likely (88%) than older adults (79%) to report having read at least one book in the previous year (Zickuhr & Rainie, 2014b). In addition, the percentage of Millennials who said they were regular book readers compares to that of the older generation who were not brought up with computers: "Some 43% of [Millennials] report reading a book – in any format – on a daily basis, a rate similar to [that of] older adults" (Zickuhr & Rainie, 2014b).

Books in the Contemporary World

The book industry, though it is becoming more competitive, is still vibrant and profitable in the 21st century, shipping more than 3 billion books in 2010 alone – "about 10 for every man, woman and child" (Schuessler, 2011). In addition, "Americans buy more than half of all e-books," and as of January 2012, "e-books accounted for nearly 20 percent of the sales of American publishers" (Cohen, 2012). Pew data from that year shows that most readers of print books or e-books "prefer to purchase their own copies of these books" (Rainie, Zickuhr, Purcell, Madden, & Brenner, 2012, p. 6); e-books are preferred when people want "speedy access and portability" while print books are preferred for "reading to children and sharing books with others" (p. 5).

Although digital works such as e-books and many other kinds of works enabled by hypertext and the Internet are on an upward trend, the print book seems to be surviving well into the Digital Age. Print books still dominate the market and are preferred by most readers, including today's college students (Robb, 2015). According to Zickuhr and Rainie (2014a):

> Though e-books are rising in popularity, print remains the foundation of Americans' reading habits: Among adults who read at least one book in the

past year, just 5% said they read an e-book in the last year without also reading a print book.

... Overall, about half (52%) of readers only read a print book, 4% only read an e-book, and just 2% only listened to an audiobook. Nine percent of readers said they read books in all three formats.

In sum, while there is a gradual decline in literary reading which is occurring at the same time as books are being increasingly produced and consumed in nonprint form, print books seem to be holding their own. Yet what people are reading is in many ways not the same kind of books as they read in the past, as the new formats for books impinge on the print book niche. The reading level of books is lower, they are shorter, the level of editing is down, and self-published books are now common. These trends are related to wider trends in who is writing and in what media. According to professors Denis G. Pelli and Charles Bigelow, there has been a writing revolution in terms of public authorship, meaning the number of self-published books in addition to published new media authors of blogs, Facebook pages, and Twitter feeds:

By 2000, there were 1 million book authors per year. ... Since 1400, book authorship has grown nearly tenfold in each *century*. Currently, authorship, including books and new media, is growing nearly tenfold each *year*. That's 100 times faster. Authors, once a select minority, will soon be a majority.

(Pelli & Bigelow, 2009, original emphasis)

The fact that nearly anyone can be an author of a book – or other published or publicly available written work – changes the nature of writing to a less privileged, more vernacular kind of activity that connects the act of writing increasingly to popular culture, making it likely that what is being written focuses on the values and practices of that culture rather than those of traditional literate culture (Pennington, 2017). While this gives great scope for innovation, at the same time it means that what is being written answers to the requirements of the new context, such as for shorter text and more attention-grabbing form and content, as imposed by the constraints of the technology and by the commercial interests that exert control of the content and form of communication.

Much of what is now published is freely available to Internet users. In other ways, the consumption of written text has changed, as more and more people are buying their books online, leading to a steep decline in bookstores, and as libraries are being repurposed to become more like Internet cafés. Changes in the nature of books and how they are read, or "consumed" in ways that incorporate other modes of perception and comprehension, have occurred as a result of electronic capabilities. Books in digital form are often not intended to replicate print books but include multimedia elements such as video or sound files, or features such as multiple plots and endings that can be accessed as desired.

Alongside new kinds of digital works (Pennington, 2013, 2017), audiobooks are both supplementing and competing with print books, as are e-books, which differ from print books in a number of ways that we will examine.

Clearly, there is more variety now in types of books and other repositories of (what was originally and primarily) written language. This would seem to be progress, as would the possibility of putting all of these books and other published material online, which Google has been seeking to do for several years and which Project Gutenberg (www.gutenberg.org/) has succeeded in doing for a great many books, especially those no longer covered by copyright. Anthony Grafton has reviewed the efforts of Google to index books all over the world, noting "the hordes of the Web's actual and potential users, many of whom will read material that would have been all but inaccessible to them a generation ago" (Grafton, 2007, p. 54). Despite all this attention to books online, Grafton concludes, "For now and for the foreseeable future, any serious reader will have to know how to travel down two very different roads simultaneously" (ibid.), the new road through the digital screen and the old road through print books.

In spite of suffering large funding cuts in recent decades, libraries remain a popular American institution (Zickuhr & Rainie, 2014b) and have maintained a presence in the era of the Internet as repositories of print books and other print material, and also as repositories of digitized information that is freely available to the public rather than being culled and curated by Google or other media companies functioning as information distillers and idea managers. For these reasons, James Palfrey believes libraries should and will survive well into the future and has given his book *BiblioTech* the subtitle *Why Libraries Matter More Than Ever in the Age of Google* (Palfrey, 2015). If so, libraries might help keep a book culture alive while also providing a counterweight to the influence of mass media aligned with corporate interests.

The Pull Away from Book Culture and the Human Arts, and the Need to Push Back

Even if we believe Grafton and Palfrey, that our shared culture will involve printed text and books for some time well into the future, it nonetheless seems clear that in most people's everyday life the ephemeral texts and nontextual artifacts of the Internet – together with other mass media, the most notable of which in the present era is still television – are overshadowing the traditional print and book culture that spawned the study of Great Books, both as a part of the standard academic curriculum and as part of a wider culture of enjoyment and learning from literature. The curriculum and culture of literature was based on the belief that knowledge of those great books reinforced a shared heritage and values among citizens while building linguistic and general knowledge. Great books held the promise of self-improvement that later led to the huge success in the United States of the Book-of-the-Month Club (Radway, 1997).

The current generation has little interest in literature as a model for shared values and a source of personal, linguistic, and general intellectual enrichment, ceding its educational functions to the practical values and skills of technology and business, and its societal position to the power and influence of mass media. The demise of bookstores, the decline of the Book-of-the-Month Club, and the overshadowing of the print and book culture by the pull of the Internet is a trend foreshadowed by the pull of television in the previous generation, when parents and educators worried that children spent too much time in front of what some referred to as "the idiot box." By the 1990s, many young people had supplemented or traded in the TV box for that other box, "the digital box," or computer, leading Luiz Costa-Lima to remark at the time that "the socialization of children takes place more through the electronic media than through reading" (Costa-Lima, 1996, p. 318).

What was a problem for reading then has only been magnified with the passage of time, as our digital devices, growing ever smaller, more portable, and more accessible, have moved people increasingly away from the literate culture of the past, with concomitant loss of the time, space, and privacy needed for solitary reading and contemplation. Michael Harris, in *The End of Absence: Reclaiming What We've Lost in a World of Constant Connection* (Harris, 2014), sees a "restless idleness" in the digital generation and fears that those immersed in a digital lifestyle will lose the ability to "access absence and solitude" in moments of internal satisfaction and inspiration which those of us in the "straddle generation, with one foot in the digital pond and the other on the shore" (p. x), have known. Being online is being constantly connected, never alone. Yet it is a superficial kind of connection, a "constant intimacy" (ibid.) which is a poor substitute for authentic – that is, offline – intimacy. Harris is also concerned about how difficult it is nowadays to lead a life offline, as he found out when he carved out a month (his "Analog August") to read *War and Peace*.

The book-centered activities of being read to or of curling up with a story or novel in bed or in a favorite comfy chair have in the present era been replaced by playing video games, watching television programs and movies, going on Facebook and other social media sites, surfing the Net, texting, and tweeting. As Jonathan Gottschall observes in *The Storytelling Animal: How Stories Make Us Human*: "Video games – and other digital entertainments – are … on the rise, drawing attention away from traditional story. The gaming industry is now much bigger than the book industry, bigger even than the film industry" (Gottschall, 2012, p. 178).

Figures from the U.S. Bureau of Labor Statistics from 2010 to 2011 (available at www.bls.gov/oes/) show huge growth in the multimedia and digital effects industry since the 1980s, as part of a general trend of entertainment industries overtaking defense as "the driving force for new technology" (Rifkin, 2000, p. 161). Gaming expert Ethan Gilsdorf makes the point that video games are an "almost $100-billion-a-year … industry soon poised to overshadow all other forms of entertainment and diversion – motion pictures, television, books and Donald Trump combined" (Gilsdorf, 2016). *Vanity Fair*'s Nick Bilton reports that "[s]ocial networks alone are more valuable than the G.D.P. of more than 95 percent of the countries around the globe" (Bilton, 2016, p. 122). While gaming, texting and tweeting, Facebooking, and other kinds of online activity – sometimes performed simultaneously in a task-juggling mode generally referred to as "multitasking" – have become primary free-time activities for children and adolescents, their school time has been reconfigured from a literate curriculum, with its focus on reading, discussing, and writing about the great themes and issues of human life through Great Books, to a competency curriculum, with a focus on technical and employment skills (Slouka, 2009).

According to Pulitzer Prize-winning journalist Chris Hedges, writing in *Empire of Illusion: The End of Literacy and the Triumph of Spectacle* (Hedges, 2009), "We have bought hook, line and sinker into the idea that education is about training and 'success,' defined monetarily, rather than learning to think critically and to challenge" (p. 95). This has affected education at all levels, right up through college. Hedges (2009) maintains that "most universities have become high-priced occupational training centers" (p. 109). Even traditionally liberal arts colleges, whose number has shrunk dramatically in the last 25 years, are under "pressure to add more practical offerings" such as engineering and business (Breneman, 2015). Economist David W. Breneman, who warned of this trend in 1990, has again come out with warnings about the decline in liberal arts education in America, reminding us of the Jeffersonian tradition that considers a liberal arts education essential for democracy:

> [W]e are drifting toward turning college into a trade school. And that is ultimately harmful. The original ethos of education was that it prepared people for citizenship, for enlightened leadership, enhanced their creativity. … If we lose an educated populace, we're open for demagogy. We need broadly educated people.
>
> *(Breneman, 2015)*

We note that trade schools, while offering the expectation of employment for graduates, are a form of education that, rather than encouraging development of the individual – which has long been a treasured value and goal of life in America and Western culture – do the bidding of the commercial sector of the economy. The American government and educational system, in Hedges' (2009) view, do the bidding of corporations in providing them technical expertise and ignoring the fact that they are not operating with any sense of moral restraint or the common good. The educational system and the government, he maintains, neither value nor promote – and are indeed fearful of – "honest intellectual inquiry, which is by its nature distrustful of authority, fiercely independent, and often subversive" (p. 89).

Giving education a foundation in business might seem to secure it with a firm footing in practical principles that have proved their merit and survived the test of time; but a business model combining competition and Darwinian "survival-of-the-fittest" principles with technological innovation is far too simple, since it ignores the diversity and complexity of human beings – the actual people who are the teachers and learners in schools (Pennington, forthcoming). A broader educational model builds instruction to suit all of the students in a class, not just the best competitors among them as measured by test scores, and includes content and instructional modes other than those which focus on technology and the Internet (e.g., in-class reading and writing groups). Bringing all of the diverse types of people and their characteristics and interests into the instructional agenda and ensuring a wide range of instructional content and approaches might offer other kinds of advantage and spur other kinds of innovation than those initiated by stereotypical high achievers or those linked to technology.[2]

As part of the present reshaping of the curriculum, the humanities and even creativity itself are rapidly being refashioned and repurposed by educational and management gurus to serve technical and commercial goals, being "promoted" to industrial status and scale. In becoming themselves "industries," they are being absorbed into vocational skills and marketable outcomes that fit their industrial status. Thus has the management guru Richard Florida, for instance, redefined "the highest order of creative work" as those "new forms or designs that are readily transferable and widely useful" (Florida, 2002, p. 69) – in particular, those which can be made into marketable products. This marketization and industrialization of aspects of life that are supposed to contribute to knowledge for its own sake, personal development, the life of the mind and the spirit, and the overall quality of experience as a human being is an enormous global trend in which all aspects of human life and culture are re-envisioned within commerce or economics, with a focus on profits and "the bottom line."

At the turn of the millennium, Jeremy Rifkin warned about the rapidly increasing consumerism of human life in his book *The Age of Access: The New Culture of Hypercapitalism, Where All of Life Is a Paid-For Experience* (Rifkin, 2000). Now, approaching the end of the second decade of the 21st century, the trend to refashion all human culture and activity in the image of the god of Mammon, according to economic values and consumerism, continues apace, with many kinds of negative effects, including not only psychological and social damage to human beings but also physical damage to us and to the planet that affects the lives of all creatures.

There Is More to Life

This book is based on our strong belief that there is more to life than the worship of Mammon, which the Merriam-Webster online dictionary (www.merriam-webster.com/dictionary/mammon) defines as:

material wealth or possessions especially as having a debasing influence <you cannot serve God and *mammon* – Matthew 6:24 (Revised Standard Version)>.

It is also based on our strong belief that there is more to life than the worship of Techné, taken to refer to technology or, as it did for the ancient Greeks, to craft or skills aimed at practical outcomes. This is not to deny that some part of life must be focused on the economic and the practical, only that there needs to be ample room for other sorts of pursuits, and that economic and practical values should not dominate all other human values. *Civilization* includes much more than this: it includes *civic duty* (acting out of a sense of moral obligation to the community); *civility* (acting out of a sense of respect and courteousness towards others); *civil rights* (the rights guaranteed to all citizens for political and social freedom and equality); and, in general, being *civilized* in all the ways that word can be taken to imply educated and self-restrained, not barbarous.

We will argue that literature and related book-centered literate behaviors are a central aspect of our civilization, of our inherited shared language and culture, and so should remain a central aspect of our shared educational and human experience, as they did for decades past – before the Internet and business, as part of the great commercialization of culture, engulfed the curriculum and gave it a utilitarian, applied skills emphasis. As university president John W. Miller and reading professor Michael C. McKenna point out in *World Literacy: Where Countries Rank and Why It Matters* (Miller & McKenna, 2016):[3]

> Societies that do not practice literate behavior are often squalid, under-nourished in mind and body, repressive of human rights and dignity, brutal, and harsh. … [V]arious forms of "barbarity" … found in all societies … are much more prevalent where literate behavior is absent. Literacy and quality of life go hand in hand.
>
> *(p. 2)*

The experience of literature and through it "*deep reading*: the slow and meditative possession of a book" (Birkerts, 1994, p. 146, original emphasis) – or a poem, a story, or any work of literature – has become urgently important as a counter-measure to the effects of our online, screen-saturated and digital-influenced lives and, more generally, to our consumerist culture and over-marketized and capitalized world. Along with the literary critic Harold Bloom, we maintain that "the struggle for literary values has to be ongoing, whatever the distractions of our moment" (Bloom, 2012).

The Education of Children

What we are advocating is a central role in people's lives and in the education of children for book culture, and specifically the reading of literature offline, and the knowledge, behaviors, and values that a culture of literary reading embodies. The American Academy of Pediatrics (2014) Council on Early Childhood recommends that children should be read to from birth, pointing out the many benefits of this practice in terms of developing language skills and interest in reading, in addition to the important social, motivational, and cognitive nurturing provided when parents read to their children. As they maintain:

> In contrast to often either passive or solitary electronic media exposure, parents reading with young children is a very personal and nurturing experience that promotes parent-child interaction, social-emotional development, and language and literacy skills during this critical period of early brain and child development.
>
> *(American Academy of Pediatrics, 2014, p. 405)*

The Academy's Council on Communications and Media policy statement on "Media and Young Minds" recommends no media use other than video-chatting for children younger than 18 to 24 months; and for children 18 to 24 months of age, they support careful introduction of selected high-quality media that is used with a child interactively and not by the child alone (American Academy of Pediatrics, 2016a). These recommendations stem from research showing that

> [c]hildren younger than 2 years need hands-on exploration and social interaction with trusted caregivers to develop their cognitive, language, motor, and social-emotional skills. Because of their immature symbolic, memory, and attentional skills, infants and toddlers cannot learn from traditional digital media as they do from interactions with caregivers.
>
> *(Ibid., p. 1)*

For children 2 to 5 years of age, the Academy recommends no more than one hour per day of high-quality programming co-viewed with assistance and scaffolding by adults to help the children understand and apply what they see onscreen to the offline context (p. 3).

Yet it is common these days to see infants and toddlers sitting alone in front of the television or in a world of their own, even within a family group or sitting on a parent's lap, engrossed in solitary activity on an iPad or smartphone. A few years ago, Christopher Bergland wrote that "61% of children under two use some type of screen technology and 43% watch television every day" (Bergland, 2013), and it is doubtful these percentages would now be lower. The Academy's own website reports that "[t]oday's children are spending an average of seven hours a day on entertainment media, including televisions, computers, phones and other electronic devices" (American Academy of Pediatrics, 2016c). According to the Academy's Council on Communications and Media policy statement on "Media Use in School-Aged Children and Adolescents":

The most common broadcast medium continues to be TV. A recent study found that TV hours among school-aged children have decreased in the past decade for children younger than 8 years. However, among children aged 8 years and older, average daily TV time remains over 2 hours per day. TV viewing also has changed over the past decade, with content available via streaming or social media sites, such as YouTube and Netflix.

(American Academy of Pediatrics, 2016b, pp. 1–2)

For children of any age, and for parents as well, the recommendation is to "develop a Family Media Use Plan for everyone" (American Academy of Pediatrics, 2016c). We suggest that this plan should incorporate print media and include initiatives for family members to read and discuss books and specifically literature together, starting in the preschool years and continuing for at least as long as children are living at home – and maybe beyond that time, as a way to maintain ties and a literate culture in the family.

Research on what preschool children learn from different kinds of media demonstrates that being read to – or watching movies – correlates with young children's ability to read other people, but television watching does not (Mar, Tackett, & Moore, 2010). It appears that there is something about television watching which (as opposed to watching films) does not engage the child's mind or emotions in relation to other human beings. There seems to be something about the television screen or content of television that encourages passivity rather than active engagement, as interaction with other people or with books does.[4] In the 1980s Wayne C. Booth was warning of the limitations of television to engage viewers, who, according to Booth (1982, 1989), tended to remain distant and isolated from the characters and actions portrayed. Booth (1982) contrasted the restricted world of television, "confined to some box or screen," with the expansive world of "printed stories, … [where] [t]he action takes place in a country somehow in my head, yet freed to occur in a space not in my head" (p. 39). In the print world, readers step into the world created on the page and make it their own; they participate in making the experience created by the story.

The positive effects of being read to or watching movies contrast sharply with the negative effects of television watching. According to a study of television watching by preschoolers carried out by the Ohio State University team of Amy I. Nathanson, Molly L. Sharp, Fashina Aladé, Eric E. Rasmussen, and Katheryn Christy, it appears that being immersed in story culture helps develop children's social skills, whereas watching television has no such effects and can also weaken development of the ability to understand others (Nathanson, Sharp, Aladé, Rasmussen, & Christy, 2013). Such understanding occurs through what has been called "theory of mind." This expression, popularized by the philosopher Daniel Dennett (Dennett, 1987), refers to the ability to take the perspective of another by imagining how their mind, and also their emotions, work – how they think and react, in particular, to other people and their minds and emotions. Theory of mind abilities are divided by some psychologists into two types – *cognitive*, the ability to infer another person's mental state, and *affective*, the ability to recognize another person's emotional state. The cognitive side of theory of mind is crucial to language use and effective communication of all kinds, while the affective side of theory of mind is crucial to emotional identification with others – that is, *empathy* – which is crucial to intimacy, relationship, and their expression through language and other means.

It appears that television viewing, and parallel aspects of digital screen viewing, lead to a reduction in theory of mind, empathy, and social competence. It can be speculated that this results, paradoxically, from desensitization, a dulling of the senses caused by an overload of a highly sensationalized mode of presentation and content, and from reduced face-to-face contact with human beings. MIT psychology professor Sherry Turkle has been warning about this in her writing, including the two books, *Alone Together: Why We Expect More from Technology and Less from Each Other* (Turkle, 2012) and *Reclaiming Conversation: The Power of Talk* (Turkle, 2015).[5] Later in this book, we examine research on how theory of mind and empathy might be enhanced in childhood and beyond by reading literature.

Research has also shown that kindergartners with good "prosocial" and emotional skills have a high likelihood of becoming successful adults. Using data from a study of children of low socioeconomic status[6] who were tracked for 13 to 19 years, starting in kindergarten, researchers Damon E. Jones, Mark Greenberg, and Max Crowley found statistically significant associations between children's social-emotional skills, as evaluated by their teachers in kindergarten, and indicators of their success later in life, as assessed by such measures as graduating high school on time, completing college, obtaining employment, avoiding criminal activity, and otherwise being a productive and healthy, contributing member of society. Writing in the *American Journal of Public Health*, Jones, Greenberg, and Crowley (2015) also review a body of research showing that IQ or test scores measuring cognitive ability are not as good predictors of future success as are measures of educational attainment that include "noncognitive characteristics such as self-discipline, academic motivation, and interpersonal skills" (p. 2283). This body of prior research supports their own research in demonstrating that "[s]uccess in school involves both social-emotional and cognitive skills, because social interactions, attention, and self-control affect readiness for learning" (ibid.).[7]

This research with children from a range of circumstances provides compelling evidence of the importance of social development for the achievement of positive outcomes in life and the avoidance of negative ones. The results are especially noteworthy given that these "noncognitive competencies … may be more malleable than cognitive skills and so may be appropriate targets for prevention or intervention efforts" (Jones et al., 2015, p. 2283). As is clear from this and other studies reviewed by Jones et al. (2015), we risk leaving out crucial aspects of education by not ensuring that all children have a strong grounding in the values and behaviors which help them get along with others, such as fairness, helpfulness, empathy, and cooperation. Luckily, these values and behaviors are highly teachable and learnable.

However, the forces of present-day consumerist, technological culture work against using school time to focus on children's emotional and social education, just as they work against giving attention in society to the culture of stories and literature in society. One consequence is that the reading of literary prose or poetry becomes a leisure-time activity of a small group – their self-indulgent "guilty pleasure." How sad that children might consider their reading a secret indulgence that must be hidden from peers and from those in authority who pressure everyone to spend time only on utilitarian pursuits, especially skill-building related to STEM and forms of reading which have the most obvious immediate relevance and practical value. These days much of the literature included in the curriculum is either part of humanities elective courses or has the practical purpose in an English (or other language) class of illustrating or teaching vocabulary and/or sentence structure. When it is included in the required curriculum, its practical value must be emphasized, especially in terms of how it makes one more employable.

Parents have become another force pushing consumerist and technological values and practices onto their children. Steven Pearlstein, Professor of Public Affairs at George Mason University, writes that the current generation of "helicopter parents" are urging their college-age children not to even consider studying literature and other liberal arts subjects (Pearlstein, 2016). He recounts many cases of parents not only advising their children not to study these subjects in college, but actually forbidding them from doing so, pushing them to major in subjects that are directly related to paid employment, typically the most practical branches of STEM fields, such as engineering and medical sciences, and of business and economics, such as accounting. Pearlstein (2016), who finds the strong pressure being put on students to bypass literature and other subjects we classify as human arts alarming, remarks that those with narrow skills and knowledge will not be competitive in the economy of today or the future. In his view, "The good jobs of the future will go to those who can collaborate widely, think broadly and challenge conventional wisdom – precisely the capacities that a liberal arts education is meant to develop" (Pearlstein, 2016).

We see the reading of literature as representing a countercultural force, a significant alternative and corrective, to that other, now dominant culture in education and society more generally. And we advocate deep reading of literature as important not only for the satisfaction it brings, but also for its benefits in: building vocabulary and general knowledge, which ground intelligence; stimulating deep thinking and deep learning, which ground creativity and innovation; and enhancing empathy and connection to other human beings, which ground morality. Such effects improve a person in ways which go beyond, and indeed which trump, any effects of education which increase employability. At the same time, it can be argued that such effects do increase employability and, beyond that, people's chances for success in life, far beyond the immediately visible effects of skills-oriented learning. In addition, recent research (as detailed in Chapter 9) suggests that reading books has survival value, increasing a person's life span (Bavishi, Slade, & Levy, 2016).

Our Goals for This Book

We aim to show the value of literature as a source and repository of human language and stories, values and culture, which can teach people about these things and about themselves. In so doing, we build the case that literature holds an invaluable place in human life that society needs to maintain as a central aspect of its heritage, and to pass on to children. We will argue that literature, and human arts more generally, can foster honest intellectual inquiry of the sort that makes people question authority and maintain an independent mind, as a basis for critical thinking and action. We will further argue that literature can be a powerful force for good, improving people who read and the lives of others whom they influence. In this sense, literature has considerable value in preparing people for life and therefore should have a central place in education.

We articulate and expand upon a view of literature and its value developed in Waxler's previous work – including Waxler (1997, 2007, 2008, 2014), Waxler and Trounstine (1999), Trounstine and Waxler (2005), Waxler and Hall (2011), and Hall and Waxler (2007, 2010) – and the Changing Lives Through Literature (CLTL) program at the University of Massachusetts at Dartmouth (http://cltl. umassd.edu/AboutPhilosophy.cfm) which Waxler codeveloped in the 1990s with Robert Kane and Wayne St. Pierre. This program was designed on the foundational view that literature has a transforming power which can be realized through reading and, further, through discussing it with others.

In our expansive view, literature:

- provides refreshing breaks and needed escape from technology, for leaving the "fast lane" and dwelling psychologically in a peaceful place away from everyday life;
- connects us to our sensuous nature;
- arouses our emotions and can both excite and calm us;
- engages the mind and the imagination in ways that go beyond other media, by painting worlds in words;
- enhances appreciation for and knowledge of well-crafted language;
- builds vocabulary and general knowledge;
- improves the ability to interpret information and think for oneself;
- cultivates understanding of the self and the development of individual identity;
- increases openness to new ideas and experiences and thus enlarges creative potentials and the possibilities for change;
- inspires appreciation for human complexity and improves the ability to read and understand others;
- fosters empathy for other human beings;

- serves as a cultural bridge to the key themes of human existence;
- raises complex ethical questions;
- provides models for human life that are inspiring and that help people create positive aspirations for the future; and
- helps to construct a road map in the journey from birth to death.

We illustrate these points with reference to selected literature, including classics such as John Keats' "Ode on a Grecian Urn" and John Steinbeck's *East of Eden*, stories by Kate Chopin and James Baldwin, and contemporary works by Junot Díaz and Gary Shteyngart, in addition to poems and stories by other authors. Other than some Biblical stories about brothers that provide a foundation for 20th- and 21st-century works addressing similar themes of sibling love and rivalry, our illustrations are all English-language works, specifically, poetry and literary fiction rather than plays (which are arguably less properly considered as a read rather than a performed medium). We also consider ways in which digital works differ from those born of print culture.

We cite research showing that the kind of deep concentration and reading which literature promotes is good for the brain and plays an important role in structuring its network of connections and keeping them functioning well. This argument, and the science that supports it, may be for some an especially convincing demonstration of the value of literature and the culture of reading that surrounds it. We also summarize a growing body of scientific research demonstrating the power of literature to widen people's perspectives and to promote empathy and tolerance. In this, literature can have an especially significant role in improving social relations and encouraging cooperative and peaceful coexistence among people. We go beyond a discussion of social issues to argue that many contemporary problems in the physical world are connected to a cultural decline which literature and human arts can help to reverse.

From these different perspectives, our book builds a case for the value of literary culture as a needed counterbalance to prevailing cultural forces, especially those related to mass media and digital culture, but also involving the current stress on competitive achievement and consumerism. We describe the downside of these prevailing cultural forces and suggest ways in which education and society can support literature and human arts to balance the focus on STEM, achievement and economic advantage, and all things digital. We seek to make the case that strengthening the culture of literature, of books, and of human arts more generally offers a means of improving people so that they are both willing and able to apply all of their knowledge – including their knowledge of science, technology, and business – to make the world a better place.

Notes

1　The website of the ProQuest company Bowker that provides ISBN numbers for books shows fiction as the book category with the most new ISBNs (over 50,000) for 2013, maintaining a rising trend for fiction against some other categories of traditional print books (www.bowker.com/news/2014/Traditional-Print-Book-Production-Dipped-Slightly-in-2013.html).

2 As argued in Pennington (forthcoming), in focusing on survival of the fittest competitors, with fitness defined by certain kinds of achievement and skills within an emphasis on technology and utilitarian outcomes, this business model reduces the opportunities that can occur in educational contexts for a kind of natural social evolution which exploits diversity in the characteristics and abilities of the human population as well as in curriculum content and modes of delivery for teaching that content.

3 Based on multiple measures of what the authors view as characteristic literate behaviors – including not only literacy test scores but also money spent on education, prevalence of computers, number and holdings of libraries, and number of newspapers – Miller and McKenna (2016) rank the United States in 7th place worldwide, behind 1st-place Finland and other Scandinavian countries as well as Switzerland, and just ahead of Germany.

4 Part of this may be the lack of continuity, as television has increasingly tended to be designed to be digestible in relatively self-contained short scenes or small bits of humor, information, or story that catch a viewer's momentary attention but do not require sustained attention so that programs can accommodate commercial breaks. It seems that television may in fact be training people to watch it in a non-concentrated, non-continuous way. As technology writer and educator Marc Prensky reports, "Research done for *Sesame Street* reveals that children do not actually watch television continuously, but 'in bursts.' They tune in just enough to get the gist and be sure it makes sense" (Prensky, 2011/2001, p. 18).

5 Human interaction through face-to-face discussion is a powerful force that can even apparently counteract the potentially "de-empathetic," emotionally disconnected and deadening, effects of watching television. Nathanson et al. (2013) report that their overall finding, which is of a negative relationship between television watching and the children's development of theory of mind, did not apply in cases in which parents and children talked about the television that the preschoolers were watching.

6 The children came from rural Pennsylvania and three cities in different parts of the country (Seattle, Nashville, and Durham, North Carolina).

7 In their own research, Jones et al. (2015) used a measurement instrument (the Prosocial–Communication subscale of the Social Competence Scale) with eight items that teachers rated on a five-point Likert (degree of agreement) scale in order to judge children's social interaction with others. Items included such attributes as "cooperates with peers without prompting," "is helpful to others," "very good at understanding feelings," and "resolves problems on own" (Jones et al., 2015, p. 2284). In the follow-up studies, the researchers assessed participants' lives up to age 25 in the categories of education/employment, public assistance, crime, substance abuse, and mental health. Significant positive statistical relationships were found between the children's prosocial communicative skills as judged by their kindergarten teachers and a number of desirable outcomes, including whether participants later graduated from high school on time, completed a college degree, obtained stable employment in young adulthood, and were employed full time in young adulthood. The positive statistical relationships indicate that those who were rated high on social skills in kindergarten tended to achieve these outcomes, whereas those who were rated low on social skills tended not to. These results can be contrasted with a set of significant negative statistical relationships found between the children's prosocial communicative skills and a range of later undesirable outcomes, including:

- the number of years of special education services;
- the number of years of repeated grades through high school;
- the likelihood of living in or being on a waiting list for public housing;

- the likelihood of receiving public assistance;
- any involvement with police before adulthood;
- ever being in a detention facility;
- being arrested in young adulthood;
- appearing in court in young adulthood;
- the number of arrests for a severe offense by age 25;
- the number of days of binge drinking in the past month;
- the number of years on medication for emotional or behavioral issues through high school.

The negative statistical relationships mean that the lower the children were rated in their prosocial communicative skills, the more likely they were to experience these outcomes, whereas the higher they were rated, the less likely they were to experience them.

References

American Academy of Pediatrics (2014). Literacy promotion: An essential component of primary care pediatric practice. Council on Early Childhood Policy Statement. *Pediatrics*, *134*(2), 404–409. doi:10.1542/peds.2014–1384.

American Academy of Pediatrics (2016a). Media and young minds. Council on Communications and Media Policy Statement. *Pediatrics*, *138*(5), 1–6. doi:10.1542/peds.2016–2591.

American Academy of Pediatrics (2016b). Media use in school-aged children and adolescents. Council on Communications and Media Policy Statement. *Pediatrics*, *138*(5), 1–6. doi:10.1542/peds.2016–2592.

American Academy of Pediatrics (2016c). Media and children communication toolkit. Retrieved on December 22, 2016 from www.aap.org/en-us/advocacy-and-policy/aap-health-initiatives/pages/media-and-children.aspx.

Bavishi, Avni, Slade, Martin D., & Levy, Becca R. (2016). A chapter a day: Association of book reading with longevity. *Social Science and Medicine*, *164*, 44–48. doi:10.1016/j.socscimed.2016.07.014.

Bergland, Christopher (2013). One more reason to unplug your television set. *Psychology Today* website. November 23, 2013. Retrieved on October 15, 2015 from www.psychologytoday.com/blog/the-athletes-way/201311/one-more-reason-unplug-your-television.

Bergland, Christopher (2014). Reading fiction improves brain connectivity and function. *Psychology Today* website. January 4, 2014. Retrieved on October 15, 2015 from www.psychologytoday.com/blog/the-athletes-way/201401/reading-fiction-improves-brain-connectivity-and-function.

Bilton, Nick (2016). The Rand pack. *Vanity Fair*, The New Establishment. November 20, 2016, pp. 120, 122.

Birkerts, Sven (1994). *The Gutenberg elegies: The fate of reading in an electronic age*. Boston: Faber and Faber.

Bloom, Harold (2012). Gardens of unearthly delights. Review of Stranger magic: Charmed states and the Arabian Nights by Marina Warner. *The New York Times*, Book Review. March 25, 2012, p. 9.

Booth, Wayne C. (1982). The company we keep: Self-making in imaginative art, old and new. *Daedalus*, *3*, 33–61.

Booth, Wayne C. (1989). *The company we keep: An ethics of fiction*. Los Angeles: University of California Press.

Breneman, David W. (2015). Liberal arts, lost cause? *The New York Times*, Education Life. August 2, 2015, p. 6.

Cohen, Joshua (2012). Means of delivery. *The New York Times*, Book Review. January 15, 2012, p. 27.

Costa-Lima, Luiz (1996). *The limits of voice: Montaigne, Schlegel, Kafka*. Palo Alto, CA: Stanford University Press.

Dennett, Daniel C. (1987). *The intentional stance*. Cambridge, MA: MIT Press.

Florida, Richard (2002). *The rise of the creative class… And how it's transforming work, leisure, community and everyday life*. New York: Basic Books.

Gilsdorf, Ethan (2016). Players gonna play: Three books on games, their appeal, purpose and often addictive qualities. *The New York Times*, Book Review. October 2, 2016, p. 16.

Gottschall, Jonathan (2012). *The storytelling animal: How stories make us human*. Boston, New York: Houghton Mifflin Harcourt.

Grafton, Anthony (2007). Future reading: Digitization and its discontents. *The New Yorker*. November 5, 2007, pp. 50–54.

Hall, Maureen P., & Waxler, Robert P. (2007). It worked for criminals: It will work for middle schoolers. *The Journal of Urban Education: Focus on Enrichment*, *4*(1), 122–132.

Hall, Maureen P., & Waxler, Robert P. (2010). Engaging future teachers to reflect on how reading and writing can change lives. *Writing & Pedagogy*, *2*(1), 91–101. doi:10.1558/wap.v2i1.91.

Harris, Michael (2014). *The end of absence: Reclaiming what we've lost in a world of constant connection*. New York: Current.

Hayakawa, S. I. (1990/1939). *Language in thought and action* (5th edition). New York: Harcourt Brace & Company.

Hedges, Chris (2009). *Empire of illusion: The end of literacy and the triumph of spectacle*. New York: Nation Books.

Honoré, Carl (2004). *In praise of slowness: How a worldwide movement is challenging the cult of speed*. New York: HarperCollins.

Jones, Damon E., Greenberg, Mark, & Crowley, Max (2015). Early social-emotional functioning and public health: The relationship between kindergarten social competence and future wellness. *American Journal of Public Health*, *105*(11), 2283–2290. doi:10.2105/AJPH.2015.302630.

Mar, Raymond A., Tackett, Jennifer L., & Moore, Chris (2010). Exposure to media and theory-of-mind development in preschoolers. *Cognitive Development*, *25*(1), 69–78. doi:10.1016/j.cogdev.2009.11.002.

Miller, John W., & McKenna, Michael C. (2016). *World literacy: Where countries rank and why it matters*. New York: Routledge.

Nathanson, Amy I., Sharp, Molly L., Aladé, Fashina, Rasmussen, Eric E., & Christy, Katheryn (2013). The relation between television exposure and theory of mind among preschoolers. *Journal of Communication* *63*(6), 1088–1108. doi:10.1111/jcom.12062.

National Endowment for the Arts (2004). *Reading at risk: A survey of literary reading in America*. July 2004. Retrieved on May 1, 2013 from www.nea.gov/pub/ReadingAtRisk.pdf.

National Endowment for the Arts (2007). *To read or not to read: A question of national consequence*. November 2007. Retrieved on May 1, 2013 from http://arts.gov/sites/default/files/ToRead.pdf.

National Endowment for the Arts (2009). *Reading on the rise: A new chapter in American literacy*. January 2009. Retrieved on May 1, 2013 from www.nea.gov/pub/ReadingonRise.pdf.

National Endowment for the Arts (2013). *How a nation engages with art: Highlights from the 2012 Survey of Public Participation in the Arts*, Research Report # 57. September 2013. Retrieved on June 28, 2014 from http://arts.gov/sites/default/files/highlights-from-2012-sppa-revi sed-jan2015.pdf.

Palfrey, James (2015). *BiblioTech: Why libraries matter more than ever in the age of Google*. New York: Basic Books.

Pearlstein, Steven (2016). Meet the parents who won't let their children study literature. Post Everything, *The Washington Post* website. September 2, 2016. Retrieved on September 3, 2016 from www.washingtonpost.com/posteverything/wp/2016/09/02/meet-the-pa rents-who-wont-let-their-children-study-literature/?utm_term=.0807b8d51c09.

Pelli, Denis G., & Bigelow, Charles (2009). A writing revolution. *Seed magazine* website. April 7, 2009. http://seedmagazine.com/content/article/a_writing_revolution/.

Pennington, Martha C. (2013). Trends in writing and technology. *Writing & Pedagogy, 5*(2), 155–179. doi:10.1558/wap.v5i2.155.

Pennington, Martha C. (2017). Literacy, culture, and creativity in a digital era. *Pedagogy, 17*(2), 259–287. doi: 10.1215/15314200-3770149.

Pennington, Martha C. (forthcoming). *Teacher–Student Relationship: Key to Effective Teaching and Learning in Contexts of Diversity*. New York and London: Routledge.

Prensky, Marc (2011/2001). Do they really think differently? In Mark Bauerlein (ed.), *The digital divide: Arguments for and against Facebook, Google, texting, and the age of social networking* (pp. 12–25). New York: Jeremy P. Tarcher/Penguin.

Radway, Janice A. (1997). *A feeling for books: The Book-of-the-Month Club, literary taste, and middle-class desire*. Chapel Hill: University of North Carolina Press.

Rainie, Lee, Zickuhr, Kathryn, Purcell, Kristen, Madden, Mary, & Brenner, Joanna (2012). The rise of e-reading. *Pew Internet and American Life Project* website, April 5, 2012. Retrieved on October 15, 2015 from http://libraries.pewinternet.org/2012/04/ 04/part-2-the-general-reading-habits-of-americans/.

Rifkin, Jeremy (2000). *The age of access: The new culture of hypercapitalism, where all of life is a paid-for experience*. New York: Tarcher.

Robb, Alice (2015). 92 percent of college students prefer reading print books to e-readers. Technology section. *New Republic* website, January 14, 2015. Retrieved on May 15, 2015 from www.newrepublic.com/article/120765/naomi-barons-words-onscreen-fate-reading-digital-world.

Schuessler, Jennifer (2011). Shelfless. *The New York Times*, Book Review. January 30, 2011, p. 22.

Slouka, Mark (2009). Dehumanized: When math and science rule the school. *Harper's Magazine*. September 2009, pp. 32–40.

Trounstine, Jean, & Waxler, Robert P. (2005). *Finding a voice: The practice of changing lives through literature*. Ann Arbor: University of Michigan Press.

Turkle, Sherry (2012). *Alone together: Why we expect more from technology and less from each other*. New York: Basic Books.

Turkle, Sherry (2015). *Reclaiming conversation: The power of talk*. New York: Penguin Press.

UNESCO (2006). *Education for all: Literacy for life*. Paris: UNESCO.

UNESCO (2011). Factsheets. www.uis.unesco.org/FactSheets/Documents/FS16-2001-Li teracy-EN.pdf.

Waxler, Robert P. (1997). Why literature? The power of stories. In Megan McLaughlin, Jean Trounstine, & Robert P. Waxler (eds.), *Success stories: Life skills through literature* (pp. 2–5). Washington, DC: Office of Correctional Education, U.S. Department of Education.

Waxler, Robert P. (2007). In honor of Rassias: What literature and language mean to me. In Mel B. Yoken (ed.), *Breakthrough: Essays and vignettes in honor of John A. Rassias* (pp. 125–130). New York: Peter Lang.

Waxler, Robert P. (2008). Changing lives through literature. *Publications of the Modern Language Association (PMLA)*, *123*(3), 678–682. doi: 10.1632/pmla.2008.123.3.678.

Waxler, Robert P. (2014). *The risk of reading: How literature helps us to understand ourselves and the world.* New York: Bloomsbury.

Waxler, Robert P., & Hall, Maureen P. (2011). *Transforming literacy: Changing lives through reading and writing.* Leiden and Boston: Brill.

Waxler, Robert P., & Trounstine, Jean (eds.). (1999). *Changing lives through literature.* Notre Dame, IN: Notre Dame Press.

Zickuhr, Kathryn, & Rainie, Lee (2014a). A snapshot of reading in America in 2013. *Pew Research Center* website. January 16, 2014. Retrieved on February 13, 2015 from www.pewinternet.org/2014/01/16/a-snapshot-of-reading-in-america-in-2013/.

Zickuhr, Kathryn, & Rainie, Lee (2014b). How those under 30 engage with libraries and think about libraries' role in their lives and communities. *Pew Research Center* website. September 10, 2014. Retrieved on August 8, 2016 from www.pewinternet.org/2014/09/10/younger-americans-and-public-libraries/.

Zickuhr, Kathryn, & Rainie, Lee (2014c). Younger Americans' reading habits and technology use. *Pew Research Center* website. September 10, 2014. Retrieved on February 13, 2015 from www.pewinternet.org/2014/09/10/younger-americans-reading-habits-and-technology-use/.

2

A SKETCH OF OUR WORLD, CURRENT AND FUTURE

Art is the nearest thing to life; it is a mode of amplifying experience and extending our contact with our fellow-men beyond the bounds of our personal lot.
— George Eliot, "The Natural History of German Life" (Eliot, 1856, p. 145)

The Human Impact on the World: Degrading the Physical Environment

As Yuval Noah Harari argues in *Sapiens: A Brief History of Humankind* (Harari, 2015), the human impact on the world was relatively insignificant until about 100,000 years ago, when *Homo sapiens* "jumped to the top of the food chain" (p. 11), "ascend[ing] to the top so quickly that the ecosystem was not given time to adjust" (pp. 11–12).

> Moreover, humans themselves failed to adjust. Most top predators of the planet are majestic creatures. Millions of years of domination have filled them with self-confidence. Sapiens by contrast is more like a banana republic dictator. Having been so recently one of the underdogs of the savannah, we are full of fears and anxieties over our position, which makes us doubly cruel and dangerous. Many historical calamities, from deadly wars to ecological catastrophes, have resulted from this over-hasty jump.
>
> (Harari, 2015, p. 12)

In the afterword to his book, subtitled "The Animal That Became a God," Harari observes that over time, *Homo sapiens* has become "the terror of the ecosystem" (p. 415). As he sees us:

> We are more powerful than ever before, but have very little idea what to do with all that power. Worse still, humans seem to be more irresponsible than

ever. Self-made gods with only the laws of physics to keep us company, we are accountable to no one. We are consequently wreaking havoc on our fellow animals and on the surrounding ecosystem, seeking little more than our own comfort and amusement, yet never finding satisfaction.

Is there anything more dangerous than dissatisfied and irresponsible gods who don't know what they want?

(Harari, 2015, pp. 415–416)

The dominance of *Homo sapiens* over the planet is the result, as Harari (2015) points out, of our highly developed mode of communication, our language, which made possible most of the culture that was created on a pre-existing, two-million-year-old platform of our ancestor humans' super-large brain, "superior learning abilities and complex social structures" (p. 11), and tool use. However, this great capacity married to *H. sapiens*' less-than-majestic qualities[1] has put us in the place where we now find our species, becoming increasingly selfish and greedy, biting the very hand of Mother Nature that has always fed us. The great difficulties we are now experiencing with climate change, the extinction of plant and animal species which provide crucial parts of our ecology, and the pollution of the air and water which we need to survive can be seen as Mother Nature getting angry enough to bite us back, with a vengeance.

As we will seek to convince you, making better use of our great trump card of language and bringing literature out of the margins of society and into the mainstream is a practical approach to improving the physical world and to getting Mother Nature off our backs, through first improving the intellectual and spiritual life of Sapiens, making us more satisfied and less restless creatures, and improving our social and physical world in the process. The route to this better world is through the imagination, paradoxically the same route which leads to our restlessness and dissatisfaction with whatever is our current state and so fuels all of our desires for "more and better" ways to be. The specific route through the imagination that we propose is one focused on literature and the human arts.

The present era combining rapid technological change with global connectivity and the harnessing of data is sometimes referred to as the Anthropocene era in order to emphasize the impact that humans are having on the planet. Besides incorporating the Digital Age, the Anthropocene is a time of widespread and rapid extinctions in the world which humans have both inherited and created. These include not only the great biological losses affecting the physical world in which *H. sapiens* and all other species live, but also the great cultural losses affecting the intellectual, emotional, and social world that is the unique ecology of human life.

Evidence of the first type of extinction, its human causes, and its dire consequences now and going forward is mounting. As the biological world has been and continues to be altered by human habitation and engineered to human purposes, we can see an increasingly "unnatural history" of the physical world as it has intersected human history and progresses towards ever more global warming and the planet's sixth mass extinction – the first in many millions of years and the only one caused by humans (Kolbert, 2014). Species are disappearing both as a direct effect of human actions, such as hunting and pollution of habitats, and as an indirect effect of changes we have made to the natural world. Donovan Hohn raises an alarm regarding "the trade routes and flight paths and navigable waterways with which we stitched continents and basins together. Thanks to us, species that evolved in isolation now collide, at times with devastating effects on ecosystems" (Hohn, 2015, p. 12). A prime example given by Hohn is of the man-made canal system in the American Great Lakes, which has made it possible for an invasive species with no predators (other than humans), the aggressive and rapidly reproducing Asian carp, to quickly spread and threaten to overwhelm native species. And, as Hohn warns, this is but one of hundreds of worrying species invasions in the Great Lakes area alone.

Naomi Klein, in *This Changes Everything: Capitalism vs. the Climate* (Klein, 2014), blames capitalism – essentially human greed and the desire for ever more profits – for destroying our planet and argues for a radical change in direction. Klein goes after the powerful voices pronouncing that competition and market forces can solve our climate woes, showing how those very market forces brought us to the place where we now find ourselves and how they are continuing to destroy our planet, pillaging its resources and treating it as our "waste dump." She argues that the current economic model, driven by perpetual growth, cannot work on a finite planet and needs to be replaced by a more realistic one. The current unworkable economic model, and the corporate forces that maintain its dominance, must be countered, she proposes, by citizens' actions to create a new world based on democratic values and sustainable, local economies. Klein is optimistic about the possibilities and gives many examples of the actions of local governments and citizens' groups that are aimed at wresting control from the corporatocracy and improving the environment.

We agree that capitalism unbridled, operating on a global, mass-market scale, is harming our physical world and making things worse on an ever larger scale and at an ever more rapid rate. We also contend that it is harming our psychological and emotional world as it narrows our culture, promoting capitalism as the universal model for all areas of human life, including art and education, and devaluing the life of the mind, the spirit, and the emotions. We further maintain that it is capitalism's huge scale and unbridled nature – its great speed and all-encompassing reach – which is making the problem so great and so serious. We would go so far as to remark that it is the very nature of capitalism, driven by maximizing profits, to expand and to ultimately become all-encompassing and unbridled, unless countered by other forces.[2] This is not to say that capitalism, in and of itself, is bad, but rather that it can easily do harm if allowed to dominate over other human values and needs. It is the dangers of the big corporations – what we might call "Big-C" or Giant Capitalism – that Klein rails against, noting that the global corporations are often monopolistic and anti-democratic; and what can be labeled "little-c" or local capitalism, tempered by other values and activities, might be part of the solution to our climate trouble and myriad ecological woes.

A similar point was made in the first chapter of Honoré's (2004) book, where the author attributes many of the problems the world is facing to the devastating effects of the increasing speed at which human life is being paced, under the influence of survival-of-the-fittest competition and what he calls "turbo-capitalism":

> Modern capitalism generates extraordinary wealth, but at the cost of devouring natural resources faster than Mother Nature can replace them. ... Then there is the human cost of turbo-capitalism. These days, we exist to serve the economy, rather than the other way round. Long hours on the job are making us unproductive, error-prone, unhappy and ill. Doctor's offices are swamped with people suffering from conditions brought on by stress: insomnia, migraines, hypertension, asthma and gastrointestinal trouble, to name but a few. The current work culture is also undermining our mental health.
>
> (Honoré, 2004, pp. 4–5)

The voice of Jonathan Crary, writing in *24/7: Late Capitalism and the Ends of Sleep* (Crary, 2013), can be added to these other voices in noting how the forces of global capitalism are wrecking people's lives and the planet in driving a kind of hyperactivity:

> [I]t is like a state of emergency, when a bank of floodlights are suddenly switched on in the middle of the night, seemingly in response to some extreme circumstance, but which never get turned off and become domesticated into a permanent condition. The planet becomes reimagined as a permanent worksite or an always open shopping mall of infinite choices, tasks, selections, and digressions. Sleeplessness is the state in which producing, consuming, and discarding occur without pause, hastening the exhaustion of life and the depletion of resources.
>
> (p. 17)

Digital connectivity is an enabler of mass-scale, "Big-C" or "turbo-" capitalism in which the Internet offers a highly effective and cost-effective delivery system for reaching the most consumers in the shortest time. This is not to say that digital connectivity and the Internet in and of themselves are bad – and in fact they can offer aid in facilitating solutions to climate change and can be harnessed to help seed and spread "little-c" capitalism as well as values and activities other than capitalism. At the same time, the extent to which our digital world has been captured by turbo-capitalism suggests both how well-suited it is to the purposes of buying and selling on a gigantic, global scale, and the difficulty of wresting it back to other ends and values. With the added bonus not only of being able to buy and sell anything anywhere and anytime, globally, but also of being able to do so at warp speed, the Internet enables a type of capitalism which we will refer to as *hyper-capitalism*, adapting Rifkin's (2000) term, in order to emphasize both vast size and great rapidity, and also its dynamic of continual and potentially unlimited expansion which, unchecked and untempered, can lead to debilitating excess. Jeff Bezos' driven, high-speed, all-encompassing vision for Amazon, which, with his leadership and command of digital technology, has become a model of business of truly Amazonian proportions, can stand as an example of the breathtaking power, the expansive potential and boundless reach, of hyper-capitalism. The flip-side of this Internet-enabled, supercharged form of capitalism is the Internet-enabled, supercharged form of consumerism represented in a life of "pop" and "bling."

Degrading the Cultural Environment

You may be more aware of and more willing to accept the evidence of the negative effects of human activity on our physical than on our cultural environment, though people have been warning of cultural losses at least since World War II. You may also be more likely to accept the warnings of scientists about destruction and loss in the physical environment than the warnings of nonscientist humanists such as philosophers, artists, and English professors about destruction and loss in the cultural environment. Yet, as we will argue in this book, the effects of cultural destruction and loss are just as serious – maybe even, ultimately, more serious – in the ways they impinge on our future.

The widespread and rapid extinctions in the physical world owe much to the impact of technology and, in recent times, to the combined effects of technology and globalization. In like manner, the widespread destructive effects in the cultural world that we inherited from previous generations are due in large part to the combined effects of media technology and global connectivity. These combined forces are like a black hole that absorbs everything near it into its own gravitational pull, making it into a bigger and bigger consolidated culture. This consolidated culture is one that worships quickness, immediate sensation, and consumerism – the elements that help to build an always changing, media-fueled "pop-and-bling" lifestyle.

The roots of such a culture were identified in the 1960s by the historian Daniel J. Boorstin, writing in *The Image: Or What Happened to the American Dream* (Boorstin, 1961). In the introduction to that book, subtitled "Extravagant Expectations," Boorstin took Americans to task for "[using] our wealth, our literacy, our technology, and our progress, to create the thicket of unreality which stands between us and the facts of life" (p. 1). The thesis of his book is that this "thicket of unreality" is the product of Americans' "extravagant expectations," which create an ever-expanding demand for illusions that we are being satisfied. Rather than offering real satisfaction, "the illusions which flood our experience" (ibid.)

represent a world of self-delusion – of self-deception combined with self-hypnosis – a world, in Boorstin's view, of image rather than reality.

The expectation of ever new and spectacular experiences is perhaps woven into American history and our sense of optimism and exceptionalism. As Boorstin (1961) observed, Americans' unrealistically high expectations for novelty are exploited by news media and television in creating "pseudo-events," fabricated "happenings" designed to be ready-made special occasions that will make the audience take notice. The example he gives is of a hotel attempting to increase its prestige by creating a 30th anniversary celebration as a high-profile public relations event. In being a newsworthy event, the celebration of the hotel's anniversary becomes a self-fulfilling prophecy in that it does indeed increase its prestige. Boorstin noted that his use of the prefix *pseudo* implies the deception and falseness behind these occasions as they are created specifically to have an intended effect by getting noticed and reported. We note that these engineered, high-profile events are similar to rituals performed for the sake of appearance or show.

Boorstin's (1961) book is important for bringing to public attention how widespread these pseudo-events were becoming in an age of mass media and also for connecting them to a kind of "pseudo-celebrity" in the sense of the celebration of people for their "well-knownness" rather than for any specific achievements. His observations more than half a century ago about how image was becoming reality identified a major social phenomenon that has continued to be remarked in the new millennium. Boorstin's themes are taken up again in Hedges' (2009) *Empire of Illusion*. In his first chapter, Hedges compares American culture to the pseudo-event of big-time wrestling, which, fueled by the medium of television, is all about gaining ratings and keeping the audience happy and entertained, substituting spectacle and ritual for real content and action. Other kinds of "simulated reality" events making up our "empire of illusion" are so-called television "reality" shows and on-air discussions and interviews between reporters or commentators and media figures such as actors or politicians that unfold according to agreed purposes, topics, questions, and agendas. Even those which are more spontaneous and unpredictable are still highly restricted and artificial compared to events that occur outside those media and entertainment contexts. As Hedges describes it, American culture is becoming increasingly false, all flash and no substance, and increasingly a "celebrity culture."[3]

New York Times editorial writer Frank Bruni, reflecting on the popularity of Donald Trump, notes that journalists have fed an American taste for entertainment-and-celebrity culture, encouraging people to prefer it over a culture of substance or even to take it as reality: "We now utterly conflate entertainment and politics, routinely confuse celebrity with authority and regularly lose sight of the difference between a cult of personality and a claim to leadership" (Bruni, 2015). From the perspective of this "pop-and-bling," entertainment-and-celebrity culture, the American public craves larger-than-life figures and events, in comparison to which "real life, our own life, is viewed ... as inadequate and inauthentic" (Hedges, 2009, p. 19). Hedges (2009) expresses a concern which we share, that "celebrity culture plunges us into a moral void [in which] [n]o one has any worth beyond his or her appearance, usefulness, or ability to 'succeed,'" with success defined in terms of fame and indicators of power such as wealth and sexual conquest, "[no] matter how these are obtained" (p. 32).

The world of the American media culture which Boorstin (1961) drew attention to in the 1960s, and which others such as Hedges (2009) and Bruni (2015) continue to draw attention to, has only been enlarged with time and increasingly exploited for both growing and showing wealth and power. In the era of the Internet, it is rapidly becoming the dominant culture worldwide. Whether we are talking about the consolidated global media culture or specifically about American culture, media-saturated, consumerist culture offers a weak basis for human life, providing poor nutrition for the intellect, the emotions, and people's relationships with others, thus leading to negative effects on individual achievement and on human society. It is therefore an inadequate basis for continuing, long-term progress in all spheres of human life.

A solid future simply cannot be built on a life of high-speed consumption centered on "pop" and "bling" – a life of illusion and spectacle, attentive to only the immediate context and momentary sensation, where "bells and whistles" and "shiny objects" both real and metaphorical (Leibovich, 2015) distract the observer from what is important. This is a life not of limitless possibilities driven by individual initiative and imagination, as our extravagant American expectations should lead us to strive for, and paced by personal characteristics and priorities. It is rather a life in which experience is severely limited, having been strongly filtered and constrained by the overriding agendas and methods of the people driving global business and the digital and media universe to direct our attention, our ambitions, and our actions to their will.[4] The forces of mass media together with hyper-capitalism have put blinders on our eyes and are – to a much greater extent than we might have realized – running our lives and putting us through our paces, defining our running space as a narrow lane on a cultural fast track that does not fit our natural speed or inclinations to find our own way.

Renewing the Physical World by Strengthening the Cultural World

Both kinds of loss – in the natural world and in the cultural world – are highly destructive to human ecology, reducing the richness and diversity of the environment and posing great risks to human health and survival. As Elizabeth Kolbert argues in *The Sixth Extinction* (Kolbert, 2014), mass biological extinctions have been precipitated by the extreme and rapid environmental changes wrought by humans, as other species do not have time to adapt and so are dying out at an alarmingly rapid rate. Yet it is in fact the *other* type of extinction, the cultural losses, that pose the greatest threat going forward, as our weakened culture is not up to the task of righting the planet. The cultural decline is in fact a prime cause of the precarious situation in which we find ourselves. Only through renewing and strengthening human culture can *H. sapiens* muster the collective will to save the physical world and ensure the ongoing cooperative efforts that are going to be required to sustain a healthy planet over the long haul. Without these, humans risk backsliding and even imminent destruction.

We are in large part responsible for this destruction and loss, and so we hold the key to undoing our own destructive forces – those of human selfishness, short-sightedness, and greed, which can perhaps be linked to Sapiens' innate fears and anxieties as a species (Harari, 2015) and which the Internet and hyper-capitalism exploit. The Me Generation – which is essentially that of the Media Generation raised in the age of screen-based mass media and Internet-enabled computers and other digital devices – shows "an empathy gap" (Kristof, 2015) towards fellow human beings that is both cause and effect of the dangerous situation we find ourselves in now. In a number of commencement addresses and other speeches he gave as Senator and as President, Barack Obama commented on the "empathy deficit" in American life, often connecting this to young people's self-absorption and superficial values. He warned repeatedly of the lack of

> ability to put ourselves in someone else's shoes; to see the world through those who are different from us – the child who's hungry, the laid-off steelworker, the immigrant woman cleaning your dorm room. … [W]e live in a culture that discourages empathy. A culture that too often tells us our principal goal in life is to be rich, thin, young, famous, safe, and entertained. A culture where those in power too often encourage these selfish impulses.[5]

The "selfish impulses" which, Obama maintains, threaten democracy and limit American influence abroad are also driving the focus on consumption and mega-profits which, we maintain, is threatening the biological health of the planet.

Human action to restore the biological health of the planet is an urgent and necessary condition of the continued existence of our own among other species. It may not be a sufficient condition, however. Acting to overcome and reverse the forces of our own destruction may depend on prior action to rejuvenate and enrich human culture, thereby nourishing the constructive forces – those of wonder, honesty, and empathy – that build understanding and community. Although restoring our world's biological health will not be possible without science – without the STEM disciplines – it will also not be possible without the human arts.

As Mark W. Roche argued in *Why Literature Matters in the 21st Century* (Roche, 2004), the humanities ensure that morality maintains a central position in society, and literature supports morality by teaching virtue and wrestling with ethical challenges. We are in agreement with Roche and argue, as he did, that literature provides a crucial counterweight to the values of information, the marketplace, and technology that have come to dominate contemporary culture and have made people lose their sense of who and what they are as human beings. In this work, we continue to build the argument for the value of humanities, literature, and a culture of books as critical to society – and also critical *of* society – now and in the future. We will at the same time go considerably beyond Roche in reviewing not only the philosophical basis of the argument but also the science supporting our position and in seeking to *show* the power of literature to move and improve human beings.

In *The Road to Character*, David Brooks urges us all to focus less on our "résumé virtues" and more on our "eulogy virtues" (Brooks, 2015). As the label implies, "résumé virtues" are those qualities such as intelligence and ambition which are revealed in the "high-achiever" accomplishments of high test scores, prestigious college entry, impressive employment titles, and other accomplishments that people associate with competitiveness and success, and that would be listed on a person's résumé. "Eulogy virtues," also as the label implies, are those qualities such as honesty, kindness, bravery, and humility that people associate with goodness and character, and that would be recalled about a person at a funeral. Although they are not necessarily mutually exclusive, as high achievers may also have many or most of the eulogy virtues listed, the competitiveness, aggression, and self-centeredness that is often associated with high achievement can run counter to the altruism – the empathy and compassion – and the morality – the sense of what is just and fair, or right and wrong – that is required for eulogy-worthy behavior.

It is not uncommon in the pursuit of a "competitive edge" for people to edge out – that is, push to the side or even disregard entirely – some or all altruistic or moral behavior – that is, what normally would go under the unmodified heading of *virtues* (as in listing traits individually), or *virtue* (as a general category of behavior). For in fact, high achievement is often gained, at least in part, by disregarding the needs or welfare of others, figuratively stepping over or even on them in climbing the ladder of success. It is also often gained by refusing, or being afraid, to do the right or the brave thing because of negative résumé consequences or the pressure of the majority in maintaining, within the status quo, one's power and status. And high achievement is often won by cutting moral corners off the truth or ethical behavior, as recently documented by economist Sam Wilkin in *Wealth Secrets of the One Percent: A Modern Manual to Getting Marvelously, Obscenely Rich* (Wilkin, 2015) – if not through outright lying and cheating one's way to the top. The different forms of cheating to get ahead that are now commonplace in American schools, businesses, sports, and virtually all aspects of personal and professional life have been amply documented by David Callahan, cofounder of the Demos public policy group, in *The Cheating Culture: Why More Americans Are Doing Wrong to Get Ahead* (Callahan, 2004).

Wilkin's true tales of the highly self-centered, self-serving, and often ruthless and amoral, if not immoral, behavior of many among the "marvelously, obscenely rich" stand as reminders of why it is so difficult, as the saying goes, for a rich man to get into Heaven, while Callahan's true tales of massive lying and cheating in American society make clear how much we need a cultural adjustment. As he documents in his book:

> Widespread cheating is undermining some of the most important ideals of American society. The principle of equal opportunity is subverted when those who play by the rules are beaten out by cheaters, as happens every day in academics, sports, business, and other arenas. The belief that hard work is the key to success is mocked when people see, constantly, that success comes faster to those who cut corners. The ideal of equal justice under the law is violated when corporate crooks steal tens of millions of dollars and get slapped on the wrist, while small-time criminals serve long mandatory sentences.
>
> (Callahan, 2004, pp. 24–25)

Both of these books underscore the need for action to counter the competitive, hyper-achievement and hyper-capitalist mentality which dominates present-day culture and which has created the values and practices of an outwardly measured, shiny-object, "pop-and-bling" lifestyle and, in so doing, left the values and practices of an inwardly measured, moral life behind. The highest level of human need is not after all the need for esteem, the regard of others, but the need, according to Maslow's (1943) hierarchy, for self-actualization – for an inwardly satisfying, fully realized life as the best person one can be. As Callahan (2004) reminds us in the concluding thought of his book, "Integrity, as the famous saying goes, is what you do when no one is looking" (p. 308).

Even though the received wisdom (at least since Adam Smith) is that stressing competitiveness and going after one's individual benefit also benefits the society, this is not as axiomatic as many economists, businesspeople, and politicians would have you believe. There is increasing evidence, as reviewed in the previous chapter (Jones et al., 2015), that social skills developed at an early age may be more predictive of success than résumé virtues. And evidence is also accumulating that aggressive, self-centered, and blinkered effort focused on achieving to the max, disregarding risk to others and the ethics of the route taken and the means employed to get to desired ends, though it can yield great material rewards and high success at an individual level (as amply demonstrated in Callahan's and Wilkin's books), can be devastating on a societal level. It can in fact be argued that, far from ensuring positive washback for the society, the more people are selfish in putting their own individual benefit ahead of any consideration of the effects on the society and ignoring the eulogy virtues, the more they destroy the society that nurtures them. This is because, according to evolutionary biologist and psychology professor David P. Barash, "[t]he basic concept of society assumes give-and-take, a social contract whereby individuals make a deal, with each forgoing certain selfish, personal opportunities in exchange for gaining the benefits of group association" (Barash, 2008, p. B13). There is a parallel here with the natural world as the more individuals compete for and thus destroy its resources, the more they harm society and ultimately themselves and their offspring. An emphasis on the eulogy virtues is therefore needed to remind people that the welfare of each individual is linked to the welfare of the community.

That the things we list on our résumé are in fact considered virtues is a testament to the contemporary egocentric Me Culture, which Brooks (2015) believes was created following World War II (though a similar effect can be noted following World War I in the liberal excesses of the "Roaring 20s"). In his view, that self-centered culture, which has its roots in 18th-century Romantic ideals of the fully realized self, was formerly tempered by a "moral realism" that prevailed up to the mid-1940s and that aimed to keep individuals in check by emphasizing their limitations and the dangers of sin. Whatever social forces were involved – including, we suggest, mass media – it is widely agreed that our society has become highly self-centered in the "Age of the Selfie," as Brooks (2015, p. 236) calls it. Brooks suggests trying to create a culture to counter the excessive focus on Me-ness and résumé virtues, offering a "Humility Code" of principles for a more virtuous life. We are less sanguine in believing that just willing it to be so is not likely to make a big difference in our morality, or to make our "morality toggle switch," as Harvard psychology professor Stephen Pinker conceives of it in "The Moral Instinct" (Pinker, 2008), become active. Nurturing altruistic and community-oriented values is something that needs to be tackled on a societal level, through the educational system and other kinds of efforts focused on modifying our current achievement-driven and self-obsessed culture.

Human Arts Sidelined in Education

Within education, there is a long history of battles between those who support a traditional arts and sciences curriculum and those seeking curricular reform through a lesser emphasis on arts and humanities and a greater emphasis on science and practical pursuits. In the middle of the 19th century, Cardinal John Henry Newman, in *The Idea of a University* (Newman, 2008/1852), mustered a defense of the humanities against the opposing forces which has often been repeated: that the humanities are crucial for teaching morality, cultural knowledge, and critical thinking. In the 20th century, an influential scientist, C. P. Snow, who was also a novelist and a British civil servant, argued that the gulf between literary intellectuals, or humanists, and scientists, especially physical scientists, was bringing education into decline and was a major hindrance to solving the world's problems. Snow, who first presented his ideas in 1959 in a high-profile lecture (the Rede Lecture), "The Two Cultures," later published in book form as *The Two Cultures and the Scientific Revolution* (Snow, 1961), described these opposing groups as forming essentially different cultures within modern society. Social scientists Richard E. Lee and Immanuel Wallerstein describe the battle between the humanistic and scientific cultures of the modern day as "a sort of cultural hurricane or earthquake" (Lee & Wallerstein, 2004, p. 5).[6]

The same gulf – though perhaps not the same "cultural hurricane or earthquake"[7] – continues today and divides literary intellectuals or humanists, essentially those in the human arts disciplines, from those in the STEM disciplines. It is a gulf that also divides humanists from economists and businesspeople, and that continues to have negative effects on education and to interfere with progress in addressing the great problems facing the world. In spite of continuing arguments from humanists about the need for what they know and teach, those pushing a science-heavy and skills- and career-oriented curriculum at the expense of arts and humanities subjects have been increasingly winning battles for control of education. Instead of the kind of cultural integration of humanities and sciences which Snow (1961) proposed, the STEM-heavy, utilitarian curriculum is leaving little space for human arts and important matters of human values having to do with what is good and what is right, and what is not simply useful but beautiful.

The lack of attention to these values of human civilization is getting us into trouble. Yale law professor Anthony T. Kronman, in *Education's End: Why Our Colleges and Universities Have Given Up on the Meaning of Life* (Kronman, 2007), argues that we have a great need for the humanities to counter the tendencies to greed and fraud that caused the financial disaster of the early years of the current millennium. If this was true then, how much more would the humanities be needed in the years following, and how much more are they needed now to counter the same hyper-capitalistic tendencies that are leading to destruction of our planet? Yet the humanities are on the decline. According to Patricia Cohen, "During the second half of the 20th century, as more and more Americans went on to college, a smaller and smaller percentage of those students devoted themselves to the humanities" (Cohen, 2009). Pearlstein (2016) reports that following the Great Recession, degrees in humanities have "fallen sharply" and are now approaching a low of 6 percent. Writing scholar Lil Brannon reflects that over the past 30 years, "[t]enure-line faculty positions have moved out of the humanities to other areas or have been eliminated [entirely]" (Brannon, 2015, p. 521). In her view, this is a sign of the humanities becoming irrelevant outside of English departments and other humanities fields.[8]

We have seen in our lifetime a growing imbalance in education between arts and humanities on the one hand and science and business on the other. Part of what is needed to redress this imbalance, and what can help enrich and nourish human life and life more generally on our planet, is, we maintain, a return to literate culture – a culture of literature, of books, and of ideas and the discussion of ideas engendered by that culture. The heavy emphasis on STEM, especially on the TE part of STEM (i.e., the emphasis on technology and the related field of engineering) without an equal emphasis on human arts disciplines, far from ensuring a rosy future, is in fact putting our species and the world in danger. The overemphasis on STEM has meant an underemphasis, first of all, on language, which is crucial for understanding and communicating about and within all STEM fields, crucial for understanding and expressing ideas and sharing them with others, and crucial for making intricate and deep conceptual connections. Humans not only communicate largely through language; they also think and learn to a great extent through language. Downplaying language puts the human capacity to communicate, to learn, and even to think at risk, thereby making it less likely that people will be able to innovate to solve problems and make advances. In short, it makes it hard to progress. And an emphasis on STEM will amount to very little beyond paying "lip service" to it without a recognition that teaching and learning about STEM, or anything at all, requires a strong co-emphasis on language and specifically reading and writing.

Leaving aside the matter of whether STEM can be conceptually and practically divorced from language, we question the position that it is largely STEM which will ensure the best education for children to maintain a competitive advantage and prepare them with the tools they will need to succeed in life and to solve the world's problems. We can first mention again the research findings of Jones et al. (2015) showing that children's social skills are a strong predictor of their future success or lack of success in school, employment, and life as contributing members of society. Even those who are extremely skeptical about the value of literature would have to admit that there is nothing in STEM that specifically relates to building social skills. And evidence is already accumulating that the emphasis on STEM is not in fact solving the world's problems – such as all of the ecological problems identified by Honoré (2004), Klein (2014), Kolbert (2014), Harari (2015), Hohn (2015), and many other scientists – and so continuing to go down the same road, only more so, would seem on the face of it to be a risky course of action.

A parallel argument against doing more of the same can be made for profit-oriented, business solutions to the world's problems. Because these tend to equate "more" and "bigger" with "better," they are not leading to solving ecological problems but instead accelerating the rate of depletion of resources and pollution of the environment, while also increasing competition and making it less likely that companies and countries will cooperate in finding solutions. In addition, far from trickling down to the poor or even those in the middle class, the huge material and capital gains of global business are tending to make the rich get richer, the poor get poorer, and the middle class get smaller and less affluent. Rather than raising all boats, the mega-success of hyper-capitalism has con-solidated and enhanced the power and wealth of the Elite One Percent class while lowering the water level for others to the point where many are finding it hard to float their boats, thereby fueling discontent and social unrest among those facing reduced resources and life chances.

The overemphasis on STEM, business, and practical skills has meant an underemphasis on aspects of life and education that build social competence and nurture interpersonal relationships and linkage to other human beings via language and prosocial behaviors, which are essential for maintaining a strong social culture in which each individual can become a successful contributing member. There is much in the reading of literature – and, in general, in arts and humanities education – that builds social competence and reinforces linkage to other human beings, thereby improving people's lives and their chances to make positive contributions to their communities and to the world at large. Such positive outcomes have been reported not only in CLTL literature reading and discussion initiatives which improved the life chances of prisoners and at-risk teens, but also in experimental research in which literature increased readers' empathy and ability to read others' social cues as well as their openness to change, as will be reviewed later in this book (see Chapters 9 and 10).

The overemphasis on STEM, business, and practical skills has meant an underemphasis in the educational curriculum on human arts disciplines, which:

- teach about human culture (anthropology) and its great creative expressions (literature, fine art, and music);
- inculcate the lessons of the past (history) and of great thinkers (philosophy); and
- raise questions of human values and morality (religion and ethics) and encourage prosocial attitudes such as sympathy and empathy.

The human arts are the place in the curriculum where students tackle controversial subjects that open their minds by revealing new perspectives and taking them out of their "comfort zone"; where critical thinking and argumentation are taught; where they are continually reminded to consider alternatives and the meanings and agendas that lie beneath the surface of what they read, hear, and see; and where they are encouraged to explore their aesthetic responses and their values. In these different emphases, human arts disciplines provide a counterweight to STEM, business, and practical subjects, while also ensuring that what is presented as an impersonal, "objective" curriculum of STEM or "life skills" is not in fact tied to the agendas and values of global capitalism, but rather becomes practical or scientific knowledge infused with the highest and best human values and purposes.

New Yorker writer David Denby, in his new book, *Lit Up: One Reporter. Three Schools. Twenty-Four Books That Can Change Lives* (Denby, 2016), argues the need for young people to read great and challenging books in the form of literature in order to develop their minds and critical sense, to be able to engage with challenging ideas, and to understand the world and other people. Denby (2016) points out that all great civilizations have had great literature, so that "[i]f literature matters less to young people than it once did, we are all in trouble" (p. xvi). Like us, Denby maintains that an emphasis on reading and discussion of literature can help to sustain our own great civilization by balancing the strong emphasis in education on STEM and in society on electronic media. By observing 10th grade classrooms at three high schools, Denby discovered how today's students can be stimulated to read, enjoy, and learn from literature mediated by enthusiastic and dedicated teachers. As Denby (2016) came to know about American teens:

> Yes, they want a way of earning a living, of fitting in and having a good life, but they want a way of being, too. Basic ethical and philosophical questions of right and wrong, acting and doing, belief and skepticism, acquiescence and critical thinking fascinate them, and nothing is more effective than reading literature for churning up such questions. ... Conversations that uncover the moral issues lodged in narrative have a good chance of meaning something special to fifteen-year-olds. ... Fifteen-year-olds will read seriously when inspired by charismatic teachers alert to what moves adolescents.
>
> *(p. 233)*

Denby's book offers an inspiring view of what is possible in teaching through literature.

In reflecting on the significance of what he observed, Denby (2016) makes points that echo many of those we are making here:

> Teens are entering a media-Internet world of infinite choices, manifold but chaotic, decentered, even incoherent. But if there is little or no authority anywhere in the public atmosphere of assertion and counterassertion, they can at least try to gain a little authority of their own. They can hope for the dignity of knowing something, understanding something. They can know math and the sciences; and they can also know things that, by their very nature are unquantifiable but help create three-dimensional human beings. Children, elementary reason would suggest, need that chance more than anyone, and to abandon children and teenagers to the tumult of screens and to lessen the value of literature and the humanities in favor of STEM subjects, as many powerful men reforming education now want to do, is almost certainly a mistake and very possibly a disastrous mistake. ... For this dubious end we are changing the nature of education, downplaying the humanities, shunting to the side literature, the arts, and much else.
>
> *(pp. 229–230)*

He adds the further point that the market for STEM graduates is "glutted" and many "can't find jobs or, if they do find them are quickly replaced by younger men and women willing to work at lower pay" (p. 230).

Pearlstein (2016), in his article about parents trying to make sure they receive a direct return on their investment in education by pushing their children to major in STEM and business fields, comments that salary differentials are not strictly a matter of what one majors in, but reflect a person's diligence, drive, and native intelligence. He notes, for example, that the top majors in history and English have higher earnings than the average student majoring in science and math. We might also point out that since reading and studying literature builds vocabulary, reading and writing skill, general language competence, and general knowledge, it offers valuable knowledge-building and skill-building for many different kinds of employment as well as for further study.

Others have realized the limitations of STEM, and a new STEAM movement aims to add Arts, referring to fine arts, to STEM and to place art and design at the heart of all education. According to Susan Riley, an "arts integration specialist," the push to STEAM is part of the push towards integrated learning, "adding the arts to the mix – as a way of further integrating creativity and artistic skills and processes across content areas. ... [T]here is also the arts integration approach to education, which teaches the selected content in and through the arts" (Riley, 2013). In this new STEAM orientation, a main goal of education is to encourage innovation through art combined with engineering or with design, as in the Rhode Island School of Design STEAM initiative (http://stemtosteam.org/).

It is encouraging that Riley's blog appears on the Edutopia website of the George Lucas Educational Foundation, which promotes an innovation-centered view of education under a vision of "a new world of learning based on the compelling truth that improving education is the key to the survival of the human race" (www.edutopia.org/mission-vision), a point of view which we heartily endorse. It is likewise encouraging to see that JP Morgan Chase is sponsoring an Arts Integration Solutions website (www.artsintegration.com/). This new focus on art as a key aspect of design and as a way into science and STEM, and in general into all content areas of the curriculum, is to be applauded. Yet we are discouraged to note that the arts-integration and STEAM initiatives do not necessarily include or stress literature as an "art," much less any of the other humanities fields that sometimes go under the heading of Arts (i.e., when contrasted with Sciences).

The Road Ahead: Correcting the Lack of Attention to Literary Culture and Human Arts

In Helen Vendler's opening chapter (subtitled "How the Arts Help Us Live") of *The Ocean, the Bird, and the Scholar: Essays on Poets and Poetry* (Vendler, 2015), the author, a professor of literature at Harvard, argues for a more prominent position for the arts in the humanities and education more generally, in order to provide a crucial person-focused and individual perspective to counter the broader group-oriented and impersonal perspectives of other disciplines. There she "propose[s] that the humanities should take, as their central objects of study, not the texts of historians or philosophers, but the products of aesthetic endeavor: art, dance, music, literature, architecture, and so on" since "it is by their arts that cultures are remembered" (Vendler, 2015, p. 15). Vendler goes on to propose that the other humanistic disciplines, both history and philosophy, which have usually been considered the "core" of humanities, in addition to the study of religion, would then be set "at the periphery" (ibid.). In Vendler's (2015) view, a focus on arts can underpin wider study in humanities, as

[t]he arts would justify a broad philosophical interest in ontology, phenomenology, and ethics; they would bring in their train a richer history than one which, in its treatment of mass phenomena, can lose sight of individual human uniqueness – the quality most prized in artists, and most salient, and most valued, in the arts.

(p. 16)

The humanities, which are in dire straits at the moment, might do well to consider this radical idea of putting the "aesthetic arts," and through them "arts" in the broader sense that encompasses the humanities, at the center of their educational objectives, especially given the interest in STEM fields and throughout education on innovation and creativity, which it is widely agreed are central to the arts.

Vendler's arguments for giving pride of place to the aesthetic arts eloquently express our own view of the value of literature within what we prefer to reference by the collocation of "human" and "arts":

What would be the advantage of centering humanistic study on the arts? The arts present the whole uncensored human person – in emotional, physical, and intellectual being, and in single and collective form – as no other branch of human accomplishment does. In the arts we see both the nature of human predicaments – in Job, in Lear, and in Isabel Archer – and the evolution of representation over long periods of time (as the taste for Gothic replaces the taste for Romanesque, as the composition of opera replaces the composition of plain-chant). The arts bring into play philosophical and historical questions without implying the prevalence of a single system or of universal solutions. Artworks embody the individuality that fades into insignificance in the massive canvas of history and is suppressed in philosophy by the desire for impersonal assertion. … The case histories developed within the arts are in part idiosyncratic, but in part they are applicable by analogy to a class larger than the individual entities they depict. Hamlet is a very specific figure – a Danish prince who has been to school in Germany – but when Prufrock says, "I am not Prince Hamlet," he is in a way testifying to the fact that Hamlet means something to everyone who knows about the play.

(Vendler, 2015, p. 16)

Vendler (2015) further argues in Chapter 1 of her book for the need to educate children to their artistic heritage, observing that "[o]ur students leave high school knowing almost nothing about American art, music, architecture, and sculpture, and having only a superficial acquaintance with a few American writers" (p. 17). In focusing on the human condition, highlighting diverse perspectives, and educating people about their artistic heritage, the arts offer a different kind of education from one that is geared to STEM, to learning a trade, or to amassing wealth. Like a broader human arts curriculum, it is a more personal kind of education, directed at creating a satisfying interior and exterior life as a human being among other human beings, and also an education that aims to ensure continuing connection with our heritage and a strong cultural base. An arts-focused education thus incorporates features that we see as essential to the project of rejuvenating and enriching human culture and nourishing the constructive forces needed to counter the current superficial life of the mainstream and the destructive course that humanity is on. We therefore support an emphasis in education on aesthetic arts within a human arts curriculum that aims to foster the traditional goals of a humanities or liberal arts education, centering on: individual expression and creativity, critical thinking and in-depth analysis, and prosocial and ethical behavior, in addition to broad-ranging knowledge of history, culture, and the self.

We would at the same time argue that literature is unique among the arts in having language, especially written language, as its medium, a medium which links literature to the other humanities disciplines and which also bridges arts and sciences. Literature holds a unique place among the arts in communicating through the vehicle of language, which virtually all members of our species have in common and which is our richest resource for human expression and for both the passing on and the creation of knowledge. As both art and language, literature stands out within the human arts not only for furthering the goals of education in both arts and humanities as reviewed above, but also for playing a vital role in maintaining and continually innovating language at its highest level, thereby sustaining intellectual progress. Literature encompasses a particularly significant type of design, which is *textual design*, the design of words into a complex "linguistic landscape" or "langscape" (Pennington, 2016) of sound and meaning. Literature therefore has an important role of creating products of human imagination that reveal both our intelligence and our human sensibility. In all of these ways, literature can be seen as essential to a vibrant human culture and a positive future for *H. sapiens* that has ramifications for all other species on the planet.

We have written this book to make the case for building back up the side of the house which has been in decline, the human arts side, that of Great Books culture and the reading of literature. We aim to convince you of the value of the human arts, good books, and the reading of literature by presenting information about the nature of reading and literature, both prose and poetry, and by giving examples of the power of literature – of story and of language itself – to move us as human beings, and to change people in ways that improve them and help make the world a better place. We will bolster our case by raising your awareness of the problems that come of ignoring these human arts and instead letting your agenda and values, and those of your children, be set by the interests behind global business, science and technology, and the culture of mass media and the Internet – all of which are intimately connected in our current era.

The Power of Literary Writing: An Example from Junot Díaz

Literary writing has an effect on the reader that goes beyond that of reading for comprehension and also beyond an appreciation we might have for nonliterary writing such as informative or argumentational prose. It penetrates our psyche and emotional armor, hitting us down deep. It creates a disturbance in us and may in fact disturb us in the ordinary sense of this word, as Martha Nussbaum, in *Poetic Justice: The Literary Imagination and Public Life*, has noted:

> Good literature is disturbing in a way that history and social science writing frequently are not. Because it summons powerful emotions, it disconcerts and puzzles. It inspires distrust of conventional pieties and exacts a frequently painful confrontation with one's own thoughts and intentions. One may be told many things about people in one's own society and yet keep that knowledge at a distance. Literary works that promote identification and emotional reaction cut through those self-protective stratagems, requiring us to see and to respond to many things that may be difficult to confront – and they make this process palatable by giving us pleasure in the very act of confrontation.
>
> *(Nussbaum, 1995, pp. 5–6)*

Junot Díaz's story "How to Date a Browngirl (Blackgirl, Whitegirl, or Halfie)" (Díaz, 1996/1995) illustrates the power of a literary work to both disturb us and connect us as human beings. We believe this story, which was first published in *The New Yorker* (www.newyorker.com/magazine/1995/12/25/how-to-date-a-brown-girl-black-girl-white-girl-or-halfie) and can now be found in a number of story collections, gives a good idea of both the power and the complexity of literature that we wish to champion.

In the story, writer and MIT Associate Professor of Writing and Digital Media Junot Díaz speaks through the voice of a teenage boy who has observed and experienced much in his short life, imbibing the patterns of authority and control that people are caught up in. He offers this experience through the character of a naïve yet in some ways all too worldly wise adolescent, Yunior, a Dominican-American living in a poor, tough neighborhood. Yunior's story is revealed as he ostensibly gives his audience instructions on how to "score" with the different kinds of girls that he knows in the neighborhood. The put-on machismo style of the language he uses gives a sense of his life there and the role models he has had for growing into a man:

> Give one of your boys a shout and when he, Are you still waiting on that bitch? Say, Hell yeah.
>
> *(Díaz, 1996/1995, p. 144)*

On another level, this language and the entire account that Yunior gives reads as the author's cynical view of a world of falseness and manipulation, and of how a young person can be drawn into that world.

The narrative reflects the kind of behavior that Yunior recommends – calculated and controlling, as if each girl can be slotted into a specific stereotypical category in terms of key information that a male audience would need to know in order to be successful:

> If the girl's from around the way, take her to El Cibao for dinner. Order everything in your busted-up Spanish. Let her correct you if she's Latina and amaze her if she's black. … A local girl won't need stories about the neighborhood but the other ones might. Supply the story about the loco who'd been storing canisters of tear gas in his basement for years, how one day the canisters cracked and the whole neighborhood got a dose of the military-strength stuff. Don't tell her that your moms knew right away what it was, that she recognized its smell from the year the United States invaded your island.
>
> *(Díaz, 1996/1995, pp. 145–146)*

This excerpt speaks volumes about this young man, and tells the reader much more than Yunior's ostensible purpose of giving advice about dating, as one who has grown up in a context of immigration and cultural mixing, racial and linguistic diversity, and of social manipulation and political control. As is often the case in a great literary narrative, the story overflows its own boundaries, creating a unique human voice that readers can connect with as its plaintive cries, its desirous yearning to be heard, reach out to those who pay attention to it, beyond its apparent intention, through the direct as well as the indirect communication built into the story by the author's skilled writing.

Yunior's narrative can be read as an amusing instruction manual on dating written by a young man who is posing as an expert but who actually doesn't have a clue. This is enough to make it an enjoyable read. However, it has a deeper and darker satirical purpose, which is to lead readers to journey into Yunior's world through discovering the powerful messages that he hints at in his words. Those who read deeply will feel both admiration and sympathy for this plucky yet vulnerable adolescent who has learned how to survive against the odds, while also identifying and empathizing with him as a representative of human nature and experience, including their own. In bringing this boy's experience to life, the story raises issues involving gender and sexuality, race and ethnicity, social status and power, thus functioning as a form of social commentary and critique.

The experience of literature, illustrated in this story by Díaz, goes far beyond the enjoyment which engaged reading can provide. A literary work opens readers to new perspectives and experiences and teaches them things they need to know, not by informing or telling, but by taking them on a journey in which the truth is gradually revealed to them. As educator and linguist S. I. Hayakawa put it in *Language in Thought and Action*,

> the reason that novels, poems, dramas, stories, allegories, and parables exist [is] to convey such propositions as "Life is tragic" or "Susanna is beautiful," not by telling us so, but by putting us through a whole series of experiences that make us feel toward life or toward Susanna as the author did.
>
> *(Hayakawa, 1990/1939, p. 158)*

Readers of literature gain insight or wisdom not through statements or propositions but through going on the emotional journey which the writer has created for them. Readers of this story by Junot Díaz, for example, are reminded of a proposition which they already knew, that "Life is tragic," while also coming to understand a new proposition, that "Yunior is a survivor." These two propositions, taken together, elevate the character of Yunior into a literary archetype, that of a tragic hero. In opening readers' eyes and affecting them on both an intellectual and an emotional level, this journey into literature changes them: a literary work, like this story by Junot Díaz, has the power to teach lessons and to make people more perceptive, more thoughtful, more sensitive, and more empathetic human beings. In some readers, it might also inspire the kind of moral outrage that can lead to social or political action.

Notes

1 An Australian filmmaker and independent scholar, Danny Vendramini, having reviewed the genetic and archaeological record, proposes that modern human physiology, sexuality, aggression, and propensity for intergroup violence – characteristics of "human nature" – emerged as a direct consequence of systematic long-term predation by Eurasian Neanderthals, who hunted, killed, and cannibalized early humans in the Middle East, also abducting and raping human females. In the scenario he imagines in *Them and Us: How Neanderthal Predation Created Modern Humans* (Vendramini, 2012), the death toll and selection pressure resulting from Neanderthal aggression and predation created a tiny survivor population of early humans and transformed these into modern competitive humans, as those who survived Neanderthal aggression reproduced and became the ancestors of all humans living today.

2 Economist and social philosopher Karl Polanyi, writing in the 1940s, argued in *The Great Transformation* (2001/1944) that a purely capitalist economy will ultimately destroy the physical and the social world by commodifying both nature and human beings, perverting them to economic purposes. He speculated about human society becoming an "accessory to the economic system" (p. 79), with a human life reduced to its value and function as labor. We agree with Polanyi's argument and the danger of commodification of human life, the reduction of human life to its value and function in terms of labor or, more currently, employability and (actual) employment. We also fear the reduction of a human being to a consumer or a datapoint that companies can aggregate and exploit to their benefit – or, possibly even worse, reduction of a human being to a machine or machine-enabler, the mere context within which a machine holds sway.

3 We might note that professional wrestling is, ironically, entirely *un*professional – as *faux* or fake as it is possible to make it. As compared to the real culture of wrestling and what it is supposed to be, pro wrestling is a joke or a satire – and, we might say, intentionally *uncultured*. Following this line of reasoning, we might observe that the "culture" of American government has in large part become similarly uncultured and unprofessional, exhibiting a very negative kind of "pop" tendency in the attention-seeking behavior of many of those sitting in Congress or running for office and a worrying need for both political and material "pop" and "bling" in order to survive.

4 The extent to which digital technology and mass media are the drivers of both the business and the social worlds of today is suggested by *Vanity Fair*'s November 2016 list of most influential people (The 2016 New Establishment, 2016). This list has Jeff Bezos of Amazon in the number 1 position, followed by Mark Zuckerberg of Facebook in 2nd place and Evan Spiegel of Snapchat in 3rd place, with screen media giants Bob Iger of Disney (4th place), Reed Hastings of Netflix (6th place), and Rupert Murdoch (8th place) also making the top 10, and seven other digital or media moguls making the top 20 in this list of movers and shakers of the current era.

5 These words can be found in a number of speeches which Obama gave in 2006 and 2007, such as his commencement addresses at Northwestern University (June 16, 2006) and Southern New Hampshire University (May 19, 2007) as well as at the Campus Progress Annual Conference (July 12, 2006), all excerpted at the Center for Building a Culture of Empathy website (http://cultureofempathy.com/obama/SpeechIndex.htm).

6 According to Lee and Wallerstein (2004), in pre-modern times, there was no differentiation between knowledge in the sense of facts, or knowledge of what is true, and knowledge of what is good and what is beautiful. In modern times, they say, "as the 'scientific' culture [became] the putative realm of 'truth' and 'facts,' … a humanistic culture devoted to 'willing the good' was constructed at the opposite pole of the consolidating structures of knowledge" (p. 4). As a consequence, in their view, "in the nineteenth century, the humanistic culture, or perhaps we should say a humanistic counterculture, was constructed defensively against the imperialistic claims of the scientific culture," which "was able to impose itself socially as the dominant culture in the world of knowledge of the modern world-system" (ibid.).

7 It seems that humanists have in recent times been overwhelmed and have lost ground which they once occupied, as they have increasingly tended to seek shelter from this storm rather than to face it head-on.

8 We have seen entire humanities departments, such as in history and many foreign languages – even those recognized as outstanding – disbanded or, in only a slightly better alternative, merged into conglomerates with other departments with which they do not logically or comfortably sit together. Areas of academic work which used to be considered humanities are now being reimagined in guises that give them an existence – and relevance – outside of humanities per se. For example, movement of English and Applied Linguistics departments into units of Communication or Education is common, and movement of those disciplines into what is often a newly created School of Design is on the rise. We know of at least one case in which a group of Applied Linguistics scholars were moved to a College of Business, where a strong emphasis was developed on language testing, with substantial income generated through the development and administration of language tests at overseas locations. While such movement may ensure that at least some humanists have ongoing employment, at the same time it adds pressure for them to shift their emphasis, catch-22 style, to areas of work that are not essentially within humanities.

References

Barash, David P. (2008). How did honor evolve? *Chronicle of Higher Education*. May 23, 2008, pp. B11–B13.

Boorstin, Daniel J. (1961). *The image: Or what happened to the American dream*. New York: Atheneum.

Brannon, Lil (2015). Unintended consequences: A comment on the CCCC Position Statement "Scholarship in Composition: Guidelines for Faculty, Deans, and Department Chairs." *College Composition and Communication, 66*(3), 516–522.

Brooks, David (2015). *The road to character*. New York: Random House.

Bruni, Frank (2015). We invited Donald Trump to town. *The New York Times*, Sunday Review. August 2, 2015, p. 3.

Callahan, David (2004). *The cheating culture: Why more Americans are doing wrong to get ahead*. Orlando, FL: Harcourt.

Cohen, Patricia (2009). In tough times, the humanities must justify their worth. *The New York Times*. February 24, 2009. Retrieved on February 25, 2009 from www.nytimes. com/2009/02/25/books/25human.html?_r=2&pagewanted=1&th&emc/.

Crary, Jonathan (2013). *24/7: Late capitalism and the ends of sleep*. New York: Verso Press.

Denby, David (2016). *Lit up: One reporter. Three schools. Twenty-four books that can change lives*. New York: Henry Holt.

Díaz, Junot (1996/1995). How to date a browngirl (blackgirl, whitegirl, or halfie). In *Drown* (pp. 143–149). New York: Riverhead Books. Originally appeared in *The New Yorker*, December 25, 1995, pp. 83–85.

Eliot, George (1856). The natural history of German life. *Westminster Review*. July 1856, pp. 51–56 and 71–72. Accessed in Nathan Sheppard (ed.), *The essays of George Eliot*, Ch. V (pp. 141–177). Transcribed from the 1883 Funk and Wagnalls edition by David Price. Ebook, March 9, 2009. Retrieved on October 31, 2016 from www.gutenberg. org/files/28289/28289-h/28289-h.htm#page141.

Harari, Yuval Noah (2015). *Sapiens: A brief history of humankind*. New York: HarperCollins.

Hayakawa, S. I. (1990/1939). *Language in thought and action* (5th edition). New York: Harcourt Brace & Company.

Hedges, Chris (2009). *Empire of illusion: The end of literacy and the triumph of spectacle*. New York: Nation Books.

Hohn, Donovan (2015). Reverse engineering: Can we undo the damage of our environmental hubris? *The New York Times Magazine*. February 8, 2015, pp. 11–13.

Honoré, Carl (2004). *In praise of slowness: How a worldwide movement is challenging the cult of speed*. New York: HarperCollins.

Jones, Damon E., Greenberg, Mark, & Crowley, Max (2015). Early social-emotional functioning and public health: The relationship between kindergarten social competence and future wellness. *American Journal of Public Health, 105*(11), 2283–2290. doi:10.2105/AJPH.2015.302630.

Klein, Naomi (2014). *This changes everything: Capitalism vs. the climate*. New York: Simon & Schuster.

Kolbert, Elizabeth (2014). *The sixth extinction*. New York: Henry Holt & Company.

Kristof, Nicholas (2015). Where's the empathy? *The New York Times*, Sunday Review. January 25, 2015, p. 13.

Kronman, Anthony T. (2007). *Education's end: Why our colleges and universities have given up on the meaning of life*. New Haven, CT: Yale University Press.

Lee, Richard E., & Wallerstein, Immanuel (2004). Introduction: The two cultures. In Richard E. Lee & Immanuel Wallerstein (eds.), *Overcoming the two cultures: Science vs. the humanities in the modern world-system* (pp. 1–7). New York: Paradigm/Routledge.

Leibovich, Mark (2015). Dazzled. *The New York Times Magazine*. September 6, 2015, pp. 11–13.

Maslow, Abraham H. (1943). A theory of human motivation. *Psychological Review, 50*(4), 370–396. doi:10.1037/h0054346.

Newman, John Henry (2008/1852). *The idea of a university, defined and illustrated in nine discourses delivered to the Catholics of Dublin.* Published as an e-book by Project Gutenberg, February 5, 2008. Retrieved on July 24, 2015 from www.gutenberg.org/files/24526/24526-pdf.pdf.

Nussbaum, Martha C. (1995). *Poetic justice: The literary imagination and public life.* Boston, MA: Beacon Press.

Pearlstein, Steven (2016). Meet the parents who won't let their children study literature. *The Washington Post* website, Post Everything. September 2, 2016. Retrieved on September 3, 2016 from www.washingtonpost.com/posteverything/wp/2016/09/02/meet-the-parents-who-wont-let-their-children-study-literature/?utm_term=.0807b8d51c09.

Pennington, Martha C. (2016). *Writing at the creative edge: Tracing the evolution of a new idea in language.* Invitational talk. School for Oriental and African Studies, University of London. November 29, 2016 Video available at www.youtube.com/watch?v=vW5FZxFwgvA&t=6s.

Pinker, Stephen (2008). The moral instinct. *The New York Times Magazine.* January 13, 2008. Retrieved on July 15, 2015 from www.nytimes.com/2008/01/13/magazine/13Psychology-t.html?pagewanted=all&_r=0.

Polanyi, Karl (2001/1944). *The great transformation: The political and economic origins of our time* (2nd edition). Boston: Beacon Press. Originally published by Farrar & Rinehart, New York, 1944.

Rifkin, Jeremy (2000). *The age of access: The new culture of hypercapitalism, where all of life is a paid-for experience.* New York: Tarcher.

Riley, Susan (2013). Pivot point: At the crossroads of STEM, STEAM and arts integration. *Edutopia*: George Lucas Educational Foundation, Education Trends blog. December 18, 2013. Retrieved on July 21, 2015 from www.edutopia.org/blog/pivot-point-stem-steam-arts-integration-susan-riley.

Roche, Mark W. (2004). *Why literature matters in the 21st century.* New Haven, CT: Yale University Press.

Snow, C. P. (1961). *The two cultures and the scientific revolution.* New York: Cambridge University Press.

The 2016 New Establishment (2016). *Vanity Fair.* November 20, 2016, pp. 124–143.

Vendler, Helen (2015). *The ocean, the bird, and the scholar: Essays on poets and poetry.* Cambridge, MA: Harvard University Press.

Vendramini, Danny (2012). *Them and us: How Neanderthal predation created modern humans.* Armidale, Australia: Kardoorair Press.

Wilkin, Sam (2015). *Wealth secrets of the one percent: A modern manual to getting marvelously, obscenely rich.* Boston: Little, Brown.

3

THE DIGITAL WORLD

Are we, paradoxically, less connected to each other now than we were before being, as we are told we are, connected with the world?

[…] Is the computer not broadening but in fact narrowing experience?

[…] Are our personal communities shrinking even as the world is becoming networked? If the computer causes human society to contract, will this also cause human culture and our highest cultural products, including language and art, to contract?
— *Martha C. Pennington, "Writing Minds and Talking Fingers: Doing Literacy in an Electronic Age" (Pennington, 2001)*

How the Online Environment Shapes Experience

Marshall McLuhan's famous dictum that the medium is the message (McLuhan, 1964) stressed the importance of particular media (he was especially concerned with television) in shaping human consciousness. This insight is still relevant today when we consider how mass media and electronic devices are quickly reshaping our human environment, our culture, our way of thinking, and our whole way of being. In each case of change in communication modality or technology, something is lost even while something is gained, such as the loss of face-to-face contact that is the price paid for gaining the capability of communicating without having to be in the same place at the same time. In every type of new communication technology — and, more generally, all kinds of new technologies — we should not simply assume progress or inevitability but rather ask, what is gained, what is lost, and is the trade-off between gain and loss acceptable?

With new technologies, people may at first equate novelty with quality or, as noted by Leon Wieseltier, give new technologies a "pass" when it comes to evaluating their value in comparison to the older technologies (Wieseltier, 2015,

p. 15). People tend to welcome new technologies without careful consideration of their benefits and drawbacks, and to readily incorporate them into their world. This is an aspect of the mainstream response of naturalizing or normalizing technologies and the changes they bring as inevitable and natural, as seems to be occurring with all things digital (Pennington, 2001, 2004). Part of this normalization or naturalization requires personification of our computing machines, analogizing their functioning to that of human beings, and making metaphorical connections of the online world to the offline one. Another aspect of this normalization/naturalization is to regard the great advance of the new technologies into every corner of human life as, by definition, progress. We wish to argue, however, that we need to continually be on our guard against and resist any negative effects, help raise awareness of these, and offer alternatives.

Like Harris, we feel the need to alert people to some negative effects of digital and mass media technologies married to the Internet, the culture that they represent and promote, and what humanity is losing in the wholesale adoption of digital, new-media technology. We agree with Harris (2014), who begins Chapter 1 of his book with the following reflection:

> Soon enough, nobody will remember life before the Internet. What does this unavoidable fact mean?
>
> For those billions who come next, of course, it won't mean anything very obvious. Our online technologies, taken as a whole, will have become a kind of foundational myth – a story people are barely conscious of, something natural and, therefore, unnoticed. Just as previous generations were charmed by televisions until their sets were left always on, murmuring as consolingly as their radios before them, future generations will be so immersed in the Internet that questions about its basic purpose or meaning will have faded from notice. Something tremendous will be missing from their lives – a mind-set that their ancestors took entirely for granted – but they will hardly be able to notice its disappearance.
>
> However, we have in this brief historical moment, this moment between these two modes of being, a very rare opportunity. For those of us who have lived both with and without the vast, crowded connectivity the Internet provides, these are the few days when we can still notice the difference between Before and After.
>
> *(p. 7)*

Like Harris (2014), we are in the "link generation" straddling the digital and pre-digital eras and so are able to "notice the difference between Before and After" (p. 7). Noticing and describing this difference is a main motivation behind our book.

As can be seen in the tendency of all things digital to be normalized or naturalized, it is characteristic of technologies to become seamlessly integrated into the contexts in which they are usually employed (Pennington, 2001, 2004). Technologies then disappear into the background as they become the context rather than the focus of activity:

As technologies embed themselves in everyday discourse and activity, a curious thing happens. The more we look, the more they slip into the background. ... This disappearance effect is evident when we consider whether a technology empowers people to do things that would be difficult, or even impossible otherwise.

(Bruce & Hogan, 1998, p. 270)

All aspects of human experience – our cognition, our consciousness, our identity, and our culture – have been altered by technology. This includes our language and our literacy. Yet we may not notice these changes.

In making certain tasks easier and quicker, and in adding new activities and functions to life, technologies change the pace of life and redirect time and energy to new tasks. The computer, the Internet, and the marriage of the two in hand-held devices are speeding up people's lives as they also channel and focus their attention in new directions.

Exploiting the Sensationalism and Immediacy of Modern Media

In addition to gearing humans' reality towards all things technological and digital, the online world privileges image and immediacy. On the Internet, people are driven by their immediate human need to *notice* things rather than a deeper need to *know* things. Internet text is designed less to be informative and more to be eye-catching, such as headlines that are "hyperbolic" or "begin with dangling participles and end with prepositions" (Marantz, 2015, p. 26). Ian Leslie argues that the Internet appeals to humans' "diversive curiosity," the type of curiosity that draws people's attention to perceptual prominence or novelty and that is easily satisfied, while threatening their "epistemic curiosity," a deeper desire to know things that takes much longer and much more effort to satisfy (Leslie, 2014). This type of curiosity, and people's efforts to satisfy it, is nurtured in the "absence" and "solitude" which Harris (2014) is so concerned is being lost in the contemporary digital life. We note that it is this epistemic curiosity – the desire to know and to understand – that drives effortful and time-consuming goals for learning, such as learning how to read or learning a body of knowledge in school or in one's area of interest. It is also the form of curiosity that leads a reader not only to the first line of text in a poem or a story – diversive curiosity may be enough to do this – but beyond the first line and into the body of a poem or story, all the way to its very last line. Thus does epistemic curiosity motivate the reader to read on, to go on a mental journey and find out where the poem or story, once begun, ends up.

The immediacy of visual media focuses the user's attention on the here and now:

Because the past and the future cannot be directly experienced but can only be conceptualized, the present is the only dimension of time that offers direct sensory stimulation to the nerves. The choice of pleasure, therefore, speaks through lips of the present.

(Bertman, 1998, p. 31)

With the Internet, like television and video, centering on sounds and images, the focus is on immediate sensation, with the effect, as asserted by Marshall T. Poe, in *A History of Communications: Media and Society from the Evolution of Speech to the Internet*, of "sensationalization of social practices and values" to emphasize "the consumption of 'cheap thrills,' that is, stimulating, low-cost entertainments" (Poe, 2011, p. 230).

In *Transforming Literacy: Changing Lives through Reading and Writing*, Robert P. Waxler and colleague Maureen P. Hall observe that young people consume spectacle as a superficial type of stimulation on the Internet: "Unlike spectacle, deep reading and discussion are always two-way (at least) exchanges, dialogic interactions. Spectacle is a one-way event without a 'live' interaction; spectacle is consumption without reflection" (Waxler & Hall, 2011, p. 68). Driven by the speed of the computer, and drawn to the images and spectacle on the electronic screens, young people leap without looking or thinking and live primarily in the emotional moment. Living moment to moment, they contemplate less and less deeply, not taking the time to upload impressions to long-term memory nor to process current experiences in relation to past memories. In substituting sensation for self-reflection, they lose a fundamental connection with their own voice and imagination. In this way, human beings become increasingly ahistorical, disconnected from their own history and life story.

Because it is an extremely high-volume medium, the unconstrained network of the Internet is, in the view of Poe (2011), "hedonizing" social practices: "people are pleasure-seeking. Thus, if a medium has extra bandwidth, people will use it for the purposes of pleasure. The Internet has ample spare capacity and has, as a result, hedonized social practices and values" (p. 233). In their widespread presence and immediacy, visual media and the Internet provide excellent vehicles for making direct appeals to potential customers that rely on sensory stimulation and pleasure-seeking to create desire. The hedonizing potential of these screen media, coupled with their direct access to enormous numbers of people, has created a "brave new world" of economic opportunities.

Writing in the late 1990s, classics professor Stephen Bertman stressed the negative side of such "opportunities," noting that modern media both enhance and exploit materialism and consumerism. Bertman (1998, pp. 37–38) commented that as people take on a primary role of consumers, the senses become all-important – both "the socially preferred avenue to gratification" and a "readily available … avenue of economic and political exploitation" – and reason is accordingly subverted "because the senses respond to things spontaneously and rapidly, whereas, by comparison, reason is slow and deliberate." On the Internet, businesses large and small exploit these tendencies in trying to lure consumers to their products by appealing to their senses and desires in ways that bypass considered judgment. Luiz Costa-Lima (Costa-Lima, 1996) and later Tony Schirato and Jen Webb (Schirato & Webb, 2004) argued that modern media have been too much controlled by commercial interests that seek to make all users into consumers and that compete with use of the Internet as a site promoting non-consumerist values and practices and the spread of "disinterested" information. This trend to commercialization of the Internet continues apace.

As personal information about users goes into a database, advertisers rush to have access to all that information. Given the efficiency of finding and sorting information about potential customers from a computerized database, computers and the Internet are invaluable resources for data mining by commercial concerns. Computers and the Internet make it possible for companies to target their products and advertisements based on data which they can capture not only from demographic information about themselves that users have deliberately shared (e.g., by entering it online) but also from users' online activity, such as which websites they visit – not to mention all of the personal information they share about themselves in their postings on social media. Product placement and advertising have an ever-expanding online dimension, even as offline, "real-world" product placement and advertising draw on computerized and Internet-derived data on consumers.

Computers and the Internet, in making so much data so easily available, fan an obsession with data that is connected to unbridled hyper-capitalism and that is also promoted by computerized data and the connectivity and reach of the Internet. An article by Bill Wasik in *The New York Times Magazine* Tech & Design issue devoted to the effects of American technology around the world expresses concerns about loss of privacy, as "all the resulting revelations then get rolled up as data that can be offered to governments and corporations – which feel practically compelled, once they know they can obtain it, to parse it all for usable intelligence" (Wasik, 2015, p. 20). Nicholas Carr, who has written in an article in *The Atlantic* titled "Is Google making us stupid?" (Carr, 2011/2008) and in his two books *The Shallows: What the Internet Is Doing to Our Brains* (Carr, 2010) and *The Glass Cage: How Our Computers Are Changing Us* (Carr, 2014) about the dangers which the Internet poses to our intellectual skills, also worries that the Internet makes us more susceptible to surveillance.

In the era of the Internet and Big Data, competition has become fierce and companies ignore these realities at their peril, as even a high-quality product can fail to ever reach or to sustain profitability unless its developers and marketers master online advertising, product placement, and often product delivery as well. In today's world, a product developer cannot have confidence that "if you build it, they will come" – in other words, that a good product creates its own market and so guarantees customers and thus profitability. Creation of a high-quality product may in fact be less important than how the product is advertised and distributed – to the extent that a product recognized to be of lesser or "modest" quality may easily capture a much larger market share through deft placement and advertising using Big Data and the Internet. In an article in *The New Yorker*, Andrew Marantz (Marantz, 2015) notes that excelling at finding and presenting the news – what we might call "news-capture" – no longer guarantees audience share or "reader-capture." Marantz goes so far as to state: "In our data-obsessed moment, it is subversive to assert that the value of a product is not reducible to its salability" (p. 26). This is truly Capitalism Gone Wild, a world in which quality equates to sales volume.

A similar phenomenon can be seen in the judgment of value based on the number of "hits," even for an artifact that is a not a commercial product such as a personal blog or YouTube video, where the size of the audience is taken as prima facie evidence of value. And in fact, it is usually only a matter of time, and a rather short time, that such artifacts, or their creators, because they attract so many Internet users, become monetized and commercialized. Thus the value of whatever is on the Internet equates to the volume of people who are aware of it; and when this is a high number, there is a slippery slope to capitalizing on all those people and turning them into customers. There is furthermore a growing "secondary market" creating commercialized products from non-original Internet content, such as compiling thematic information that has gone viral – so-called "memes" – and then showing this on a website that requires paid subscriptions or receives money from advertisements displayed there. Marantz (2015) observes that the creators of the original content are typically cut out in the process, receiving no share of any revenues, and sometimes not even being credited or cited.

This is a form of hyper-capitalism unbridled in the extreme: creating an Internet product from the efforts of invisible and unpaid others and distributing this product quickly and efficiently to a very large number of consumers based on digital capabilities of Big Data and electronic distribution. The product is created without having to pay for its component parts, in effect removing the middleman, and without having to wait for those parts to be produced, thus making both creation and placement cheap and quick; and it also is created with a guarantee (from online hits and with digital distribution) of a very large market. This digitally enabled product is in this sense an instance of hyper-capitalism at its most perfect, creating a product which is both cheap – virtually free, at least in terms of its core content – and quick – virtually instantaneous – to produce, and which contains within itself a market-driven mechanism for continued product renewal (i.e., based on Internet-captured content and user data) and (like an addictive product such as cigarettes, liquor, coffee, or many kinds of drugs) ever-escalating demand.

Clearly, modern media are opportunistic, providing the means for those so inclined to move rapidly into arenas where media capabilities can be exploited to economic, political, and indeed, other kinds of advantage that come from being the first one to do something by means of the available media technologies or from being an early-stage convert or adopter of innovations involving media.

Living in the Shadow of the Machine

Humans live in a world that is, Wieseltier (2015, pp. 1, 14) observes, increasingly defined by "technologism," driven by quantification, "idolatry of data," and "the most unimaginable data-generating capabilities of the new technology." In this "idolatry of data," a new form of currency or "bling" has arisen. As described by Sven Birkerts, writing in *Changing the Subject: Art and Attention in the Internet Age*, "Letters, numbers, codes [have become] the new coins of the realm" (Birkerts, 2015, p. 69). Where data and quantification become the dominant values, people pay the price with their individuality and human complexity. This is a world that does not include the Measure of Man to a sufficient degree but rather the Measure of the Machine.

In *Terms of Service: Social Media and the Price of Constant Connection* (Silverman, 2015), Jacob Silverman suggests that the major platforms controlling people's interaction with the digital screen today – Amazon, Facebook, Google, Twitter, Pinterest – are primarily engaged in "dataveillance" (p. 131), a powerful and effective strategy to measure, quantify, and manipulate the desires and behaviors of all those who spend time online. Every "like" button users click on, every algorithmic alert they respond to, gives the platform moguls and other unknown and undetected others hovering in the vast Internet Hive information about those users which they then package and sell or use for other – sometimes nefarious and illegal – purposes. At the same time, these simple responses reinforce users' sense that they are somehow still "connected" to the online world, the world that supposedly really matters. They begin to feel left out, off the grid, if they disconnect. Turkle (2012) reflects that "with constant connection comes new anxieties of disconnection, a kind of panic" (p. 16) about being offline:

> I find people genuinely terrified of being cut off from the "grid." People say that the loss of a cell phone can "feel like a death." One television producer in her mid-forties tells me that without her smartphone, "I felt like I had lost my mind."
>
> *(Ibid.)*

It is not substantive meaning that users of digital media seek, but visibility, someone or something acknowledging that they still exist. They withdraw from living in the immediate environment, preferring to check their smartphones, looking for the best selfie to post on Facebook, "the one that will draw the most comments and 'likes'" (Silverman, 2015, p. 61). Those immersed in online culture celebrate the digital self as the privileged self, best displayed through activity performed on the electronic screen. In this way, three-dimensional people become reduced to digital nodes on the grid and begin to live a restricted remote-control existence that is dictated by the ingenuity and power of those platform moguls interested primarily in accumulating profits and monetizing everything that people do – every movement, every gesture.

According to Conor Dougherty, a technology reporter writing about smart-phones, people's attention is increasingly focused on checking their mobile screens, with many admitting to keeping the mobile device with them in bed at night (Dougherty, 2015). Dougherty (2015) maintains that the smartphone satisfies "two fundamental human impulses ... our quest to find new and interesting dis-tractions, and our desire to feel that we have checked off a task." Smartphone use becomes self-reinforcing as it literally rewires the brain to be constantly questing for the kinds of satisfying "quick-fix" experiences which the device delivers. Observers are becoming alarmed at this kind of habitual activity, bordering on dependence, which many people pursue on their smartphones. As Dougherty (2015) observes, "Those habits have prompted enough soul searching that a slew of new companies see a business opportunity in helping people cut back." It is perhaps ironic that the same "smart" technology which created this powerful instrument of distraction is now being used to pull people away from using it as much as they tend to – in effect, to train them to check their phones less.

A life lived online is a life lived in a rush to do whatever is there to do – to email, to text, to tweet, to post on Facebook, to check the news, and to buy. The Internet, in urging people to act, and to act quickly, turns out to be the perfect vehicle to encourage people to give in to temptation and to consume – "to shop till they drop." The very quickness of media is antithetical to deliberation and rationality. On the Internet, speed is a driver of consumerism and part of the warp and woof of digital capitalism, Judy Wajcman argues in *Pressed for Time: The Acceleration of Life in Digital Consumerism* (Wajcman, 2014). The lure of a "pop-and-bling" lifestyle, as the consumer side of what we have been calling hyper-capitalism, digitally delivered and digitally enhanced, exploits people's rush to stay busy, to live life in the fast lane, and to keep up with, or ahead of, the Joneses.

In this media era, people's attention has become a commodity which businesses aim to exploit. Raffi Khatchadourian (Khatchadourian, 2015) observes that "attention – at least, the kind worth selling – is becoming increasingly scarce, as people spend their free time distracted by a growing array of devices" (p. 58). This has created a market "in the mining of consumer cognition" (ibid.). The new frontier for the mining of consumers' attention and more broadly their cognition is, as Khatchadourian (2015) reports, to capture their emotions: "By scanning your face, computers can decode your unspoken reaction to a movie, a political debate, even a video call with a friend" (p. 51). Thus are computers being programmed to read our very thoughts, and to do so outside our awareness, without either our knowledge or consent.

The Internet as a Technology of Distraction

Those who inhabit the digital world learn to divide their focus and to regulate their mental energy in short bursts that result in limited spans of attention. Spending a lot of time on the Internet buys speed and trains attentiveness and mental agility in short-term, or working, memory at the expense of sustained attention, concentration, and the continuous mental processing needed for deep thinking or deep reading, and for consolidating meaning in long-term memory. Carr (2010) observes in *The Shallows* that the plasticity of the brain makes it possible for humans to adapt to the demands of new situations, such as repeated exposure to websites, and to "train" the brain to respond in certain ways to those new stimuli. On the downside:

> The influx of competing messages that we receive whenever we go online not only overloads our working memory; it makes it harder for our frontal lobes to concentrate our attention on any one thing. The process of memory consolidation can't even get started. And, thanks ... to the plasticity of our neuronal pathways, the more we use the Web, the more we train our brain to be distracted – to process information very quickly and very efficiently but without sustained attention. That helps explain why many of us find it hard to concentrate even when we're away from our computers. Our brains become adept at forgetting, inept at remembering.
>
> *(Carr, 2010, p. 194)*

As Carr (2010) further notes, "Our uses of the Internet involve many paradoxes, but the one that promises to have the greatest long-term influence over how we think is this one: The Net seizes our attention only to scatter it" (p. 118). Daniel J. Levitin refers to an evolved perceptual system, "the attentional filter" (Levitin, 2014), which helps humans decide what they need to pay attention to as well as what they "can safely ignore." While no doubt useful for warning people of potential danger, this attentional system can become overloaded: "The constant flow of information from Twitter, Facebook, Vine, Instagram, text messages and the like engages that system, and we find ourselves not sustaining attention on any one thing for very long – the curse of the information age" (Levitin, 2014).

Levitin observes that the human brain becomes exhausted by too many attentional switches. Moreover, all of this attention to the phenomena and attractions of the digital world – and thus to the momentary satisfaction of what Leslie (2014) has termed "diversive curiosity" – takes time and attention away from other matters which may be of greater importance and also keeps people from taking the time needed to become immersed in a single task – and so to patiently pursue things which can satisfy, in Leslie's terms, "epistemic curiosity." Levitin (2014) argues for the value of time spent offline in relaxation and daydreaming, or mind-wandering, as promoted for example by taking a walk or listening to music. Such activity helps to reset the brain to its off-task (or what Levitin calls its "task-negative") mode and thus encourages a "flow" of thoughts and "connections among disparate ideas" that can trigger insight and creativity. We note that highly engaged reading may similarly invoke this free-associating off-task mode of mental activity that stimulates new thoughts and connections.

Ultimately, Carr makes a point about the economic considerations behind the new Internet mode of reading geared to fast consumption of information in a form of scattered attention and multitasking:

> Every click we make on the Web marks a break in our concentration, a bottom-up disruption of our attention – and it's in Google's economic interest to make sure we click as often as possible. The last thing the company wants is to encourage leisurely reading or slow, concentrated thought. Google is, quite literally, in the business of distraction.
>
> *(Carr, 2010, p. 157)*

Humans are prone to the distractions of the moment. Alex Soojung-Kim Pang has written about how much we are distracted by our electronic devices. He describes smartphones as "weapons of mass distraction, these interruption amplifiers" (Pang, 2015, p. 15), observing in his book *The Distraction Addiction: Getting the Information You Need and the Communication You Want, Without Enraging Your Family, Annoying Your Colleagues, and Destroying Your Soul* that

> [w]hen you're constantly interrupted by external things – the phone, texts, people with "just one quick question," clients, children – by self-generated interruptions, or by your own efforts to multitask and juggle several tasks at once, the chronic distractions erode your sense of having control of your life. They don't just derail your train of thought. They make you lose yourself.
>
> *(Pang, 2013, p. 47)*

Although he argues that we can control this addiction, turning smartphones "into filters that protect your attention rather than compete for it" (Pang, 2015, p. 15), as the term "addiction" implies, this may be easier said than done. He agrees with us that the danger is indeed great, suggesting that "[t]he habits we develop to make our smartphones more mindful can help us keep from losing our minds in a future that threatens to be even more distracting" (ibid.). While we applaud his optimism and his very real and practical attempts to help people use their smartphones more wisely, we are more pessimistic about people's ability or willingness to control their use of electronic devices and avoid losing their minds and themselves in what promises to be an "even more distracting" future.

People think they are doing so much more with the Internet and technologies than was possible in the past, making so many more connections and connecting at such greater distances. They assume that this makes their lives richer and deeper. However, Paul Virilio, in *The Futurism of the Instant: Stop Eject* (Virilio, 2010), points out that going "out far" does not mean going "in deep." Indeed, as he says, "The proximity of the far away greatly favors exteriority to the detriment of all conscious interiority" (p. 45). Thus is the human world turned inside out, as the outer life increasingly takes over all of people's time and attention. In the digital culture, the distant journey made possible by electronic devices is not one that encourages going *in deep*; instead, the farther people journey through the electronic network, the more they spread themselves thin. Rather than going deep, they go surface, probing not the depths of human thought and emotion – the greatest things we are capable of – but what Carr (2010) labeled "The Shallows." It is the difference between a deep dive, the diver going fully into the water, becoming totally immersed and thoroughly saturated, and someone staying almost entirely out of the water, boogie boarding for the thrill of speed, of whizzing across a flat space, the water only the medium on the surface of which the board is made to move.

Part of our argument is that words (language), especially when shaped into literature, carry richly sensuous meaning that arouses and inspires readers in a way that other forms of language not cast in literary or story form or images streaming across a screen cannot, by offering the rare opportunity these days "to go in deep." The encounter with aesthetic, literary language excites the imagination of the reader, who is in continuous dialogue with it. Such language calls to every reader, connecting to each person's story. In this way, story creates story, as every story invokes, and evokes, other stories. As readers help to create the stories they read by mapping their own stories onto literary narratives, the process draws on their memories and desires, and draws them into the depths of their linguistic knowledge, imagery, and past and present physical experience. The journey into the territory of literary narrative thus takes the reader into the depths of the self. We question whether such a journey can be made either through the kinds of language that typify digital contexts or through images on a screen.

Life Reduced in the Digital Environment

In the case of audiovisual media and electronic devices, even as they add new dimensions to life they also reduce its dimensionality in different ways. Digital information is reduced from the full complexity – the irregularity, the novelty, and the unpredictability – of phenomena generated outside digital contexts. As Jaron Lanier, the father of virtual reality technology and author of *You Are Not a Gadget: A Manifesto*, has noted, "A digital image captures a certain limited measurement of reality within a standardized system that removes any of the original source's unique qualities" (Lanier, 2011/2010, p. 132), and the same is true of digital music and art. Digital artists create perfect replications of sunflowers, or deliberate non-replications, and computer programmers program the computer to "perform" a concerto with no imperfections.

As people are finding out, the computer versions are often not as enjoyable, and so, in human terms, not as good, as the originals. The originals are more complex because they contain features and imperfections that reveal the nature of their human creators. There is something about people's individual traits as conveyed in a work of art or music, and also their human imperfections, that makes the offline and analog versions better by the standards of other human beings who share traits and imperfections with the artist. It is only natural that this should be the case as the computer versions are unnatural by comparison.

Digitizing information requires certain other kinds of reductions:

> Information systems need to have information in order to run, but information underrepresents reality. … Under the No Child Left Behind Act of 2002, for example, U.S. teachers are forced to choose between teaching general knowledge and teaching to the test. … What computerized analysis of all the country's school tests has done to education is exactly what Facebook has done to friendships. In both cases, life is turned into a database.
>
> *(Lanier, 2011/2010, p. 67)*

Moreover, as Lanier observes: "Personal reductionism has always been present in information systems" (Lanier, 2011/2010, p. 66), as the person is reduced to whatever categories of information are asked for.

The Internet and the electronic devices by which we access it are reducing the dimensionality of life in another sense, by moving so much of our time and so many of our activities online. We now work online, shop online, carry out a large part of our communications online, and increasingly perform many of our leisure activities online as well. A great deal of our reading and accessing of information is now also done online.

The dimensionality of life is also reduced by the ready online access to attention-grabbing stimuli, which can easily become "time sinks," as well as the ready access to like-minded people. The great knowledge gateway of the Internet can channel a person's life in ways that narrow or "silo" experiences and perspectives. As remarked by Bruni (2014):

> The Internet … opens up an infinite universe for exploration, but people use it to stand still, in a favorite spot, bookmarking the websites that cater to their existing hobbies (and established hobby horses) and customizing their social media feeds so that their judgments are constantly reinforced, their opinions forever affirmed.

This narrowing or "siloization" of focus by the Internet can lead, paradoxically, to less diversified knowledge and social experience and more polarization of society in a medium which is aimed at widening access to people and information. It can have significantly negative effects on communication, when like-minded and like-voiced individuals come together in ways which reinforce only certain perspectives and types of information, insulate them from competing worldviews, and embolden them to disseminate misinformation and hate speech, and to interfere with the communication of others.

The World as a Reflection of the Machine

Our world is increasingly a digital one which, when compared to our offline world, is a very different world, one that makes available many affordances not available in the offline world. In this sense the online world is to be celebrated as offering new opportunities and aids for human beings. Yet more than providing new affordances and tools, as the digital world increasingly becomes the unremarked backdrop – the backgrounded context or framing – of our lives, it defines a new culture. This is a culture which builds on and in some ways supersedes, at the same time as it contrasts with and in some ways conflicts with or distorts, the culture that existed prior to the development of computer and Web technology and the great linked network of the Internet. It is a culture reflecting the characteristics of digital tools and contexts and how these have been developed, sometimes in ways that are less than optimal for us as humans and can be seen as limitations or distortions of the richness and potentials of human life.

In several senses, the digital world is a degraded or false reflection of the non-digital world outside. Far from capturing the full depth and breadth of human experience, it is a world of managed access and presence, as can be seen in the posting of staged selfies and other photos on Facebook, and in general the filtered information posted by people on social media sites and individual websites, as well as the strong bias of the Internet to commercial purposes. Moreover, beyond being a limited version of the human world, the digital world can be a version of the human world skewed to negative practices, such as the expressions of hatred and bullying that take place in some online communities, the self-destructive behaviors (e.g., anorexia and bulimia) supported on some websites, or the violence and obsessive behavior promoted by many online games.

In such a world, humans become disconnected from their memories, which have been outsourced to the Internet. When they see these flickering screens, they begin to believe that these images, already manipulated by others, are really them, although they are in fact stereotypes at best, totally unreal simulacra (Baudrillard, 1994) at worst. Popular culture, starting with television perhaps, makes people's lives into this kind of dream or hallucination. What is manufactured as media content becomes what people believe and dream about, as in advertising creating what can be considered false reality, false desire, and false memory. Hedges (2009) argues that people are losing the ability to tell the difference between the real and the pseudo, such as the pseudo-events which pass for entertainment on television, and that this is putting us in grave danger: "The more we sever ourselves from a literate print-based world, a world of complexity and nuance, a world of ideas, for one informed by comforting, reassuring images, fantasies, slogans, celebrities, and a lust for violence, the more we are destined to implode" (pp. 189–190), as "cultures that cannot distinguish between illusion and reality die" (p. 143).[1]

Ease and comfort have always defined the dream of modernity, the Machine Age and progress, but the user-friendly world of the Digital Age suggests the danger lurking just beneath the surface of those well-oiled and humming machines. The world which technology is creating is a pseudo-human, machine-geared, Stepford world: a simulacrum of the life which technology can never replicate in all its depth and complexity – a life built on human physiology, cognition, and language; on human needs and desires; on morality defined in human values; and on human history and culture. Where is the human in a world geared to and gauged by the efficiency and effectiveness of machines? As implied by the statement made in the title of Lanier's (2011/2010) book *You Are Not a Gadget*, when machines become the measure of a person, they reduce people and their lives. As Lanier (2011/2010) elaborates:

> [W]hen we [technologists] deploy a computer model of something like learning or friendship in a way that has an effect on real lives, we are relying on faith. When we ask people to live their lives through their models, we are potentially reducing life itself. How can we ever know what we might be losing?
>
> *(p. 70)*

It is alarming to observe people so easily modeling themselves on their machines and gearing their lives to what those machines offer and emphasize. It is both surprising and distressing to realize the extent to which people are reducing themselves and their lives by giving in to the power of their technologies, allowing their time and attention to be directed to the purposes of texting, Facebooking, and surfing the Net, and allowing their behavior to be shaped as well by online mega-companies like Amazon and Google that are expanding their commercial activities and the products they offer as they continually refine their algorithms and strategies for selling those products. It is not too far-fetched to describe it as people allowing themselves to be shepherded – that is, herded and guided like sheep – by the powers of the computer, in all its manifestations of digitized information, computational capability and capacity, and electronic transmission, which they now have at their fingertips, as realized especially in the delivery system of mass media married to the Internet. And it is especially alarming to realize the extent to which all this technological power is under the service of business and especially serves the interests of some very large corporations. When we allow machines, and the businesses that employ them to do their bidding, to direct us to this extent, we are allowing them to take over our *agency*, a matter of great concern to Birkerts (2015, pp. 53–54) and to us.

People often think of the computer or their digital devices as their helper or "friend." And because they believe in the power of the machine, they put their faith in its ability to outperform any human being. This leads to problems when the human being relies on the machine even when there is evidence that it is not working well, having been "lull[ed] … into a false sense of security" that Carr (2014), in *The Glass Cage*, calls "automation complacency" (p. 67). In our view, this is part of a larger form of "media complacency" surrounding all that the computer and digital devices offer through mass media and the Internet, as people seem very prone to complacency about the loss of privacy and control and the commercial purposes behind so much of what they are doing through their machines – even to the extent of losing awareness of these realities of the digital context.

The Internet is an environment custom-made for companies to lurk in the background, gather information about us, and bombard us with ads and enticements to buy their products. While sellers encourage people to see this as positive – in terms of shopping convenience and customization of offers, for instance – we again want to ask what is gained and what is lost, and whether the trade-off is worth it. Besides letting oneself be led by the commercial interests controlling the Internet, there are dangers inherent in making personal information available online, of being surveilled and targeted by unseen and unknown others. This includes the various and sundry "baddies" that we are all constantly being warned of – the online bullies, thieves, and people posing as other than who they are, trying to steal our peace of mind, our identity, and our money: the Internet, with its cloak of anonymity, is an environment custom-made for meanies and charlatans.

A twin problem of "automation bias" is identified by Carr (2014):

> It creeps in when people give undue weight to the information coming through their monitors. Even when the information is wrong or misleading, they believe it. Their trust in the software becomes so strong that they ignore or discount other sources of information, including their own senses. If you've ever found yourself lost or going around in circles after slavishly following flawed or outdated directions from a GPS device or other digital mapping tool, you've felt the effects of automation bias.
>
> (p. 69)

Like lemmings, we follow the lead of our machines, accepting the fact of our powerlessness as an "underlying – [albeit] veiled – truth" (Birkerts, 2015, p. 57). In effect, the machines – and the businesses behind them – end up running the people, as human beings serve their purposes and become *their* slaves and enablers rather than the other way around.[2]

We are allowing machines to take over whole areas of activity that used to be performed by human beings and trusting in their power to do things better than we can do them ourselves. We are personifying our dumb machines as "intelligent beings" that are able to lead and also to partner us, even to participate in (to create and to understand) human meaning or meaningful activity. We have gone too far in the way we are humanizing our Great Brains, our computers, our electronic devices, and putting our trust in them. For after all, they have no living parts, no self-awareness, no emotions, no ability to empathize or to return our trust. They are missing all of our "animal parts" – and indeed, any sort of actual soft-tissue, chemically fed brain. Human beings are *alive*: we have a beating heart, and our parts are warm and soft. We should not forget that all of this equating of us to our machines, and them to us, is based on analogy and metaphor.

The comparison of humans to machines is at best simplistic and at worst dead wrong. So is the equating of human language to machine language, or *its* language, that of binary code. In naturalizing machines as human and vice versa, we are losing awareness of the ways in which we are so much more than they are, and so very different. Literature and book culture can help us regain the sense of humanity's gifts and special nature as a species, our superiority over our machines, and help us regain the vision and the strength of character needed to reimagine a better world, a better future, with machines as our aids rather than leading the way or taking over. Literature and book culture can help people regain a sense of their own agency and control.

The Need for a Course Correction

Digital media intensify a way of living and behaving that reduces the complexity of human life and changes the human experience to the kinds of experience which can be processed and represented electronically. As Alva Noe reflects, "Brain, body, and world form a process of dynamic interaction. That is where we find ourselves" (Noe, 2009, p. 95). This integrated whole is threatened by our online culture. Richard Kearney warns that we may now be entering a disembodied and immaterialist culture, one in which experience is increasingly removed from real bodily sensation, "vicarious, by proxy, and often voyeuristic" (Kearney, 2014). Kearney characterizes the world of the Internet as one in which "[t]ouch screen replaces touch itself. The cosmos shrinks to a private monitor; each viewer a disembodied self unto itself." Kearney suggests that in this disembodied, immaterialist culture, we sense our own bodies more as image than as flesh. Thus are our real, flesh and blood bodies "excarnated," as the opposite of "incarnated": "if incarnation is the image become flesh, excarnation is flesh become image" (Kearney, 2014).

This is yet another way in which humans come to resemble their technologies, as the Internet is less its physical embodiment than its immaterial embodiment in the fleeting images and visceral experiences which digital technology produces. This kind of digital experience, fragmented and disembodied, reduces the physicality of human life even as it interferes with "the [human] ability to perpetuate by mind and language a nonphysical continuity, that fragile continuity of ideas that we know as civilization" (Bertman, 1998, p. 29). In our extreme information era, our technologies are interrupting our history and the continuity of ideas in our culture and ways of being, breaking up our coherence.

The digital world is an increasingly familiar one for human beings but in many respects remains foreign and even hostile to our species. It is a world obsessed with speed, one that is always on, a world of 24/7 activity that keeps people plugged in from dawn to dawn, encouraging them to spend all of their money by shopping round the clock and also to spend all of their time doing something – anything – as long as they stay online. At the same time, it is a world which for human beings represents a pared down and highly managed environment – a world of illusion and manipulation, of instant gratification and an endless present, without a past or a future. Those who live in this world are caught in a great consumer web of buying and selling everything and anything, and in an endless flow of insignificant activity geared to the mechanical, electronic, and digital world – a world without origins or horizons, devoid of the sense of temporal duration or spatial rootedness.

Without realizing it, people are taking on the characteristics of the online world as driven by the Great Machines, both the capitalist one and the technological one, behind it. It is as if the electronic screen and online network now represents the reality of the world, reflected back to those who live in it a new kind of onscreen, online, disembodied consciousness in which living, breathing human beings become practically inert, the Sitting Dead, unable to move or to do anything but shop and search, text and tweet, all day and all night long. In such a disembodied environment, there is little room for risk or adventure, little opportunity to create unique lives and life stories. In this world of "mass amnesia sustained by the culture of global capitalism" (Crary, 2013, p. 34), the great danger is that we lose our minds, or part of our minds, in the sense of reducing our intelligence as individuals and as a species – our collective memory and thus our culture – and also in the sense of losing or reducing our rationality, that is, our sanity.

It is not that digital culture is alone responsible for these effects, but that digital power and control makes it increasingly difficult to break free from them. It supports information at the expense of wisdom, browsing for fragments of knowledge and experience rather than exploring the mind and the inner self in deep thinking and reading. It flattens people out rather than making them well-rounded; it breaks them up and makes them lose their sense of coherence. Is it possible to return to a way of experiencing life in a fuller, more coherent, and more meaningful way? Roche (2004) argues for the value of reading and literate culture in maintaining and reinforcing a sense of human value and coherence:

> [T]he technological age does not easily lend itself to a sense of coherence, but in reading literature and understanding the unfolding narrative of a human life and the developing whole of an artwork, we are encouraged to gain a deeper sense of coherence that may be transferable to reflection on our selves, on the hidden logic of our own development.
>
> *(p. 211)*

By experiencing through literature the behaviors, the feelings, and the values of a fully realized and fully articulated human life and culture – those supported by literary text rather than the vapid texts of information and digital screens – people are able to gain back a sense of who and what they are as civilized human beings.

Note

1 The inability to distinguish reality from illusion and fakery in what people say, such as real news from fake news, truth from "truthiness," is a sign of disintegration of the very foundation of the human social order, which is established on a baseline of truth, trust, and shared understandings of what words mean.

2 Carr (2014), near the end of *The Glass Cage* (pp. 224–227), rejects "the master-slave metaphor" (p. 226) for the relationship of humans to technology as a distortion, since in his view, tools do not have an agency that is independent from the tool user. As our discussion here makes clear, we believe the master-slave metaphor captures something important in that relationship.

References

Baudrillard, Jean (1994). *Simulacra and simulation* (trans. Sheila F. Glaser). Ann Arbor: University of Michigan Press.

Bertman, Stephen (1998). *Hyperculture: The human cost of speed*. Westport, CT: Praeger.

Birkerts, Sven (2015). *Changing the subject: Art and attention in the Internet age*. Minneapolis, MN: Graywolf Press.

Bruce, Bertram C., & Hogan, Maureen P. (1998). The disappearance of technology: Toward an ecological model of literacy. In David Reinking, Michael McKenna, Linda Labbo, & Ronald D. Kieffer (eds.), *Handbook of literacy and technology: Transformations in a post-typographic world* (pp. 269–281). Hillsdale, NJ: Lawrence Erlbaum.

Bruni, Frank (2014). Demanding more from college. *The New York Times*, Sunday Review. September 7, 2014, p. 3.

Carr, Nicholas (2010). *The shallows: What the Internet is doing to our brains*. New York: W. W. Norton & Co.

Carr, Nicholas (2011/2008). Is Google making us stupid? In Mark Bauerlein (ed.), *The digital divide: Arguments for and against Facebook, Google, texting, and the age of social networking* (pp. 63–75). New York: Jeremy P. Tarcher/Penguin. Originally appeared in *The Atlantic*, July/August 2008.

Carr, Nicholas (2014). *The glass cage: How our computers are changing us*. New York: W.W. Norton & Co.

Costa-Lima, Luiz (1996). *The limits of voice: Montaigne, Schlegel, Kafka*. Palo Alto, CA: Stanford University Press.

Crary, Jonathan (2013). *24/7: Late capitalism and the ends of sleep*. New York: Verso Press.

Dougherty, Conor (2015). Put down the phone. *The New York Times*, Sunday Review. July 12, 2015, p. 3.

Harris, Michael (2014). *The end of absence: Reclaiming what we've lost in a world of constant connection*. New York: Current.

Hedges, Chris (2009). *Empire of illusion: The end of literacy and the triumph of spectacle*. New York: Nation Books.

Kearney, Richard (2014). Losing our touch. *The New York Times*, Sunday Review. August 31, 2014, p. 4.

Khatchadourian, Raffi (2015). We know how you feel. *The New Yorker*. January 19, 2015, pp. 50–59.

Lanier, Jaron (2011/2010). *You are not a gadget: A manifesto*. New York: Vintage Books. Also excerpted in Lanier, Jaron (2010). The serfdom of crowds. *Harper's Magazine*. February 2010, pp. 15–19.

Leslie, Ian (2014). *The desire to know and why your future depends on it.* New York: Basic Books.

Levitin, Daniel J. (2014). Hit the reset button in your brain. *The New York Times*, Sunday Review. August 10, 2014, p. 5.

Marantz, Andrew (2015). The virologist: How a young entrepreneur built an empire by repackaging memes. *The New Yorker*, Annals of Media. January 5, 2015, pp. 20–26.

McLuhan, Marshall (1964). *Understanding media: Extensions of man.* New York: Mentor.

Noe, Alva (2009). *Out of our heads: Why you are not your brain, and other lessons from the biology of consciousness.* New York: Hill and Wang.

Pang, Alex Soojung-Kim (2013). *The distraction addiction: Getting the information you need and the communication you want, without enraging your family, annoying your colleagues, and destroying your soul.* New York: Little Brown and Company.

Pang, Alex Soojung-Kim (2015). Hacking the great distractor: How to use your smartphone to project your attention, rather than squander it. *The Pennsylvania Gazette*, *113*(3), 14–15.

Pennington, Martha C. (2001). Writing minds and talking fingers: Doing literacy in an electronic age. In P. Brett (ed.), *CALL in the 21st century* (CD-ROM). Barcelona: ESADE Institute (Idiomas) and Hove, U.K.: IATEFL. Papers from a conference sponsored jointly by ESADE Institute (Idiomas), Barcelona, and IATEFL CALL SIG, June 30–July 2, 2000.

Pennington, Martha C. (2004). Cycles of innovation in the adoption of information technology: A view for language teaching. *Computer-Assisted Language Learning*, 17, 7–33.

Poe, Marshall T. (2011). *A history of communications: Media and society from the evolution of speech to the Internet.* New York: Cambridge University Press.

Roche, Mark W. (2004). *Why literature matters in the 21st century.* New Haven, CT: Yale University Press.

Schirato, Tony, & Webb, Jen (2004). *Understanding the visual.* Thousand Oaks, CA: Sage Publications.

Silverman, Jacob (2015). *Terms of service: Social media and the price of constant connection.* New York: HarperCollins.

Turkle, Sherry (2012). *Alone together: Why we expect more from technology and less from each other.* New York: Basic Books.

Virilio, Paul (2010). *The futurism of the instant: Stop eject.* Oxford: Polity Press.

Wajcman, Judy (2014). *Pressed for time: The acceleration of life in digital consumerism.* Chicago: University of Chicago Press.

Wasik, Bill (2015). Welcome to the age of digital imperialism. *The New York Times Magazine*, The Tech & Design Issue. June 7, 2015, pp. 16–20.

Waxler, Robert P., & Hall, Maureen P. (2011). *Transforming literacy: Changing lives through reading and writing.* Leiden and Boston: Brill.

Wieseltier, Leon (2015). Among the disrupted. *The New York Times*, Book Review. January 18, 2015, pp. 1, 14–15.

4

LIVING LIFE ONSCREEN AND ONLINE

All the things that bind us together and make life worth living – community, family, friendship – thrive on the one thing we never have enough of: time.
– *Carl Honoré,* In Praise of Slowness: How a Worldwide Movement Is Challenging the Cult of Speed *(Honoré, 2004, p. 9)*

Internet Overload: Creating an Extreme Type A Society

Over the past 50 years, we have become increasingly aware of the extent to which our inventions shape us as much as we shape them. In *Future Shock*, Alvin Toffler had already suggested that people would be overwhelmed with information overload in the fast-approaching future (Toffler, 1970). More recently, Poe (2011) has described the trend to amass increasing amounts of information, noting "how audiovisual media engendered the practice of pervasive (and often intrusive) documentation. The Internet continues this trend" (p. 243).

Since at least 1996, the Internet has been recording a good percentage of the *new* spoken, written, printed, recorded, photographed, or filmed messages that passed over it. ... But just as significantly, the Web is assimilating the pre-Internet past as well. For well over a decade now, institutions of every shape, size, and purpose have busied themselves with the digitization and posting of artifacts that were not "born digital." The scope of this project is mind boggling: every government record, every corporate record, every clerical record – pretty much everything ever written, printed, or photographed by an agency of one sort or another. Google and a consortium of academic libraries alone plan to scan and make available somewhere around

32 million books. This may seem like a lot of information, but it may be exceeded as individuals and their families get into the act.

(Poe, 2011, p. 243, original emphasis)

Assured that all this information is useful to someone at some time, and fearful that we may in the future need or want to know something that is contained in some information source somewhere, we are being led to collect it all, every last bit of information. However, as Teddy Wayne maintains, "in the midst of the streaming era" of 24-hour news, availability of "entire seasons of TV shows" and "most movies ... at any time," and "the [ceaseless] flow of the Internet and social media, ... this eternal retrievability of anything online ... panics us" (Wayne, 2015). Only our computers can keep up with all this information and flow of content, while only individual human beings can decide what information or content is in fact worth knowing about – or writing about. Humans understand that communication must be selective to be significant: saying anything, or everything, is not the same as saying something.

Isn't it better to have all the information there is available, ready for access as needed or desired? Perhaps not. In the words of David Shenk, "As we have accrued more and more of it, information has emerged not only as a currency, but also as a pollutant" (Shenk, 1997, p. 30). Shenk described the condition of modern humans at the end of the 20th century as engulfed in

> "data smog," ... the noxious muck and druck of the information age. Data smog gets in the way; it crowds out quiet moments, and obstructs much-needed contemplation. It spoils conversation, literature, and even entertainment. It thwarts skepticism, rendering us less sophisticated as consumers and citizens. It stresses us out.
>
> Data smog is not just the pile of unsolicited catalogs and spam arriving daily in our home and electronic mailboxes. It is also information that we pay handsomely for, that we *crave* – the seductive, mesmerizing quick-cut television ads and the twenty-four hour up-to-the-minute news flashes ...; it is also the Web sites we eagerly visit before and after dinner, ... and the dozens of channels we flip through whenever we get a free moment.
>
> The blank spaces and silent moments in life are fast disappearing. Mostly because we have asked for it, media is everywhere.
>
> *(Shenk, 1997, p. 31)*

As the "blank spaces and silent moments in life are ... disappearing" (Shenk, 1997, p. 31), so are the opportunities for the "digressive wanderings" (Percy, 2015) of the human mind that occur when the brain is not otherwise occupied. Making time and space for such digressive wanderings not only helps maintain stress at a healthy level but also promotes the formation of new mental connections that result in "*aha!* moments" of insight and creativity which Oprah

Winfrey is so fond of pointing out. These digressive wanderings occur not only in the shower, in bed on first awakening, or when taking a leisurely stroll, but also in the other moments people spend alone and in solitary contemplation with a good book. Such moments allow book readers to create time and interior mental space to explore the depth of themselves, so that they might reflect on who they are and who they might become.

Now well into that distant future predicted by Toffler, those living today find that change is happening so fast that even the present is disorienting. "[T]he blinding speed and overwhelming power of digital technology in its relentless march to engulf the entire human sensorium" (Waxler & Hall, 2011, p. 151) threatens human experience, limiting people's ability to discover and explore the vast possibilities of their interior landscape. Writing in 1991, Jerry Mandler observed:

> In our society, speed is celebrated as if it were a virtue in itself. And yet as far as most human beings are concerned, the acceleration of the information cycle has only inundated us with an unprecedented amount of data, most of which is unusable in any practical sense. The true result has been an increase in human anxiety, as we try to keep up with the growing stream of information. Our nervous systems experience the acceleration more than our intellects do. It's as if we were all caught at a socially approved video game, where the information on the screen comes faster and faster as we earnestly try to keep up.
>
> *(Mandler, 1991, p. 64)*

Within the same decade that Mandler had warned against celebrating speed as a virtue unto itself, Bertman took up this argument in his book, *Hyperculture: The Human Cost of Speed* (Bertman, 1998). In Bertman's view, people's constant interactions with computers are in fact changing the human reality to be more computer-like and so less hospitable or comfortable for human beings in terms of our natural rhythms: "the more our society depends upon electronic information flow and entertainment, the more our everyday lives need to keep up with its speed-of-light pace, since our economic and emotional existence is wired into its circuitry" (Bertman, 1998, p. 4).

This was almost two decades ago, when Bertman (1998) could only see the situation getting worse: "The media we use, rather than allowing us to relax as a result of their efficiency, will instead keep revving us up with their infectious speed" (pp. 4–5), making it harder and harder to keep up. Honoré (2004) makes the point that

> the human brain is hardwired for speed. We get a kick from the danger, the buzz, the thrilling, throbbing, heady surge of sensory input that comes from going fast. Speed triggers the release of two chemicals – epinephrine and norepinephrine – that also course through the body during sex.
>
> *(pp. 33–34)*

A society built on speed is both self-reinforcing and ever accelerating, becoming one in which the pace of life keeps increasing, continually reinforcing a sense of the need to stay busy and to keep up. Such a society can be described as one with a Type A personality, or, to use Bertman's (1998) term, a "hyperculture":

> A hyperculture is a culture that is easily bored and readily distracted, one in which entertainment is transformed from an occasional personal and group diversion to a way of life, occupying all the interstices between periods of work. Quickly exhausting its energy reserves, a hyperculture continually demands refuelling. Rejecting the acquisition of perspective as necessarily too time-intensive an activity, it craves instead to be injected with doses of short-term stimulation. For the hyperculture is a society of "busy bodies," frenetically striving to keep up, not simply out of economic necessity but out of psychological preference.
>
> *(Bertman, 1998, p. 123)*

Bertman's insights echo those of Boorstin (1961) about Americans' escalating desires for immediate satisfaction and are also echoed in Harari's (2015) conclusion that we humans are constantly "seeking little more than our own comfort and amusement" (p. 416).

Honoré (2004) comments that the cost of hyper-speed may be especially high for children, who suffer effects in the quality of their lives and in their physical and mental health:

> Living like high-powered grown-ups leaves little time for the stuff that childhood is all about: messing around with friends, playing without adult supervision, daydreaming. It also takes a toll on health, since kids are even less able to cope with the sleep deprivation and stress that are the price of living hurried, hectic lives.
>
> *(p. 10)*

Honoré (2004) reports that psychologists who would normally be treating adolescents for anxiety are now treating "children as young as five suffering from upset stomachs, headaches, insomnia, depression and eating disorders" (p. 10). He also notes the high rate of teenage suicides in industrial societies. Honoré is one of many now advocating a much slower pace to society, following a "Slow philosophy" that includes walking instead of riding, and doing things like eating dinner and reading without interference from electronic media. We agree that people need more time and space to make sense of the unfolding of their lives, more time and space to dream and to reflect on their experiences *as they are occurring*.

Bertman's analysis of the human costs of speed in an Internet era is especially relevant to a discussion of literary or deep reading, which requires serious time for contemplation and evolution of ideas. His voice can be added to those of others sounding warnings about the fact that "reflection and meditation are functions inconsistent with the computer's nature" (Bertman, 1998, p. 23). Waxler and Hall (2011) maintain that "the rhythm of human life and the human heart" does not match "the rhythm of the flow of electricity and digital bits on an electronic screen" (p. 161). The computer, together with its connected electronic hardware and software, while doubtless aiding many aspects of accessing and creating information, does not have the right natural speed nor the affordances for deep reading of literature. The act of reading literature offline allows readers to set the rhythm and the pace of their activity as their own natural rhythm, giving them a sense of their own human agency instead of ceding control to that ever-accelerating "brakeless car [of technology] rolling downhill" (Bertman, 1998, p. 24).

You Call This Living?

Crary (2013) reinforces the point that people now live an online life in public view whose activities and rhythms are dictated by an always-on digital pulse animated by Big Media and Big Business that threatens to close off people's options for a fully realized human life and sense of self. As Crary (2013) puts it, "24/7 steadily undermines distinctions between day and night, between light and dark, and between action and repose. It is a zone of insensibility, of amnesia, of what defeats the possibility of experience" (p. 17). The 24/7 digital world creates people who are only half awake, going through life as if anesthetized or sleepwalking. Even when asleep, those who are trapped in digital time seem awake to the electronic flow of networked systems running through their consciousness. Caught within the digital flow of never-ending activity, they wake to check their email messages, to browse the latest stock quotes, to get the very latest news bulletin – carrying out these tasks with attention scattered, only half sensate.

Digital die-hards and wannabes can never catch up with the demand for them to stay involved in these activities – to acquire the hot new app or digital device, or to connect to the new or best online group or source – because each new product or context is devised to keep people wanting more. The masters of such apps, devices, and online groups and sources – those behind Microsoft, Apple, Amazon, Google, Facebook, and many other companies – are engaged in "the relentless capture of time and experience" (Crary, 2013, p. 40). In the quick-paced age of mobile devices, huge segments of the population in virtually every country have become online addicts who respond to the apparatus at the expense of almost everything else. Like other kinds of addicts, these people forget their humanity, lose their rationality, and border on incoherence, as they stumble and stutter through life in a digital maze. Their personal identity likewise loses its coherence and is, as Crary (2013) states, "reconfigured so as to facilitate the fabricating of oneself into a jumble of identities that exist only as effects of temporal technological arrangements" (p. 59). Thus do humans become fragmented and disoriented – and, ultimately, distressed by their fraught state and unsatisfying, less-than-full lives.

Those who are immersed within these electronic arrangements are forced to reconfigure themselves as if they were the same as the commodities that these mobile devices relentlessly promote – another sense in which human beings are being redefined in nonhuman (economic, mechanical or machine-enabling, and data-oriented) terms. If one is not to be left out, declared incompetent, or perceived as a dinosaur, one must, it seems, be part of this endless stream of commodified online activity in order to optimize participation in the new world of relentless possibilities. Crary (2013) suggests, echoing points made by Boorstin (1961) some time ago and by Hedges (2009) more recently, that this does not give pleasure but, at best, a temporary sensation – like the fleeting effect of violent games, porno images, or hard drugs.

Being drawn into the "pop" and "bling" mechanics of the machine and the culture that surrounds it, unwary users find themselves caught up in a process that can only lead to "a flattening of response and the replacement of pleasure with the need for repetition" (Crary, 2013, p. 87) as a poor substitute, a form of reinforcement rather than excitement. It is a process that reduces experience and draws those living in the online world into the dynamic of the machine as their way of interacting, robbing human beings of their rootedness in language as a way of connecting directly with other human beings and of conveying their particular lived experience. In Crary's view, this is not a transitional phase that will eventually return to stability as we used to know it, but an apparently permanent dimension of a new order of things. While we find Crary's discussion powerful, we are not ready to agree on this point, as we remain optimistic about the possibilities for a brighter future, one that will return those who are living only half-alive and doing the bidding of Big Business and Big Media to a state of wholeness and agency. The answer is to stop giving pride of place to the Internet and mass communication, reserving a most special place for interaction on a more human scale.

The Digital Lifestyle

We live in an era when those born after 1980, the "Digital Natives," to use terminology popularized by Prensky (2011/2001), experience and interact with the world in ways that differentiate them from a contrasting group of "Digital Immigrants" (ibid.) born earlier who were not exposed to digital devices at a young age. Those who were born in the heyday of the Digital Age find electronic gadgets compelling and easy to use: the devices are to them entirely normal, part of the "real world" as they know it – more so than the technologies of the prior age. Harris (2014) illustrates this "brave new world" in relating that his 2-year-old nephew, when given a print magazine, seemed to become frustrated when he tried to swipe a picture on the page with his fingers and nothing happened.

The native inhabitants of the online world interact with their environment and those around them in new, digitally influenced ways that are impacting what they spend their time doing, the ways they play, learn, and socialize. These digital natives are texters, gamers, app users, and Facebook friends. They are the so-called "multitaskers" who simultaneously check and work on their text messages, emails, and web pages as they also browse the Internet and listen to their iPod and perhaps a class lecture all at the same time. They are proud of this skill set and involvement with technology that sets them apart from their parents' and grandparents' generations.

But what does all this multitasking really amount to? As Patricia M. Greenfield notes, "Divided attention," which is part and parcel of digital culture, "is the precursor and prerequisite for multitasking, defined as carrying out more than one task simultaneously" (Greenfield, 2009, p. 70). Research shows that when attention is divided, tasks are performed superficially and often incorrectly or with an error-filled result, using a holistic, scanning mode or a selective, skimming mode of taking in information, in which even short-term memory is only lightly engaged, long-term memory hardly at all. We therefore question whether multitasking can be seen as a form of skilled behavior, based on the impossibility of doing multiple tasks well simultaneously. To perform multitasking means doing the individual tasks with degraded attention and skill – that is, in point of fact, performing the tasks in at best only a semiskilled way and at worst an unskilled way.

It is an interesting example of naturalization that we have already become used to thinking of multitasking as skilled and useful, or necessary, behavior in an online context – thus something that people can benefit from learning. Yet from another perspective, multitasking is a kind of distracted behavior that detracts from task performance as individual tasks remain unfinished or are handled superficially. Moreover, those used to keeping many kinds of activity going at the same time and to the frequent interruptions of being constantly online find it difficult to concentrate on just one thing. In scattering people's attention, breaking their concentration, and dividing the actions of their mind and body over multiple tasks, multitasking reduces their self-control and agency. Thus does the always-on-the-Internet lifestyle manipulate people to do the bidding of those controlling the Internet and all the interconnected media and business interests by making them less deeply involved in what they are doing.

People have increasingly realized the futility of trying to do many things at one time and the value of focusing attention on one task at a time, that is, of "monotasking" or "single-tasking," Verena von Pfetten reports (von Pfetten, 2016). Training attention and concentrating on one thing has long been considered something to be learned and practiced in school, and will presumably get increased curriculum time and be included on standardized tests if monotasking or single-tasking is now reconsidered as an important skill for academic and life success.

Loss of Individuality in the Internet Hive

The question "Who am I?" which has occupied philosophers and theologians through the ages and the questing for an answer which is central to the development of a healthy ego and sense of individuality and confidence is being lost in Internet users' siloized activity and also in their massively interconnected activity as part of the great social network that is the online Hive. Interacting as part of the Internet Hive can be seen as the flip-side of the obsessive solitary activity that heavy digital media users engage in. In both cases, human beings lose their depth and individuality in relation to others, as they spend much of their day disconnected or only lightly and partially connected to others. As a result, they have no coherent sense of self, as they increasingly lose deep and sustained connection with others, thereby also losing the thread of their own life story as part of a human history and community larger than themselves. Without their own story, human beings grow anxious, isolated, and dispossessed. They become nodes in a social network, like bees in a hive, rather than individual human beings on a quest to expand consciousness and enrich culture. Yet, as Socrates said, "The unexamined life is not worth living."

This big conformist Hive, which has been promoted first by television and now by the Internet, represents a lowest-common-denominator orientation that is ultimately a reduction and a dumbing down of humanity. Lanier (2011/2010) accuses "all those hundreds of millions of users of social-networking sites of reducing themselves in order to be able to use the services" (p. 53). He says, "I know quite a few people, most of them young adults, who are proud to say that they have accumulated thousands of friends on Facebook. Obviously, their statements can be true only if the idea of friendship is diminished" (p. 51).

The reduction in human life and individuality as observed in Facebook posts and Facebook friends is a manifestation of a synchronous Hive Mind that thinks it is independent but is actually operating in total concert with the rest of the Hive – like the Borg of *Star Trek*. As posting on Facebook is a degraded form of communication, so interacting with Facebook friends and adopting their views are degraded forms of human interaction. Communication via social media is regimented and constrained in ways that inhibit free and independent thought and action. The Internet therefore does not necessarily promote a diversity of ideas and opinions and in some of its more popular modes is a poor substitute for – even a parody of – democracy.

The follow-the-crowd Hive mentality has fed the increasing information overload and speed of daily life that Mandler, Shenk, and Bertman warned of in the 1990s. The situation is one made worse by people's sense that they must try to keep up with all those Joneses – all those imagined others in the Internet Hive who are supposed to be "in the know," keeping pace with what is trending on the Internet. In his "Future Tense" piece, Wayne (2015) observes that the inability to keep up with all the serials available online creates an "urgent compulsion to catch up, in case you missed" a certain show. The same sense of urgency and compulsion to catch, or catch up to, whatever you might have missed that is creating a buzz in the Internet Hive is a legacy of our increasingly technologically fueled and electronically enabled online lives. We can note in contrast how people absorbed in a book are disconnected from any hive or outside influence, in a world of their own, with no sense of missing or needing to catch up to anything or anyone else.

Especially worrying is that being a member of the massed Internet Hive seems to promote incautious and extreme kinds of follow-the-crowd behaviors that go considerably beyond what individual actors would perform in person, such as cyberbullying, trolling, and other forms of aggressive communication, including death threats and virulent "Twitter storms" (Sykes, 2016). It is as if they are being driven by a force greater than themselves to act in ways that are not their real or usual selves. This is truly Hive behavior, in which the massed energy of a large body of people fuels the behavior of its individual bodies, ultimately overwhelming the logic and the agency of every self-controlling person by the sheer force and momentum of the omni-controlling collective. It is yet another sense in which the "social" aspect of social media is not a positive thing. The promotion of both conformity and extreme behaviors in the Internet Hive, within the onscreen world of illusion, imaging, spectacle, and exploitation, are aptly captured by the in-your-face title of Internet researcher and linguist Claire Hardaker's forthcoming book, *The Antisocial Network* (Hardaker, forthcoming).

Pointing out the ways in which the Internet is an "antisocial network" can help in a project like ours, of trying to move people away from a life lived largely online and in the image of the machine, to one lived largely offline and in the fullness of human experience, interacting and learning with and from the copresence of other human beings and from the great products of human language and imagination in literature. In addition, the fact that more and more people are writing books about the dangers of the Internet reinforces the value of the book as a medium for developing and disseminating the kinds of long-form arguments and complex ideas that can be created through language to counter the short-form idea-bites and sensationalized images of the electronic screen medium. Even more can a literary work stretch the mind as it also exercises the imagination and gives the heart a good workout, too.

Obsessive Digital Activity

As Bertman (1998) observed, "Electronic technology radically contracts the interval between need and fulfillment. And therein lies its ability to amplify the power of now" (p. 23). In focusing attention visually and on the here and now, the Internet overstimulates.

In the face of overstimulation, the distinction between what is more important and what is less important can easily be lost. ... Forced to handle too much data, the individual may practice "psychological absenteeism": avoiding responsibility and decisions, chemically insulating his psyche from the reality, and seeking various forms of sensual gratification as substitutes for understanding. Just as the pupil of the eye contracts in response to excessive light, so the receptors of the mind contract in response to excessive information.

(Bertman, 1998, p. 21)

The power of now is also expanded by de-historicizing information, putting all of the information that ever was on the Internet:

Like some enormous gravitational force, the Internet is sucking the past into its vast memory banks. That digitized past will be affixed to the ever-expanding present of born-digital information, at which point the "what came before" will be one seamless digital archive.

(Poe, 2011, p. 243)

Thus will those who live on the Internet increasingly live in one place and time, or outside of any place and time, thereby losing the multidimensional connectedness and rootedness of human life.

As we have already described, a general consequence of the ways in which digital and online culture is developing is an increasing focus on the here and now. In the context of Facebook and texting, people are frequently updating their posts to tell or to show in their selfies or live-stream videos where they are, what they are doing, and how they are feeling at a given moment. Their lives are becoming increasingly self-centered, self-referential, and trivialized. Rather than probing the depths of themselves and how they fit in the world, they obsessively avoid addressing such issues by brief forays into literally locating themselves in the instant, rather than paying attention to the slow unfolding of events. This obsessive updating and publicizing of current status and activities seems to be filling an important psychological need, especially for young people, maybe because a more in-depth and long-term focus is too frightening, given the state of the world. They do not seem to have the tools they need to face the larger issues surrounding them beyond the minutiae of the trivial and the here and now – just such tools as are provided by a study of literature and other human arts.

Controlling the world of their flat screens offers, at best, a very temporary and minimal sense of being in control that is, however, an illusion: all that is controlled is the one-dimensional world of the screen, with the sense of control provided by merely manipulating images on the screen. People, and especially young people, are controlling the little space and world in front of them, what is happening on the screen – often as a substitute for control of other aspects of life. And they are controlling very little even there: the medium dictates the parameters of what they can in fact control, and it pressures to certain kinds of activity and a certain order of activity. They may think they control the tasks they take up, but these are subtly and not so subtly controlled by the forces of Big Media, often in collaboration with Big Business, and by the ginormous Internet Hive and its faddism – sweeping like a great tsunami wave across cyberspace (and hence also geographical space). They are jumping to add new content and "friends" on Facebook so they can continually expand and update their little corner of that context – but always in the terms defined by the space itself and by the social networking Hive. They think they control the order in which they multitask, but in fact, they are responding to emails and text messages, no matter how insignificant, before all else. Their online activity amounts to an obsession, or many different kinds of obsession.

In addition to consuming a lot of time and energy, all of this online activity is creating negative psychological effects, such as increased stress levels in university students related to the "endless barrage of alerts and notifications" and "higher anxiety levels and dissatisfaction with life" (Wortham, 2014) reported by university students who are heavy cell phone users. Some scientists are now speaking of "Internet addiction." Jerald J. Block, in an article in the *American Journal of Psychiatry* (Block, 2005), reports great concern about this in the United States as well as in China and South Korea. He reviews the literature on this problem, a type of compulsive-impulsive spectrum disorder with subtypes of excessive gaming, sexual preoccupations, and email/text messaging. All of these forms of Internet addiction, according to Block, are characterized by:

excessive use	loss of sense of time or a neglect of basic drives;
withdrawal	feelings of anger, tension, and/or depression when the computer is inaccessible;
tolerance	the need for better computer equipment, more software, or more hours of use;
negative repercussions	arguments, lying, poor achievement, social isolation, and fatigue.

(Block, 2005, p. 306, original emphasis)

These symptoms of Internet addiction can be found in many of those who grew up with and on the Internet, the "natives" of the digital world. Frances E. Jensen, a neurologist who wrote, with Amy Ellis Nutt, *The Teenage Brain: A Neuroscientist's Survival Guide to Raising Adolescents and Young Adults* (Jensen, 2015), notes that young people, whose brains are still developing, are especially prone to risk-taking behavior and may develop addictions as a form of learning without good impulse control.

A recent book by Mary Aiken, a psychologist specializing in cyber-forensics, titled *The Cyber Effect: A Pioneering Cyberpsychologist Explains How Human Behavior Changes Online* (Aiken, 2016), recounts numerous cases of negative effects of time spent on the Internet that can be classified as addictions, risky behaviors, and other kinds of seriously negative psychological effects involving abnormal or criminal behavior. Aiken relates these to a general tendency for "human behavior [to be] amplified and accelerated online by … an almost predictable mathematical multiplier, the *cyber effect*, the $E = mc^2$ of this century" (p. 5, original emphasis). In our view, it is the overstimulating and the desensitizing properties of the Internet and the digital screen culture that lead to impulsivity, loss of control, and disengagement. The overstimulating nature of the Internet and the digital screen culture can be seen in the time-and-attention-consuming, obsessive, and addictive behaviors of gaming, which is a major activity for many children and young adults, and texting, which has become the main focus of the time and attention of a great majority of the under-30 generation. Both the overstimulating and the desensitizing effects of the Internet can be seen in the increasing number and increasingly graphic nature of pornographic and violent images that result from the escalation built into Internet algorithms determining the content presented to viewers. Aiken (2016) describes this automatic escalation as follows:

> The essential problem lies with the search algorithms. They are designed to speedily deliver listings of the most frequently searched phrases. Extreme content and scary scenarios, which always draw the most adult eyeballs, can be presented first regardless of the searcher's age – due to the popularity of the sensational information.
>
> *(p. 146)*

The combination of extreme behavior and social disinhibition shown in online sexual exhibitionism and in cyberbullying exemplify the combined effects of overstimulation and desensitization that these algorithms promote.

Aiken raises alarms about the many dangers lurking on the Internet and in common digitally centered pursuits that can become obsessive and harmful to both psychological and physical health, even leading in some cases to death. She cites the case of a boy who jumped out the window of a tall building after continuously playing World of Warcraft for 36 hours in a gaming marathon, "having left behind a note saying that he wanted to join the heroes of the game" (Aiken, 2016, p. 71). British journalist Simon Parkin, in *Death by Video Game: Danger, Pleasure, and Obsession on the Virtual Frontline* (Parkin, 2016), presents a bird's-eye view of video gamers and gaming and why those online games are so all-consuming that they often become obsessive and dangerous – to the literal point where "people are dying to play video games" (p. 10). Parkin's book is an attempt to understand the power and dynamics of video games that can even be deadly, offering "an investigation into a slew of deaths in which young men and, occasionally, women have been found dead at their keyboards after extended periods of video-game playing" (ibid.).[1]

Aiken's and Parkin's books add to the concerns raised by Turkle in *Alone Together* (Turkle, 2012) about the serious effects of the solitary activity and "aloneness" bred of digitally focused activity and in her next book, *Reclaiming Conversation* (Turkle, 2015), about a technology-induced "crisis in empathy" resulting from focusing on the digital screen instead of on face-to-face interaction through conversation. It is a mark of addiction that people have trouble pulling themselves away from the screen and digital activity such as gaming and texting; they do not look up, much less talk, to their closest friends and family members sitting nearby. Even such intimate activities as making love to a partner or breastfeeding a child may command less attention than the digital screen. Aiken (2016) suggests the possibility of an "evolutionary blip" (p. 94) resulting from lack of mothers' eye contact with their babies as they stare instead at the screens of their hand-held devices. It seems that the increasingly all-engulfing culture of digital activity is showing signs of becoming hazardous to human life in a number of ways.

Have we reached the point where the spread of people's, especially young people's, addiction to the Internet might be termed an *epidemic*? Surely this term *can* be applied, at least metaphorically, to the rapid rise of addictive gaming and other forms of incessant online activity such as texting, tweeting, and updating Facebook posts among the digital generation. This is what might be considered the weak sense of "epidemic" as applied to the spread of incessant online activity. Given that the term "epidemic" is generally reserved for the transmission of physical illness person to person, we might ask whether its strong, non-metaphorical sense applies as well: is it an accurate factual or scientific depiction of the very rapid spread of negative psychological effects such as those described above for gaming, which it can be noted easily lead to related negative physical effects? In other words, *must* the term be applied, simply, as an accurate description of what is going on?[2]

The question as to whether the spread of Internet addiction is accurately described as an epidemic does not have an easy answer, especially given that the word "epidemic" is not a neutral term but rather one imbued with fear and suggesting serious consequences. Whether the term "epidemic" is applied in any particular case is therefore not merely a decision about the facts of the case but is also a political decision. Given the danger of an epidemic, it is also an ethical decision. In consideration of the negative consequences of epidemics, there are cases when the term *should* be applied, for the general welfare of all those who are or might be affected by the phenomenon under consideration, as a warning. We suggest that the use of the term "epidemic" may be appropriately applied in this ethical sense, in order to raise a red flag about what young people are doing online, and, moreover, to suggest the need for a cure. What we prescribe is large and regular doses of literature, combined with plenty of rest time offline. That should help cure what ails these young people: it is just what the doctor (actually, we two Ph.D. doctors) ordered.

What Young People Are Doing Online

What in fact are young people doing online? A Parent-Teen Cell Phone Survey that was part of the 2009 Pew Research Center's Internet & American Life Project (Lenhart, Purcell, Smith, & Zickuhr, 2010a, 2010b) showed American teens using the Internet for the activities of:

- connecting to a social networking site;
- getting news or information about current events or politics;
- buying things online (e.g., books, clothing, music);
- online sharing of artwork, photos, stories, or videos;
- finding content (e.g., songs, text, or images) to reuse and remix in their own artistic creations;
- searching for information about health, dieting, physical fitness, drug use, sexual health, or depression;
- creating or working on a journal or blog;
- using Twitter; and
- visiting virtual worlds such as Gaia or Second Life.

These results suggest that the Internet has fulfilled its original purpose of providing information freely, in addition to the commercial purposes behind Facebook and dot-com sites selling products. The free-access side of the Internet is, however, constantly threatened by the commercial side, so that the information which can be obtained online, just like other products and resources, is likely not to be available entirely freely – either in the sense of being offered at no charge or in the sense of being offered uncurated by some entity controlling some part of Internet access or activity. The fact that a great deal of what Internet users are exposed to is filtered and channeled by commercial interests may not be of great concern to those who grew up in an online universe, since it is what they are used to, and may in fact be below their level of awareness. That is why we in the "straddle generation" (Harris, 2014, p. x) who are concerned about such commercial filtering and channeling of Internet content need to speak up.

The 2009 Pew survey results (Lenhart et al., 2010a, 2010b) indicated that wireless connectivity using Internet and cell phones was increasing among the Millennials, and that Facebook was the social network of choice. The study reported teens spending a great deal of time texting, instant messaging, and creating content for Facebook, such as posting selfies or commenting on Facebook friends' pictures or walls. The information given in the 2009 survey can be updated based on data gathered by Pew researchers in 2013 showing that almost all (98%) of Americans under the age of 30 are Internet users and that most (90%) of the under-30s also frequent social networking sites, branching out from Facebook to also use Instagram, Snapchat, and Twitter – the latter used by over a third of young people aged 16–29 and over half of those aged 16–17 (Zickuhr &

Rainie, 2014). The 2013 Pew survey indicates a very high use of technology in all age groups, with most people having a cell phone and more than 75 percent of Americans aged 16–29 having a smartphone, over 40 percent in this age group having a tablet computer, and almost 25 percent having an e-reader. It also shows continuing high social media activity in all age groups, with Facebook still predominating even as other services gain users.

Since 2013, smartphones have largely replaced "non-smart" cell phones and are also generally preferred over tablet computers for quick and portable connection to the Internet. Facebook's acquisition in 2012 of Instagram and in 2014 of WhatsApp Messenger service, the most popular messaging service for smartphones, together with its introduction in 2016 of a "Live" feature allowing real-time video streaming, will perhaps help ensure its majority share in social media for some time into the future – although, given the rapidly changing digital landscape, this is by no means assured. At any rate, it seems certain that Facebook and other online social platforms, and the services and companies providing technical and media support, data capture and analysis, and the informational resources and products which online customers desire, will continue to exert a strong influence on the young as well as on the growing numbers of adults in both the born-digital and digital-adopter cohorts, and that they will do so with an ever greater degree of "anywhere-anytime" access. The trend seems to be for the share of people's time and attention that is directed to online activity to keep on growing while the share that is directed to offline activity keeps on shrinking.

The Need for a Culture Beyond the Internet and Popular Culture

Whether or not they stress the "always-on" interconnectivity or the solitariness of Internet activity, most critics of a life lived online agree that our so-called "social media" are causing humans to lose social capacities that are critical to interaction with other human beings in contexts outside the Internet, and some critics are pointing to the development or reinforcement of antisocial tendencies by online activity and to further harmful psychological and physical effects of living in a digital world. As we maintain, engagement with literature is a way to counter this negative redefinition of human social life. Engagement with literature can help to move young people offline and give their lives more dimensionality and depth of meaning than they are now experiencing, thus countering two kinds of trends identified in a 2014 survey of 1,200 undergraduates by the market research firm Student Monitor (www.studentmonitor.com/), as reported in *The New York Times* Education Life supplement of February 8, 2015 (Trending: A Few of Their Favorite Things, 2015). The *Times* listing of the top 15 selections of "in" things on campus by the sample of college students shows that the majority of those "in" things, 9 out of 15, involve digital devices, activities, or sites (the numbers represent rank order):

- digital devices – Apple iPhone (1), Apple iPad (5), Laptops (11);
- digitally enabled activities – texting (3), taking photos with mobile phone (15);
- digitally accessed sites – Facebook (4), Instagram (6), Snapchat (8), Twitter (10).

The only other choices reported to make the top 15 were coffee (2), drinking beer (7), working out (9), hooking up (12), going out to clubs/bars (13), and college football (14). This survey highlights the strong pull of digital technologies and activities surrounding those technologies while also painting a broader picture of college students' focus away from their studies, as the only possible connection to schoolwork is "Laptops," which is only at 11th place. It is perhaps not surprising to learn that college life centers not on the life of the mind but on social life – both that of beer drinking, clubbing, and hooking up, and the kind of circumscribed social life provided in digital media. We would nonetheless like to argue the need to counterbalance these forms of "culture-lite" by attempts to engage young people with the life of the mind, such as by reading literature.

Denby (2016) expresses his concern about the ultimate outcomes of young people living their lives plugged into their computers rather than reading and discussing Great Books offline:

> Perhaps no one can say definitively how much teenagers gain or lose by obsessively playing games, obsessively using social media and the Internet (evidence exists on both sides of the case), but we can be sure they lose an enormous amount by not reading very seriously. The ability to understand the world and other people can't be created on screens alone. The ability to recognize lies and stupidity can't be created there either.
>
> *(p. 230)*

As Denby agrees, reading literature, especially in book form, can enhance the depth of human life and understanding, as deep reading calls for full attention and evokes self-reflection and contemplation. The activity of individual readers and of communities of readers who contemplate and discuss Great Books offers an important counterculture to the popular culture mainstream – to pop culture or "culture-lite" – not only for teenagers and college students but also for all children, and everyone, helping to ensure a richer, fuller life.

A Literary Example of the Clash of the Generations: *Super Sad True Love Story: A Novel*

The difference between the digitally focused generation and those who straddle the earlier book generation is captured well in the two characters of the young Eunice Park, daughter of Korean immigrants, and the older Lenny Abramov, son of Russian immigrants, in Gary Shteyngart's best-selling satirical novel, *Super Sad True Love Story: A Novel* (Shteyngart, 2010). The story is set in America in a dystopian future that is not far from the present and that reflects some of the concerns we have now about where our world is tending.

The generation of students whom we now encounter in the classroom have grown up with digital screens. They are very much like Eunice, who majored in Images and "verbals" in Digital, spending a lot of her time scanning streams of texts on Globalteens (an advanced Facebook application). Like one of the high school students that Denby (2016) observed, who said that books smelled like old people, Eunice thinks books are smelly old artifacts, reminders of a decaying past, death itself. Reading a book is something so foreign to her that she was amazed to see Lenny Abramov, who eventually becomes her boyfriend, absorbed in a book.

By way of contrast with digital-generation Eunice, Lenny, 15 years older, whom she sees as a dinosaur, is one of the last of the long-form readers, a lover of words and books, novels by Tolstoy and Chekhov, and one of those who still keeps a book-form diary that he fills daily with his handwritten observations. Part of the link generation, Lenny uses email and is sometimes drawn further into the digital world through the advanced smartphone that he, along with everyone else in this near-future scenario, uses for online social interaction, shopping, and broadcasting of personal information. Lenny is saddened because he senses that something in language and life is fading from the world, as it becomes increasingly one geared to and managed by the omniscient and omnipresent machine – a scenario reminiscent of George Orwell's Big Brother future in *1984* (Orwell, 1949).

Lenny and Eunice's love story is set within a near future in which book culture has been replaced by obsessive screen watching, data mining, and live streaming of one's moment-to-moment activities and status on digital devices, and in which people's social and economic standing is updated continuously and automatically from information about them that is available online. The story depicts a world that is close to our present state of affairs and that seems worryingly possible as a projection of where we might be headed. The possible world Shteyngart paints is one in which conformity and consumerism not only are central values, but are encouraged by a government trying to control an increasingly chaotic situation in the face of a looming economic crisis. His novel thus proves to be a doubly "super sad" and "true" story, a human tragedy played out on both a small and a large scale, reflecting the deep truths that can be told in fiction and the sort of idiosyncratic and at the same time more widely applicable case history which Vendler (2015) maintains is the value of artistic writing.

We wonder how long it will be before the emotional depth and heartfelt connection that comes from offline reading and human interaction will be made numb by the powerful influence of the digital environment. Most of our students reading on a Kindle or a Nook may still be reading, but reading online or with a digital device is a different experience from the reading of print. Screen reading is more restricted than page reading, is a different visual experience, and makes available and so invites other kinds of online activities that interrupt the reading process. We fear that through the screen students are not reading with the imaginative and embodied depth experienced through a book that both invites and requires sustained focus and concentration. Nor will these students know what such experience signifies unless they continue to exercise what Maryanne Wolf, in *Proust and the Squid: The Story and Science of the Reading Brain*, calls the "reading brain" (Wolf, 2007) through engagement with printed books. We also believe that they need to be spending significant time offline doing other things, especially interacting face-to-face in dialogue with other human beings.

Notes

1 As Parkin (2016) concludes from his research on video gaming: "We consume a book, but a game consumes us. It leaves us reeling and bewildered, hungry and ghosted in the fug of chronoslip" (p. 24) – a state in which the player slips out of time and space, into a sort of out-of-body experience that takes place in a fantasyland of virtual reality where the player may lose awareness of physical needs. We note that gaming tends to take over and consume a person's time and attention, as texting and other online communicative activity also tend to do, but seems to "consume" the person's mind and whole being to a greater extent than other types of focal online activity, "compelling [some] young people," as Parkin (2016) puts it, "to emigrate from reality into their virtual dimensions beyond the natural limits of their well-being" (p. 10).

2 Part of the answer could be seen to lie in whether this addiction is spread by people-to-people contact. Given that some epidemics are spread by indirect people-to-people contact, as when their germs are left on surfaces that other people touch or spread by international flights, it is at least arguable that addictive digital behaviors are spread people to people – by game developers who spread the seeds of addiction to those who frequent gaming sites, by those users who compete with each other in online games, and by those who are online social media "friends" or texting and tweeting buddies. Is their spread rather a new form of machine-to-people contact that amounts to a new mode of transmission of ill-health effects? Or is it more accurately a type of machine-to-machine contact that has negative effects on humans as the users of those machines?

References

Aiken, Mary (2016). *The cyber effect: A pioneering cyberpsychologist explains how human behavior changes online*. New York: Spiegel & Grau.

Bertman, Stephen (1998). *Hyperculture: The human cost of speed*. Westport, CT: Praeger.

Block, Jerald J. (2005). Issues for DSM-V: Internet addiction. *American Journal of Psychiatry*, 165(3) 306–307. doi:10.1176/appi.ajp.2007.07101556.

Boorstin, Daniel J. (1961). *The image: Or what happened to the American dream*. New York: Atheneum.

Crary, Jonathan (2013). *24/7: Late capitalism and the ends of sleep*. New York: Verso Press.

Denby, David (2016). *Lit up: One reporter. Three schools. Twenty-four books that can change lives*. New York: Henry Holt.

Greenfield, Patricia M. (2009). Technology and informal education: What is taught, what is learned. *Science*, 323(5910), 69–71. doi: 10.1126/science.1167190.

Harari, Yuval Noah (2015). *Sapiens: A brief history of humankind*. New York: HarperCollins.

Hardaker, Claire (forthcoming). *The antisocial network*. London: Palgrave Macmillan.

Harris, Michael (2014). *The end of absence: Reclaiming what we've lost in a world of constant connection.* New York: Current.

Hedges, Chris (2009). *Empire of illusion: The end of literacy and the triumph of spectacle.* New York: Nation Books.

Honoré, Carl (2004). *In praise of slowness: How a worldwide movement is challenging the cult of speed.* New York: HarperCollins.

Jensen, Frances E. (with Nutt, Amy Ellis) (2015). *The teenage brain: A neuroscientist's survival guide to raising adolescents and young adults.* New York: HarperCollins.

Lanier, Jaron (2011/2010). *You are not a gadget: A manifesto.* New York: Vintage Books. Also excerpted in Lanier, Jaron (2010). The serfdom of crowds. *Harper's Magazine.* February 2010, pp. 15–19.

Lenhart, Amanda, Purcell, Kristen, Smith, Aaron, & Zickuhr, Kathryn (2010a). *Social media and Internet use among teens and young adults.* February 3, 2010. Washington, DC: Pew Research Center. www.pewinternet.org/~/media//Files/Reports/2010/PIP_Social_Media_and_Young_Adults_Report_Final_with_toplines.pdf

Lenhart, Amanda, Purcell, Kristen, Smith, Aaron, & Zickuhr, Kathryn (2010b). Social media and young adults. *Pew Research Center* website. February 3, 2010. Retrieved on February 20, 2012 from www.pewinternet.org/Reports/2010/Social-Media-and-Young- Adults.aspx.

Mandler, Jerry (1991). *In the absence of the sacred.* San Francisco: Sierra Club.

Orwell, George (1949). *1984.* London: Secker & Warburg.

Parkin, Simon (2016). *Death by video game: Danger, pleasure, and obsession on the virtual frontline.* London: Profile Books Ltd.

Percy, Jen (2015). The war every soldier brings home. Review of Brian Turner's My Life as a Foreign Country. *The New York Times,* Book Review. January 11, 2015, p. 19.

Poe, Marshall T. (2011). *A history of communications: Media and society from the evolution of speech to the Internet.* New York: Cambridge University Press.

Prensky, Marc (2011/2001). Digital natives, digital immigrants. In Mark Bauerlein (ed.), *The digital divide: Arguments for and against Facebook, Google, texting, and the age of social networking* (pp. 3–11). New York: Jeremy P. Tarcher/Penguin. Originally appeared in *On the Horizon 9* (October 2001), 1–6.

Shenk, David (1997). *Data smog: Surviving the information glut.* New York: HarperCollins.

Shteyngart, Gary (2010). *Super sad true love story: A novel.* New York: Random House.

Sykes, Charles J. (2016). Where the right went wrong. *The New York Times,* Sunday Review. December 18, 2016, p. 3.

Toffler, Alvin (1970). *Future shock.* New York: Random House.

Trending: A few of their favorite things (2015). *The New York Times,* Education Life. February 8, 2015, p. 2.

Turkle, Sherry (2012). *Alone together: Why we expect more from technology and less from each other.* New York: Basic Books.

Turkle, Sherry (2015). *Reclaiming conversation: The power of talk.* New York: Penguin Press.

Vendler, Helen (2015). *The ocean, the bird, and the scholar: Essays on poets and poetry.* Cambridge, MA: Harvard University Press.

von Pfetten, Verena (2016). Read this story without distraction (Can you?). *The New York Times,* Fashion & Style. April 29, 2016. Retrieved on October 6, 2016 from www.nytimes.com/2016/05/01/fashion/monotasking-drop-everything-and-read-this-story.html?_r=2#story-continues-1.

Waxler, Robert P., & Hall, Maureen P. (2011). *Transforming literacy: Changing lives through reading and writing.* Leiden and Boston: Brill.

Wayne, Teddy (2015). Lest any bit of data pass you by. *The New York Times*, Sunday Styles, Future Tense. January 4, 2015, p. 2.

Wolf, Maryanne (2007). *Proust and the squid: The story and science of the reading brain*. New York: HarperCollins.

Wortham, Jenna (2014). Trying to live in the moment (and not on the phone). *The New York Times*, Business. October 19, 2014, p. 3.

Zickuhr, Kathryn, & Rainie, Lee (2014). Younger Americans' reading habits and technology use. *Pew Research Center* website. September 10, 2014. Retrieved on February 13, 2015 from www.pewinternet.org/2014/09/10/younger-americans-reading-habits-and-technology-use/.

5

READING ONSCREEN AND ONLINE

Once I was a scuba diver in the sea of words. Now I zip along the surface like a guy on a Jet Ski.
> – *Nicholas Carr, "Is Google Making Us Stupid?"(Carr, 2011/2008, p. 65)*

Text Going Digital

The digital versions of print genres such as newspapers, magazines, and other forms of writing are typically not mere translations or simple uploadings of the offline versions to the online context. They have quickly evolved to new digital genres with interactive features – such as animated text and the ability to jump to different parts of the text and to supplementary material in textual and nontextual forms such as illustrations, music, and video – and with their own aesthetic (Pennington, 2013, 2017). New app and Web versions of stories feature animated characters, the ability to interact with these, to scroll around panoramic views or rooms and street scenes, and to hear text narration. J. D. Biersdorfer describes a website which reworks some African folk stories (Pixel Fable, www.pixelfable. com) and which includes "colorful illustrations that accompany the blocks of brief text," interactive features such as the ability to choose a location, and "augmented reality markers" that can be processed by a webcam to "reveal characters and other story elements floating on the screen" (Biersdorfer, 2015).

Biersdorfer (2015) believes that "the digital bells and whistles of literary apps" have value in attracting new readers and encouraging old readers to revisit texts that they already know, though he realizes "[s]ome may argue that [they] … distract from the already rich text at hand." In fact, these are not necessarily contradictory points, as people are no doubt attracted by "digital bells and whistles" even as these distract from attention to the accompanying text, that is, from absorbing the story in its written form, through a reading process. This process may be more or less backgrounded or even bypassed altogether in favor of optional text narration and various visual and interactive, often game-like, features. It is also notable that at least one of the story apps Biersdorfer describes includes print not in continuous and connected text but only in brief blocks. There can be no doubt that all of these features substantially change the process of interacting with a story. We note the similarity of this multifocal form of reading to multi-tasking, involving a similar scattering of attention; and we predict that reading digital texts will soon be seen, in the naturalization paradigm we mentioned before, as requiring a new type of skill set (though, as in the case of multitasking, we wonder whether this kind of image-and-information mining can in any sense be considered skilled reading).

Putting a book onscreen makes it possible to add many kinds of enhancements to printed text, such as animated words or pictures, links to other information, and video and sound files. These are all features that attract audiences to electronic versions of books and have given them a large audience, especially among the young. Putting a book online also reduces the cost of adding and reproducing such features as color and illustrations – and in general avoids the costs associated with printing on paper. This can be a reason for a publisher to prefer an electronic text, though the high cost of developing the files means that an "enhanced" e-book needs either a high price or high sales to offset the cost of developing added digital features. There is also the feature of portability, which many advo-cates of e-books point to as a major reason to adopt this new form of the book. Not only are e-readers often lighter in weight than a print book, they are able to store hundreds of books, making it much easier to travel with books and poten-tially also alleviating problems of permanently housing large numbers of books, such as the need to add bookshelves to one's living space. There is also the matter of convenience in being able to download books from online booksellers such as Amazon, thus being able to get a desired book immediately and also not needing to travel to bookstores to make a book purchase.

Yet a majority of people still prefer to read from physical books. While most people find that the various kinds of added "bells and whistles" attract their attention, many also complain that they prefer not to have these attractions, which divide their attention and pull them away from the concentrated reading act. In this sense, the added electronic features are more *dis*tractions than attrac-tions, as they interfere with the process of highly engaged reading, in which a person drifts out of the here and now and into the mental world of a story. All those bells and whistles, and the physical properties of the electronic machine, seem to tie the reader to the operation of the device, making it harder to achieve a state of deep reading. As Carr (2011/2008) observes, "The kind of deep reading that a sequence of printed pages promotes" is a form of "deep contemplation" that is "valuable … for the intellectual vibrations those words set off within our own minds" (p. 74).

Printed books help create attention and embodied experience, which enhances the depth, the complexity, and the significance of the reading experience in terms of the thoughts and emotions it triggers and the mental connections it forms to other experiences. These include both the reader's remembered experiences from the past and the immediate physical experience of reading: the touch and the smell of a book, the movement of physically turning pages, the sense of duration and location. The screen tends to work against such possibilities of deep engagement and embodied experience, making reading a less fully human experience, one that does not call on the full capacity of the reader's senses, memory, and active imagination.

The connection of past and present experience is part of the pull of reading literature in a fully engaged way: it takes the reader on a journey into her/himself. In reading literature, the reader is pulled into a story that connects to the reader's own life and becomes part of that personal journey, as it also connects through the reader's own memory and emotions to the lives and experiences of others, as supplemented and enhanced by the experiences of characters in the story. In also triggering the reader's imagination, literature extends the connections of the reader's past and present to the future, making it possible for the reading experience to have profound effects on a person's life journey going forward, literally changing one's life through literature.

Reading in a Digital Environment

Given the fact that teens are reading Facebook pages and searching information and products in online sites, can we conclude that they are doing a fair amount of reading online? It depends on what you mean by reading. How true is it, as some proponents of moving everything onto the Internet say, that people read as much, if not more, in an electronic medium? It is true that the Internet expands the potential access to texts (assuming that all texts can or will become digitized). But it is also true that the electronic medium and the whole screen and commercial culture surrounding it pressures to reduce the time spent on texts, both in writing and in reading them, and also to reduce the focus on the printed word in favor of the visual image. And it appears that the reading which people do online is rather different from the reading that they do offline.

Webtext has a number of properties that differentiate it from printed text, including its:

- *visuality* – emphasis on visual rather than textual or linguistic features;
- *multimodality* – combination of text with other modalities;
- *dynamism* – potentials for movement, action, and interaction;
- *mutability* – ability to be altered;
- *compactness* – orientation to a small space;
- *nonlinearity* – variable directionality and nonsequential properties.

Because of the nature of such texts, reading multimodal pages and digital text involves not only reading comprehension as traditionally described – the recognition and interpretation of words in sequence – but other kinds of acts connecting eye and brain, as well as hands, in the "consumption" – the recognition and interpretation – of images, which tend to take priority over the more laborious and time-consuming process of connected reading. Even linguistic text may be viewed like an image when it appears onscreen (Bruinsma, 2004).

In 1997, Jakob Nielsen of the Nielsen Norman Group began his Alertbox posting for October 1, on "How Users Read on the Web," with the simple response, "They **don't**" (Nielsen, 1997, original emphasis). Since the early 1990s, Nielsen has extensively studied and reported on how people "read" (or **don't** read) web pages (specific studies are available under the Articles tab at the Nielsen Norman Group website, www.nngroup.com), finding a tendency by most people to skim and scan websites and other onscreen pages in an "F" ("fast") pattern of reading that involves not really reading but rather scanning a text in a way that actually skips quite a bit of it (Nielsen, 2006). This F-pattern, which was investigated using eye tracking, involves both horizontal and vertical scanning. The top part of the F is formed in the first reading movement, a horizontal sweep, "usually across the upper part of the content area" (Nielsen, 2006). The middle bar of the F is formed when a user "move[s] down the page … and then read[s] across" (ibid.). The last reading movement is a vertical one scanning along the left side of the website's content to form the stem of the F.

This type of F-pattern reading may not apply to the e-book device – those devices appear to work differently – although these may have some other differences (and disadvantages) as compared to reading books in the form of printed text on paper (see discussion below). Whether as cause or effect, this F-pattern mode of reading/searching means that web pages are designed with small amounts of easily scannable text (Nielsen & Morkes, 1997), putting the main information at the left margin and employing features such as bullet points, inverted pyramid style (starting with the conclusion), and highlighting of keywords, often with live links to further information (Nielsen, 1997). The style of web pages sometimes combines features of PowerPoint, news headlines, executive summaries of long reports, and news stories that place the key information in the first (short) paragraph on the assumption that people may not read the detail of the whole story. Like those other written forms, web pages are designed with visual attraction and maximal efficiency in mind.

Baldry and Thibault (2006) describe the way people "read" multimodal text such as that which is found on the Internet as involving "two *reading paths* … : a vertical one and a horizontal one" (p. 26, original emphasis), maintaining that reading in multimodal genres may not follow "a typical linear left-right, top-down" process but

> will often follow a more complex reading path than the one we are used to when we read a novel. We can use the term *cluster hopping* … to describe the

fact that the reading process is discontinuous, defined in terms of relationships of often overlapping clusters which require the reader to "hop" backwards and forwards. Rather than following a definite linear sequence, the reader can jump to different clusters of items on the page in a fixed sequence.

(Ibid., original emphasis)

Baldry and Thibault's description of the reading of multimodal text suggests how consuming these kinds of typically hybrid Internet texts combining print with other features incline users to a certain kind of visually oriented attention.

James Inman, in *Computers and Writing: The Cyborg Era* (Inman, 2004), describes an *"individual meta-reading heuristic"* that gamers use to "scan screens for interesting words or phrases or perhaps the comments of other players with whom they are friends" (p. 114, original emphasis). The kind of reading that people do online is often selectively focused in such a meta-reading orientation – more a form of searching for information than reading in the sense of full absorption and comprehension of text. This meta-reading process of skimming and scanning for information is neither sequential nor comprehensive as in reading a continuous text. It is rather a sort of fragmented, surface-oriented, localized reading.

Stephanie Strickland and M. D. Coverley note the "surfing, sampling, multi-tasking kind of reading [which] is often elicited online" as well as the "problem-solving, focused, remembering" kind of attention with which some gamers approach reading on the screen – both of which they contrast with the "[d]eep, focused attention [that] print readers are trained to have, [as] attention itself is being reshaped, becoming a mix of deep and hyper, or focused and mobilized" (Strickland & Coverley, 2012, p. 347). All of these screen reading modes – and very likely others, such as reading a book on an e-reader – contrast in significant ways with reading print offline in an extended and continuous period of concentration with the intention of absorbing the full meaning of a text.

Poe (2011) states that we experience web pages not as discrete entities but more as a stream of information:

You "surf" through them one after another in a continuous stream. You stop when one grabs your attention, read a bit, then move on ... [in] a continuous stream of texts, sounds, and sights. In this sense, surfing the Internet is like watching captioned TV, with one crucial difference: there are millions of channels on the Web. Just how many millions, no one knows.

(p. 232)

This is a very different reading, or "visual consumption," process than reading in the traditional sense – more like sampling or browsing through a book or a line of books before settling down to actually read a book. Such unsettled or restless activity seems to be encouraged by the digital medium, its form and content. Reading performed as part of surfing the Net, multitasking, or cluster-hopping is hit or miss and fragmentary, becoming essentially a quick search for easily accessible nuggets of information. The depth of reading is the limit of one screen at best, and global features of texts – even the whole point of what is read – will often be missed.

The different kinds of reading or visual consumption done online combine some aspects of reading in the sense of comprehending the meaning of text with features of screen watching, such as in watching television, and other cognitive-visual tasks, such as zeroing in on the most eye-catching object in the visual field, looking for something specific that one has in mind, and trying to retain information for a task at hand. The kinds of reading done online require different kinds of coordinated visual and mental activity, and hence different wiring of the brain, than reading text offline (Wolf, 2007). The brain's circuitry is created by the kinds of cognitive activity in which a person engages, which develop its gray matter by increasing the number and complexity of the neural connections and branching paths through the brain and develop its white matter by strengthening the connections and paths for those activities in which it engages most often. Over time, the strength of connections in the brain can be changed by long-term potentiation, or strengthening, due to a high volume of activity, as well as by long-term de-potentiation, or weakening, due to inactivity or negatively influencing activity and "*pruning*, where the brain fine-tunes and eliminates earlier connections deemed no longer useful" (Jensen, 2015, p. 60, original emphasis). Pruning is a main manifestation of the brain's plasticity and ability to reconfigure itself in response to experience.

The human brain must be retrained and re-engineered from spoken to written language and must be retrained and rewired also for reading print and, in different ways, for attending to visual media such as television and digital screens. The television- and screen-watching brain has been trained and wired to operate with attention divided and engaged in short bursts. The reading brain that was developed through interaction with print for deep and sustained attention has given way in the online generation to a digital brain developed through interaction with electronic devices (Wolf, 2007). Prensky (2011/2001) reviews ways in which the brains of digital natives are likely to be "*physiologically different*" (p. 17, original emphasis) from those of digital immigrants, based on differing experiences that build different cognitive structure. While Prensky (2011/2001) emphasizes the positive effects on the skills of children and adolescents based on "repeated exposure to computer games and other digital media" (p. 17), other researchers express concern about cognitive losses and other negative effects on brain and behavior. Wolf and Barzillai (2009, p. 35), for example, suggest that "early immersion in reading ... largely online tends to ... habituate the learner to immediate information gathering and quick attention shifts," leading to "truncated development" of the skills needed for "deep reflection and original thought."

Not only how people are reading but what they are reading, and so what they are filling their time and their minds with, is changing. Much of the content of text online, as we have said, tends to light and popular topics as well as consumerist activities and values. In addition, people are spending more time reading short texts of a social nature, as when they read all of their social messages – their pop-up emails and text messages – before anything else. This sort of social or "hive" reading is a new kind of reading that is far from traditional or deep reading. The attentional pull of visual media and the petty detail and steady stream of Facebook posts, text messages, and tweets are replacing the power of the language and the detail of books and literary works to grab attention and to maintain a certain configuration of the brain that is associated with print reading.

What People Say about the E-reading Experience

Besides reading information posted online, many have been won over by Amazon and some other companies trying to get people to buy their e-readers and move to a total electronic reading experience using electronic books. While some people are early and enthusiastic converts, a discussion about the Kindle e-reader versus the traditional book-reading experience, taken from posts in 2012 and 2013 at Amazon.com's romance forum (www.amazon.com/forum/romance?_encoding= UTF8&cdForum=FxM42D5QN2YZ1D&cdThread=TxTSRN47M7LL5J), shows that there are many issues related to reading literature online. However, the discussion suggests that once a person buys an e-reading device, there is an attempt to learn to live with its imperfections. Of interest is the fact that most of this sample of people who have e-readers use a combination of paperbacks or library books and their e-reading device, and some use more than one electronic device to compensate for shortcomings in the e-reader.

Whether those commentators are typical or not is hard to know. Since the thread is posted on Amazon, one of the biggest sellers of e-books and e-reading devices, there are potentially more positive views expressed than there might be in other contexts, though the posts do include criticism of Amazon's control of the e-book market. They also criticize the entire e-book industry in commenting on how poorly some e-books are formatted and edited, with some being described as riddled with errors and potentially subject to deletion. At the same time, there are a lot of positive comments about reading on various electronic devices that allow e-reading, with most of the commentators preferring to read on purpose-made devices or smartphones rather than on tablet or laptop computers. Advantages mentioned include space-saving, portability, the built-in light, the possibility of enlarging the font, ease of access to books, and ease of handling – especially the ability to read with one hand free to do other things. One person also suggests that using an e-reader is especially useful for reading nonfiction because of the note-taking function that is included in the device.

Some commentators in the online discussion forum make positive comments about print books as well. One remarks that the physicality of a book helps recall the location of a specific passage, and several remark that it is easier to move around in a print book than in an e-book. While most commentators seem to have accepted what they read in e-reading as *books*, one commentator makes a point of differentiating what is read online from actual books in terms of their digital nature and the gadgetry involved. Another shares a love for the feel of a book, and yet another notes the desire to possess a bound copy of an especially treasured book. The desire to hold or possess a physical book suggests that bound copies of books may be considered more significant possessions than electronic copies, which are after all entirely ephemeral – that is, they exist within the machine in a fleeting, electronic form. If given a reality outside the machine, through printing of the pages on paper, their special nature vanishes and they move into the category of "neither fish nor fowl," becoming like a printed book, but minus the covers and the binding that seem to be important defining features of the traditional category of "book."

Of interest is an apparent tendency noted by some of the commentators to read faster and more on the surface of language, such as by noting errors rather than getting deeply into the reading experience, when e-reading. There is also mention of doing other things online ("multitasking") during the reading act, thus interrupting and changing the reading process to move it towards the process of reading or searching texts online as we described previously. The fact of being able to read with one hand that is mentioned as an advantage also suggests a lesser level of involvement in the act of reading than a person has if needing to use both hands to hold a book and turn the pages. The reduction in or loss of the physical side of reading changes the reading act, making it (literally and figuratively) more mechanical and less embodied and sensual.

The felt need mentioned in some of the comments to preview the ending of a novel and the difficulty some encountered in doing so with an e-reader, in addition to the difficulty of easily moving back and forth in the text, suggests further changes in the act of reading when performed electronically. The e-reader seems to force or encourage a diminution of the act of reading, making it a less concentrated act and shortcutting some of its usual component actions. The overall impact seems to be one of reducing the act and process of reading by making it in a sense easier and faster (requiring less labor and time) and less engaged and invested (requiring less mental and emotional involvement), and by bypassing some of the usual steps and accompanying behaviors. On the other hand, the multimodal digital reading environment described above arguably enlarges the reading context and adds both content and activities to the reading act, changing it in the process from a focused experience of linguistic comprehension and interpretation to a significantly different, multifocal multimedia experience.

Reading Light and Reading Heavy

If we accept online reading as now normal and naturalized, we might then attempt to point out its advantages – which of course the companies selling e-readers are already trying to do. From that perspective, one might argue that online texts are better because of the possibility of reading faster, of viewing wonderful color graphics and potentially animated and artistic illustrations, of following inserted hyperlinks at will to gain more information than appears on a particular page, and of being able to read and do other things online at the same time, such as catch emails, text messages, and other postings, and surf the Net. These purported advantages of e-texts are in addition to the ease of access, handiness, portability, and space-saving mentioned above for e-readers, and to savings of paper and lower cost for e-books as compared to print books. For these reasons, American consumers in huge numbers have purchased e-readers and e-books, while educators and government officials, including former U.S. President Barak Obama, have pushed for use of e-textbooks in schools.

In spite of the initial rush towards e-books for individual reading and classroom texts, evidence is accumulating that these may not have staying power. As Alice Robb reports:

> Despite the embrace of e-books in certain contexts, they remain controversial. Many people just don't like them. ... After years of growth, sales are stagnating. In 2014, 65 percent of 6 to 17-year-old children said they would always want to read books in print—up from 60 percent two years earlier.
>
> *(Robb, 2015)*

Naomi S. Baron's research with college students across several countries, as reported in *Words Onscreen: The Fate of Reading in a Digital World* (Baron, 2015), reveals that the vast majority (92%) of them, even though digital natives, now prefer reading by means of print books or other hard copy, especially for serious reading requiring concentration, rather than by means of e-readers, laptops, tablets, or cell phones – though for "light reading" they have less of a preference as to reading medium.

Although storing and reading texts on a Kindle, Nook, or other highly portable e-reading device avoids the cost of paper and printing, as Baron realizes (Robb, 2015), e-books are less environmentally friendly than paper-and-print books, given the rarity and toxicity of some of the metals used to produce the devices and the environmental cost of generating the necessary electricity and of disposing of spent electronic devices and components. While digital text has great value for information search and information-centered reading – and so considerable potential for academics, researchers, and students studying for exams – this is not the business model driving the development and sales of e-books and e-readers, which is reading for pleasure, specifically, fiction. We believe that a digital device is not optimal for reading literature and predict that, given the shortcomings mentioned above for e-books and e-reading, many people will abandon e-readers and move back to reading literature "the old way" – at least for those books that have easily available print versions, which we note would not include many of those older and out-of-print works being digitized by Project Gutenberg.

Or will they? An alternative scenario is that e-reading and the "reading-light" – or "reading-lite" – experience of the digital world, which in the current generation is a "switch-experience" (i.e., a switch from books to screens, and from print text to digital text and other digital forms) will be the established, mainstream culture for future generations – and possibly over time all they know. Inevitably, this will mean that the type of reading – deep reading – which is associated with print culture and the reading of books and which has been the core of education for centuries, the emotional and intellectual pleasure of the act of sustained reading, the pathway to the world of the imagination, and the trigger to knowledge and insight, will remain but a shadow of itself, and could be lost altogether. Paradoxically, this dimmed reading culture is that of the flash screen, which holds great attraction for our vision-oriented species yet encourages a kind of surface-oriented, hurried activity that is antithetical to reading as previous generations came to know it and had their brains structured to do it. Every medium shapes the experience of its users by its properties; we might say, recalling McLuhan's (1964) famous dictum, that the medium *is* the experience. As the reading-heavy, reading-deep culture is reconfigured into a reading-lite, reading-surface one, current and future generations are shifting their experience away from much of what that former culture represents.

As Sven Birkerts observed in *The Gutenberg Elegies: The Fate of Reading in an Electronic Age*, "Reading, because we control it, is adaptable to our needs and rhythms" (Birkerts, 1994, p. 146). The experience of reading in the way that he termed "deep reading" seems to give readers chances for what Rachel Grate calls "serendipity and sense of control" (Grate, 2014), which she suggests are limited when using an e-reading device. Part of the serendipitous as well as controlled process of reading printed text is that the reader can be surprised and yet be aware of helping to shape that surprise. Social scientists have found little evidence that touching a screen to move a page can offer both the sense of control and the kind of serendipity that Grate (2014) is talking about. Nor does it seem that reading text distanced by the screen evokes the same kind of full sensory experience and enjoyment that a book provides. In fact, the screen and its physical properties seem to work against this kind of experience, as does the way in which text is represented on the screen.

The screen culture, in favoring the visual over the textual, visuality over textuality, promotes quick absorption rather than slow processing of information. It therefore favors the use of prominent images more than text and, for text, values messages that can be easily and quickly read and understood. Reading on screen is typically a matter of scanning quickly around the page, moving between images to quick-read "text-bites" in the way of short sentences (at best) or short bursts of prose, and rapidly switching from one text-bite to the next and then one page to the next. It therefore tends to create a more restless and fragmented type of behavior than reading offscreen from a printed page, which is a slower and more linear and cumulative process. The pop-up windows and links on the screen also distract from the concentrated, slow, and cumulative reading process that moves readers deeper into the depth of their own consciousness. When reading a book, Grate (2014) also points out, longer sentences and larger bodies of text trigger deep processing of information and long-term memory connections. Book reading improves the ability to concentrate and has a calming effect that can help people relax. According to Grate (2014): "Just six minutes of reading is enough to reduce stress by 68%," and reading may help maintain "brain functioning ... as you age. One study even found that elderly individuals who read regularly are 2.5 times less likely to develop Alzheimer's."

If people are reading more, even if much of their reading is onscreen and online, isn't this a good thing? Not necessarily, because, as Grate (2014) comments, "not all forms of reading are created equal." Grate cites research suggesting that the experience of reading on an e-reader does not promote the formation of deep mental connections that make the reading event, and the content of what is read, memorable, so that a story read on a Kindle is remembered less well than one read in paperback form. Reading onscreen or online tends to foster a surface-oriented kind of attention driven by diversive curiosity rather than the deeper sort of reflection driven by epistemic curiosity that engenders deep thought and reflection.

Baron (2014), in an article entitled "How E-reading Threatens Learning in the Humanities," comments that "not all reading works well on digital screens." Reading on screens trains people to read for information, but information is not knowledge, nor does it last for more than an instant before it is consumed. On the screen, users are "power browsing," as Baron (2014) puts it, encountering "vapor text" and increasingly training themselves to read for information not knowledge. Screen readers are, at best, receiving snippets or fragments of information without much coherence. As a consequence, they don't seem to care as much about what they are reading, such as whether they miss things or read incorrectly. In Baron's (2014) summary: "The bottom line is that while digital devices may be fine for reading that we don't intend to muse over or to reread, text that requires what's been called 'deep reading' is nearly always better done in print."

What we, along with Grate (2014) and Baron (2014, 2015), are talking about is a less intellectually, emotionally, and indeed physically, involved, disembodied form of reading done when using an electronic device. We speculate that even reading a long novel on a screen is an experience that usually does not sustain deep reading or provoke the kinds of sensual images and cognitive and emotional connections that become etched in long-term memory the way reading a novel in print does. In reading a novel in print, readers have the experience of the novel inhabiting them and growing inside them, becoming a permanent part of their consciousness that connects to their sense of self, and their fully embodied past and present experience. Reading literary text in print on paper engages a person in an experience that requires more than superficial participation.

Whereas the screen trains people to watch and wait for something to happen, reading requires a person to do something to a text to make it come alive – to decode all of its elements and to work to comprehend their meanings and to take in its full significance. The Internet trains people to search and shop, and, when there is too much to search and shop, to merely browse and window-shop. This includes browsing and window-shopping for information. What it does not encourage is stopping for a while to ponder what is before the eyes: the images on the screen are set up for rapid impression, to be absorbed all at once or by quick eye movement and scanning. The screen is therefore not a medium conducive to engaged, contemplative reading. Nor does it connect the experience of reading to the body, to how it feels – in terms of sensing physically and emotionally – and to its natural speed and rhythm. As Max Bruinsma puts it succinctly, "screens are for watching, paper is for reading" (Bruinsma, 2004).

As creatures that have been fitted by nature with certain inbuilt perceptual mechanisms for coping with all the different kinds of stimuli which present themselves to our senses, we humans are drawn to the most accessible forms of stimulation. Our attention is thus drawn to the closest and quickest form of stimulation, that which draws us in by being easily available, such as when we turn on our computers to read our emails or browse the Internet, or when we turn our attention to whatever program is in progress on a nearby television screen. Beyond the ready availability of such stimuli, we are wired as humans to be drawn to forms of stimulation which are high in accessibility because of their prominence or novelty. These are stimuli which command our attention by being perceptually strong or unusual, such as bright lights or loud noises – what we have referred to before as things that "pop." Thus is our attention drawn in the supermarket checkout line to a shocking headline on the cover page of a broadsheet or to the ready sources of stimulation which are the magazines littering doctors' waiting rooms, and to the titillating celebrity gossip or "lit-lite" stories appearing in them, even though we might not deliberately or usually engage in such reading events.

So why do any readers choose to read literature, as a much weightier form of text, than flimsy gossip, "lit-lite," or "lit-free" stories matching headlines which go for shock value? It is because "reading heavy" offers satisfactions and benefits that "reading light" cannot. Although "reading light" in effect fills the mind and quickly satisfies its desire to be fed, its effect is neither lasting nor profound. "Reading heavy," in contrast, fills the mind and satisfies its desire to be fed in lasting and profound ways. Pico Iyer compares the attraction people have to, in our terms, "lightweight" forms of reading as like the desire for, and the satisfaction gained from, fast food (Iyer, 2015). He reflects on the immediate pull of such reading as a form of momentary fulfillment, a "guilty pleasure" which is easily indulged:

> I still surrender – gratefully – to the latest congressional sex scandal or celebrity memoir whenever I'm killing time waiting for a plane, even though

> I know that any book by D. H. Lawrence or Marcel Proust will leave me
> feeling more alive, more myself, more in love with the world.
>
> *(Iyer, 2015)*

At the same time Iyer reflects that what we have termed "reading light" or
"reading-lite," like other guilty pleasures such as indulging in fast food from time
to time, can in the long run affect health – in this case, the health of the mind.
"Reading heavy" is rich in health-giving benefits, providing deep nourishment
and food for the soul and the psyche, enhancing the reader's humanity, leaving
the person more energized and alive.

When people encounter literary narrative, they are invited to participate in a
kind of dialogue with the language of the story, as written by the author and as
put into the mouths and thoughts of the characters, and also with themselves.
The story will have value for them if they are willing to open themselves to it
and to respond to it, to experience it as it unfolds and to reflect on that experience.
Through such engagement with the words of the author and the story characters,
readers map aspects of their own lives onto the story in a way that allows personal
knowledge to emerge within a multidimensional interactive space between the
story and each reader. In the process, the story shapes, and changes, the interior of
individual readers even as those readers also shape the story in relation to their
personal experience.

A Short Story That Speaks Volumes: "The Story of an Hour"

The best writers are able tell a story in a way that brings readers into it, to
experience it themselves. This they do by telling stories about characters that
have recognizable connections to all people, that remind readers of themselves
and others they know or have heard about, characters whose experiences
resemble their experiences. They tell a story in a way that is memorable and
leads readers to think and feel, that connects to other things they know, and
that is a learning experience and offers valuable lessons and insights. Those
writers are able to do all this through the way they populate their story and
structure their narrative, its plot and settings, and through the particular
language they use, which is in the best case a kind of artistic, aesthetic or literary,
language. "The Story of an Hour" (Chopin, 1895/1894), originally published
in *Vogue* magazine under the title "The Dream of an Hour" and then reprinted
soon afterwards in *St. Louis Life* (January 5, 1895) under its current title, is a
recognized literary work by the American Southern writer who went by the
pen name of Kate Chopin that demonstrates how even a very short but well-
constructed story can enlarge readers and help them to understand themselves
and others.

The opening of the story is a dramatic event: the young Mrs. Mallard, who is
described as having "a heart trouble," gets news that her husband is dead.

She did not hear the story as many women have heard the same, with a paralyzed inability to accept its significance. She wept at once, with sudden, wild abandonment, in her sister's arms. When the storm of grief had spent itself, she went away to her room alone. She would have no one follow her.

After a time sitting alone in her room, Mrs. Mallard senses "something coming to her and she was waiting for it, fearfully." As she "abandoned herself" to this something, the idea takes hold that she is now "free, free, free!" Readers will be aware of the lack of freedom which some women experience in marriage and can imagine that at the time this story was published, at the end of the 19th century, many women's lives would have been substantially tied to those of their husbands. They can therefore empathize with Mrs. Mallard, who, after all, "knew that she would weep again when she saw the kind, tender hands folded in death; the face that had never looked save with love upon her, fixed and gray and dead." Readers can see both sides of this woman whom Chopin depicts as "young" and "fair," yet with "lines [on her face that] bespoke repression," and who has some-times loved and sometimes not loved her husband. They understand the irony when the writer juxtaposes her "quick prayer" now "that life might be long," when "only yesterday she had thought with a shudder that life might be long."

The reader also understands other ironies in the story, in the very short-lived free-dom Mrs. Mallard experiences that allows her to descend the stairs "like a goddess of Victory" with "a feverish triumph in her eyes," only to find her husband alive and well at the bottom of the stairs. Adding further irony, upon seeing him, she instantly dies. But the final, overarching irony of the story comes in its last sen-tence: "When the doctors came they said she had died of heart disease – of joy that kills." Perhaps the true point is that the joy which the young wife had felt in her heart, contemplating her newfound freedom during the hour of her widowhood, was taken away from her, and it was the shock of *that* great loss which killed her.

Reading a story energizes the imagination of the reader, who is called on to inhabit the world which the writer has created and to make the story his/her own. The language compels the reader to create the emotions and the sights and sounds of the scenes, to feel, to see, to smell, and even to taste and touch what the characters might be experiencing. As we have been suggesting, the Digital Age privileges the visual more than the textual, and, as a result, people seem to be losing this ability to fully imagine all that words on a page, and pages in a book, have to offer.

References

Baldry, Anthony, & Thibault, Paul J. (2006). *Multimodal transcription and text analysis: A multimedia toolkit and coursebook with associated on-line course.* Sheffield, U.K. and Bristol, CT: Equinox.

Baron, Naomi S. (2014). How e-reading threatens learning in the humanities. *The Chronicle of Higher Education.* July 14, 2014. http://Chronicle.com/articles/147661.

Baron, Naomi S. (2015). *Words onscreen: The fate of reading in a digital world*. New York: Oxford University Press.

Biersdorfer, J. D. (2015). Through a touch-screen looking glass. *The New York Times*, Book Review. April 12, 2015, p. 29.

Birkerts, Sven (1994). *The Gutenberg elegies: The fate of reading in an electronic age*. Boston: Faber and Faber.

Bruinsma, Max (2004). Words on screens. *Typotheque* website. November 29, 2004. Retrieved on January 3, 2015 from www.typotheque.com/articles/words_on_screens.

Carr, Nicholas (2011/2008). Is Google making us stupid? In Mark Bauerlein (ed.), *The digital divide: Arguments for and against Facebook, Google, texting, and the age of social networking* (pp. 63–75). New York: Jeremy P. Tarcher/Penguin. Originally appeared in *The Atlantic*, July/August 2008.

Chopin, Kate (1895/1894). The story of an hour. *St. Louis Life*, January 5, 1895. Originally published in *Vogue*, December 6, 1894, under the title "The dream of an hour." Retrieved on August 4, 2015 from http://my.hrw.com/support/hos/hostpdf/host_text_219.pdf.

Grate, Rachel (2014). Science has great news for people who read actual books. *Mic* website. Sept. 22, 2014. Retrieved from http://mic.com/articles/99408/science-has-great-news-for-people-who-read-actual-books.

Inman, James A. (2004). *Computers and writing: The cyborg era*. Mahwah, NJ: Lawrence Erlbaum.

Iyer, Pico (2015). Healthy body, unhealthy mind. *The New York Times*, Sunday Review. January 4, 2015, p. 3.

Jensen, Frances E. (2015). Plastic fantastic. *Pennsylvania Gazette*. September/October 2015, pp. 56–62.

McLuhan, Marshall (1964). *Understanding media: Extensions of man*. New York: Mentor.

Nielsen, Jakob (1997). How users read on the Web. Jakob Nielsen's Alertbox, *Nielsen Norman Group* website. October 1, 1997. Retrieved on January 25, 2001 from www.useit.com/papers/alertbox/9710a.html. Also available at www.nngroup.com/articles/how-users-read-on-the-web/.

Nielsen, Jakob (2006). F-shaped pattern for reading. *Nielsen Norman Group* website. April 17, 2006. Retrieved on January 26, 2016 from www.nngroup.com/articles/f-shaped-pattern-reading-web-content/.

Nielsen, Jakob, & Morkes, John (1997). Concise, SCANNABLE, and objective: How to write for the Internet. *Nielsen Norman Group* website. January 1, 1997. Retrieved on January 25, 2016 from www.nngroup.com/articles/concise-scannable-and-objective-how-to-write-for-the-web/.

Pennington, Martha C. (2013). Trends in writing and technology. *Writing & Pedagogy*, 5(2), 155–179. doi:10.1558/wap.v5i2.155.

Pennington, Martha C. (2017). Literacy, culture, and creativity in a digital era. *Pedagogy*, 17(2), 259–287. doi: 10.1215/15314200-3770149.

Poe, Marshall T. (2011). *A history of communications: Media and society from the evolution of speech to the Internet*. New York: Cambridge University Press.

Prensky, Marc (2011/2001). Do they really think differently? In Mark Bauerlein (ed.), *The digital divide: Arguments for and against Facebook, Google, texting, and the age of social networking* (pp. 12–25). New York: Jeremy P. Tarcher/Penguin.

Robb, Alice (2015). 92 percent of college students prefer reading print books to e-readers. Technology section. *New Republic* online. January 14, 2015. Retrieved on May 15,

2015 from www.newrepublic.com/article/120765/naomi-barons-words-onscreen-fate-reading-digital-world.

Strickland, Stephanie, & Coverley, M. D. (2012). Creativity and writing in digital media: New frontiers and cutting edges. *Writing & Pedagogy*, *4*(2), 345–354. doi:10.1558.wap.v4i2.345.

Wolf, Maryanne (2007). *Proust and the squid: The story and science of the reading brain*. New York: HarperCollins.

Wolf, Maryanne, & Barzillai, Mirit (2009). The importance of deep reading. *Educational Leadership*, *66*(6), 32–37. Available at www.ascd.org/publications/educational-leadership/mar09/vol66/num06/The-Importance-of-Deep-Reading.aspx.

6

EDUCATION AND LITERACY IN DIGITAL CULTURE

Content through the audiovisual channel is usually meant to stimulate, not educate.
– *Marshall T. Poe,* A History of Communications: Media and Society from the Evolution of Speech to the Internet *(Poe, 2011, p. 200)*

Media Shaping Education

As communications media evolved in the audiovisual era – which Poe (2011, p. 167) describes as reaching its pinnacle in 1990 – an audiovisual culture was created that was "the product of the audiovisual media and the organized interests that brought it into being" (p. 201) and that maintained control of those media as "concentrated in the hands of a relative few" (p. 200). The "sensationalist" nature of the media of radio, film, and television and the interests of those controlling them to capitalize audiovisual media to the greatest extent possible has meant that they were developed with a primary purpose of entertainment and a comparatively lesser emphasis on public service and education. Poe (2011), in summarizing the era, remarks: "Everywhere we find the audiovisual media dominated by entertainment, usually of the low-brow variety. Content through the audiovisual channel is usually meant to stimulate, not educate" (p. 200).

In the 1980s, Neil Postman was raising an alarm regarding television, arguing that we were fast becoming a culture addicted to entertainment and were in danger of "amusing ourselves to death" (Postman, 1985). He pointed out that as an educational medium, television was not a simple mode of transmission or a neutral delivery system for content but rather a dangerous one that subsumed educational purposes under entertainment and consumerist values, thereby both reducing and changing educational goals. Postman's cynicism about television as a learning environment is captured well in his statement, "Television educates by teaching children to do what television-viewing requires of them" (p. 144) – which, we maintain, is to watch in bursts for whatever catches their momentary attention yet leaves room for commercial messages and doing other things at the same time, such as eating.

Watching television seems to reduce human beings to couch potatoes: an inert and captive audience of passive observers waiting to be entertained and consumers waiting to be fed whatever the media moguls and sponsors choose to feed them. The inactivity of television watching and the lack of full engagement make people lethargic and also contribute, in combination with the relentless promotion of food products in commercial breaks, to obesity. The American Academy of Pediatrics (2016a) policy statement on "Media and Young Minds" cites research showing significant increases in BMI (body mass index) related to heavy media use by preschoolers (p. 2), and their policy statement on "Media Use in School-Aged Children and Adolescents" (American Academy of Pediatrics, 2016b) points to studies showing that television watching is a risk factor for obesity, particularly for children 4 through 9 years of age (p. 2). Harvard's T. H. Chan School of Public Health website devoted to obesity prevention (Obesity Prevention Source, 2016) points to "extensive research [confirming] the link between television viewing and obesity in children and adults, in countries around the world." It can be concluded that watching television makes both the mind and the body flabby and that this is often not so much a by-product as a central dynamic and purpose of the medium. Public television seems to be an exception, especially in its programming for preschoolers, such as *Sesame Street* (American Academy of Pediatrics, 2016a, p. 2).

Attempts to use television as a medium for education have otherwise not been very successful, and perhaps never will have much success, given the nature of the medium together with the powerful interests pressuring it to generate profits on a mega scale. To the extent that the electronic environment subsumes the media of the audiovisual era, the same arguments may apply to the use of digital media in education. In this millennium, some educators have been raising alarms about the Internet and electronic media that are similar to those raised for television. In an article in *University Business*, for example, Bob Rogers noted that "the digital wizardry now being installed in college campuses around the country was developed as the quintessential delivery system for sensations, not experience" (Rogers, 2005, p. 25). Others raise issues about the use of technology to deliver substandard educational experiences such as rote learning. The American Academy of Pediatrics (2016a) "Media and Young Minds" policy statement, for instance, maintains that most apps that are supposed to be educational are based on rote learning of academic skills and are not supported by established curricula, input from education or child development specialists, or research (p. 2).

Yet digital media and culture are different from audiovisual media and culture in some ways that offer unique capabilities for education, such as automated forms of modularized and self-paced units and courses within online learning environments. These capabilities can be described as the programmed learning of the 1950s updated to electronic environments and augmented by digital capabilities. In theory, this combination of features should offer powerful instructional technologies. In practice, they have been widely adopted for delivering standardized courses online, in the attempt to make education more profitable by reaching the widest possible audience and eliminating or reducing the need for the "middleman" – that is, the (human) teacher. Both students and faculty often find that the available learning systems and the courses developed with their aid fall considerably short of their potential.

Issues can be raised with these learning environments which have been raised as criticisms of other modular approaches to instruction, both programmed learning and all forms of test-driven instruction: that they fracture knowledge domains, focus on limited and short-term learning goals, promote education as the learning of individual items of information, and make learning a less interactive and less human process (Pennington, 2011). There has long been a tendency in education to modularize and compartmentalize complex knowledge domains, such as in the teaching of language, where

> [v]ocabulary is separated from reading, punctuation is separated from sentences, sentences from paragraphs, creativity from analysis. ... The study of language becomes entirely removed from the uses of language in and outside class. And it's the separation of the skills of literacy from their embodiments in literature and in talk that encourages students to divorce what they do in one class from another class and divorce what they do as learners from what they do as people.
>
> *(Kutz & Roskelly, 1991, p. 219)*

Such segmentation or compartmentalization of knowledge or information is often an attempt to simplify a complex domain in order to make it more learnable. There is a question, however, as to whether a domain once broken up loses the coherence necessary for it to be correctly perceived and understood. This tendency to compartmentalize and segment knowledge is encouraged by the use of online learning environments, where information is organized into learning modules and tests. The property of the medium dictates the kind of testing that is possible, and in the name of standardization, reliability, efficiency, online delivery, and – equally important – online scoring, limited responses in the way of disarticulated information nuggets and skill components (competencies) are tested rather than creative and individual responses giving evidence of integrated knowledge and skill complexes such as those of reading and writing.

Although educators continue to raise issues about standardization, restricted responses, and fragmentation of knowledge with regard to electronic delivery of courses (e.g., Remley, 2013), and although students desert online courses at a high rate and generally do not like studying in the disembodied online environment as much as they do in a whole-body environment of a class with a teacher and other students in the same room, the forces of economics (e.g., reduced teaching costs and reaching as many students as possible, no matter where they are located) continue to pressure to online modular instruction and testing. At the same time, the current push toward integrated learning in K–12 education and to interdisciplinarity at university level are pressuring the designers of online instruction to rethink how the digital environment might be redesigned to move away from segmented towards more holistic modes of learning and testing. If integrated learning and interdisciplinary approaches can be implemented in online instruction and testing, it would be heartening to once again see educational philosophy dictating teaching methods and leading the medium for delivery of instruction, rather than the other way around.

At present the increasing dominance of electronic media in education seems unstoppable, as business interests have ensured that the latest media have saturated college campuses, public and private schools, private homes, and just about all other public and private spaces, and as educators seek to make use of whatever technology is available. An "upside down" approach to education is now becoming widespread in which students study content modules online and then class time is used for Q & A and other forms of interactive learning. This seems a promising approach to the use of technology in instruction that adds new potentials to education – as word processors and online search capabilities have done. Other new potentials are added by creative use of portable electronic tools for independent and collaborative learning experiences, such as the varied applications of mobile devices for language learning (see, e.g., Díaz-Vera, 2012) or for other kinds of applications in academic contexts.

A notable example is an initiative at Duke University that gave every student an iPod, as described by Cathy N. Davidson, a professor of English there, in *Now You See It: How the Brain Science of Attention Will Transform the Way We Live, Work, and Learn* (Davidson, 2011). Davidson shows the value of this iPod giveaway, as students used these devices to record lectures and many other kinds of interactions for academic purposes which their teachers designed into their courses. Like many English teachers, Davidson is on the leading edge of advocating media and technology in both content and delivery of instruction, such as blogging, multimedia presentations, and use of gaming. Like others, she sees these uses of media as developing skills that students will need for the future, and also as potentially dealing with the tendency of students' attention to wander, arguing that these kinds of activities will keep them engaged.

Prensky (2011/2001), who pointed out that the teaching and learning approaches being used in today's educational system do not match the thinking or learning styles of those raised in the digital world, has been a vocal advocate for teaching all subjects and all types of content by "Digital Native methodologies" (p. 10), such as games and simulations. In his view, Digital Immigrant methodologies will be less successful with the current generation of students and what they need to learn of "Future" content – that which is digitally and techno-logically oriented – as well as the "Legacy" content of the "traditional" curriculum (Prensky, 2011/2001, p. 8). As examples of Digital Native methodologies for teaching "legacy content" in humanities subjects, he suggests teaching classical philosophy through "a game in which the philosophers debate and the learners have to pick out what each would say," or the Holocaust through "a simulation where students role-play the meeting at Wannsee" (p. 11).

Clearly, the available media have an important role in education, being in some ways virtually essential in today's world and in other ways offering valuable instructional tools and resources for educational innovation. Yet we emphasize that when the medium dominates, dictating what is possible or what is easiest in the curriculum, the results may not be positive. As McLuhan (1964) so forcefully articulated, the medium is not a neutral container of information but shapes and even becomes the message. We point out the danger, in particular, of electronic and digital media dominating the educational curriculum and dictating its entire content and process, since this could effectively squeeze out literature and human arts as not fully compatible with the medium.

Although education has increasingly focused on digital activities and the practical knowledge needed for working with and learning from technology, we question whether an emphasis on behaviors related to digital activity is always justified. Alan Kirby maintains that the new technologies are "the death of competence" (Kirby, 2009, p. 241), meaning real knowledge, in favor of what he sees as mere technical skill – the ability to manipulate the Machine but not necessarily to use it for the important purposes of human life. Kirby suggests that this diminished appreciation for competence and knowledge contributes to the contemporary contempt for education. We agree with Kirby's general point but question whether much of what is taught as the "technical skills" for using computers, mobile devices, and the Internet merit classification as *skilled* – or indeed *technical* – activity, as opposed to being more properly viewed as everyday utilitarian behavior. This is not a mere matter of semantics, since what is considered everyday utilitarian behavior would not normally be taught in universities, thus reserving time for other higher and deeper level curricular concerns such as those we are proposing.

Reading Online and Offline: Effects on Literacy and Education

There is no doubt that the Internet changes literacy, as reading becomes far less likely to be done either intensively or extensively. These days, students groan – they really complain! – at the thought of reading "a whole chapter" much less a whole book. Today's students often perform a kind of speed-reading or speed-browsing, as we described in Chapter 5, in which they scan quickly over a web page, or jump from one website or post to another, searching for titles and key-words, or reading the first few words of each paragraph of a short reading with short paragraphs, trying to find specific information or perhaps aiming to take in enough of the content to get the gist. Their reading is also very often a kind of "hive" activity involving their communication with friends as well as "friends" – that is, all their pseudo-friends in the great pseudo-social Web of the Internet.

What of those who say these electronically inspired skills – including the purported meshing of them in multitasking – are needed, that they will benefit the students in the world of the 21st century? The skills of connecting online such as to work on a project are surely useful, as is the ability to find information online. However, surface reading, fragmented reading, and hive reading can only take a person so far. And the reading which students are doing nowadays – whether surface, fragmented, hive, or all three (which is most likely) – is, if you really think about it, in fact pseudo-reading, non-reading, or even *anti*-reading, in the sense of working against real reading in the traditional sense. In fact, it is harming them as readers, making them handicapped, disabled as readers, as they become habituated to minimally involved textual surfing, unable to slow down and concentrate on what is in front of their eyes. And what they prefer to read, or non-read, is often quite far from text – much less literature – in the traditional sense.

How can this handicapping of our children, this diversion of reading towards the trivial and this disabling of their ability to concentrate, to slow down and read carefully and in an involved way, be equipping them for all that the future holds? On the level of the civilization as a whole, it could make it hard for *H. sapiens* to maintain a competitive advantage in terms of literacy and language. Such surface activity could significantly reduce the power of language because a lot of that power lies in the longer and the more complex units of discourse that students are now bypassing in their reading – and their writing (Pennington, 2001, 2013).

A possible countering influence with some positive effects for education is the Harry Potter phenomenon that has turned many in the Millennial and the succeeding generation into avid readers of fantasy fiction geared for children and young adults. According to Wikipedia[1] (https://en.wikipedia.org/wiki/List_of_best-selling_books), the Harry Potter books have collectively sold hundreds of millions of copies since J. K. Rowling published the first U.K. volume, *Harry Potter and the Philosopher's Stone* (Rowling, 1997), retitled for publication in the United States as *Harry Potter and the Sorcerer's Stone* (Rowling, 1998), and the last volume, *Harry Potter and the Deathly Hallows*, some ten years later (Rowling, 2007). These books have been especially popular with the Facebook generation, who as a group put them at the top of their list of books that have influenced them (Kozlowska, 2014). Interest in Harry Potter books continues today with sales of the 2016 hardcover script book for the play, *Harry Potter and the Cursed Child* (Rowling, Tiffany, & Thorne, 2016), selling over 2 million copies in the United States and Canada in its first two days in print, as reported by *The Wall Street Journal*, closing in on the sales of the best-selling script book of all time, J. B. Priestley's *An Inspector Calls*, and on the sales record of the best-selling hardcover book since 2009, Dan Brown's novel, *The Lost Symbol* (Maloney, 2016). Like

J. R. R. Tolkien's *Hobbit* (Tolkien, 1937) and *Lord of the Rings* (Tolkien, 1954–1955), which have also sold hundreds of millions of copies (https://en.wikipedia.org/wiki/List_of_best-selling_books), the Harry Potter series draws in young readers by fantastical content, quests and adventure, and innovative language in the often Celtic-sounding names of characters.

The extreme popularity of Harry Potter and the stories in which he is the central character may have influenced the young readers of today to read not only more but longer books, as the J. K. Rowling stories started growing in length after the first book, averaging close to 500 pages, with the longest being close to 900 pages (Word Counter Blog, 2016). According to Michele Debczak, writing on the Mental Floss website:

> For many readers, Harry Potter was the series that first acquainted them with stories that surpassed the 300-, 500-, and even the 800-page mark. It's been nearly two decades since the first book was released and today, lengthy children's texts have become somewhat of a norm.
>
> *(Debczak, 2016)*

She reports that since 2006, the average middle-grade book has grown from 174.5 pages to 290 pages in length. The Harry Potter books have naturally served as a model for other books aimed at tween, adolescent, and young adult readers, and so may have caused them to grow longer, as writers increased the number of words and pages in their works for these audiences and the book industry agreed to publish their longer books. The greater length is also a reflection of the nature of the fantasy genre and readers' hunger for more and more details to fuel their imaginations and powers to envision fantasy characters and worlds.

What has been termed the "Harry Potter effect" by many is seen in positive terms as bringing more young people to books and to the sustained reading of fiction. Yet another kind of Harry Potter effect may not be so positive, as young people are drawn to reading the Harry Potter books and others of a similar fantasy type instead of reading more challenging books of a literary type. According to M. Anthony Mills, this is part of a larger cultural trend of "dumbing down" and "pandering" in the attempt "to win the hearts and minds of the Millennial generation … by lowering standards and expectations" (Mills, 2014). Mills calls this the "Harry Potter Paradox," suggesting that the most extreme case is that of humanities fields, "where concerns about being 'current' 'applicable' and 'relevant' have driven these fields into irrelevance" (Mills, 2014).

Mills' (2014) discussion of the Harry Potter Paradox highlights larger cultural forces undermining art by pitting it against entertainment. In his view, the reading of the Harry Potter series and other works typically classified as juvenile or young adult fiction – such as Suzanne Collins' Hunger Games trilogy of *The Hunger Games* (Collins, 2008), *Catching Fire* (Collins, 2009), and *Mockingjay* (Collins, 2010) – is therefore not something to celebrate. He makes the further point that these books have not had the claimed positive effect on reading by children: "The *Harry Potter*s and *Hunger Games* of the world are outliers" (Mills, 2014).

It is not clear that those who have read the Harry Potter and Hunger Games books are outliers, given the hundreds of millions of Harry Potter books sold since 1997 and the surpassing of Harry Potter books sales on Amazon by those of the Hunger Games trilogy in 2012 (https://en.wikipedia.org/wiki/List_of_best-selling_books). Even if they are outliers in the sense of reading more than the average child or Millennial, the Harry Potters and Hunger Gamers are not outliers in another sense: they are squarely within the normal distribution of behaviors of children and young adults who grew up with mass media, electronic technologies, and the Internet, so that they prefer and expect these kinds of high-fantasy entertainments – if not in books then on screen. The easy movement of the Harry Potter and Hunger Games fantasy worlds – like those of the Hobbit and the inhabitants of Middle-earth before them – to the big screen, as films, and to the small screen, as games, and the great popularity of the movies and games derived from those books, suggests how well they fit within current popular media culture.

Although the interplay between good books and good movies is of long standing, it seems that the influence is increasingly from screen media representations of stories back into their representations in print media. This wash-back from screen media inevitably changes the content and language of stories written down to reflect screen properties having to do with visuality and Hollywood values. Such washback from screen media is not only from the large-screen medium of film but also, increasingly, from the smaller screen media of television, desktop and laptop computers, and smartphones. Many have noted that the plot of the Hunger Games books revolving around a televised death match has much in common with the manufactured "games" of some television "reality" series, which Collins herself has claimed (in a promotional video; www.scholastic.com/thehungergames/videos/contemporary-inspiration.htm) as an inspiration for the trilogy.

If the Harry Potter books have had a countering effect to screen culture of getting young people reading books again, this may be something to cheer.[2] At the same time, even if the touted "Harry Potter effect" is real and has increased reading among a large segment of Millennials and the succeeding generation, we feel the need to alert educators and parents to the other side of the "Harry Potter effect," which we agree with Mills represents a subtle though pervasive negative outcome in the culture that those children and young people share with all of us. Consequently, if children and teenagers read Harry Potter and other fantasy fiction books aimed at young readers, we suggest that parents and especially educators take a proactive role in trying to ensure that those books do not simply function as reinforcement of popular culture but as platforms for learning and for further reading in the genres of literary fiction.

The New Academic Literacy: Co-opting Our Human Tradition

Wolf and Barzillai (2009) are optimistic about digital potentials for reading, believing that education can harness digital technology to encourage deep reading, using software specially designed to "help readers pause and monitor their comprehension, resist the pull of superficial reading, and seek out a deeper meaning" (p. 36), and also to encourage good practice in conducting Web searches and reading online using modeling. At the same time, they underscore the importance of print literacy for developing children's deep reading and the skills and imagination that result from such engaged reading. In their view, both online and print literacies are valuable and can reinforce each other.

Technology and mass media are clearly shaping the educational experience and even *becoming* the educational experience. As Waxler and Hall (2011) note, "Increasingly, education becomes training for the digital age much as education, for too long, was training for work in the industrial sector" (p. 161). As in other contexts, our media and the effects and the values that they create are increasingly being accepted as the norm. In an article decrying the diminution of humanities in education, Mark Slouka asks "What do our kids need to know today? As far as some are concerned, whatever will get them hired by Bill Gates" (Slouka, 2009, p. 35). Media-driven education, which moves machines into the foreground and human beings into the background, is fast becoming simply the "new normal."

There is no doubt that students are becoming more "visually literate," that is, more visually oriented and visually skilled, through their exposure to screen-based media (Greenfield, 2009). Yet their higher visual orientation is not something we should necessarily applaud or seek to emulate in our educational curricula. For it appears that the strong visual orientation of the present era has been bought at a cost to "deep processing: mindful knowledge acquisition, inductive analysis, critical thinking, imagination, and reflection" (Greenfield, 2009, p. 71). We wonder whether this visual skill born of exposure to screen-based media should in fact be considered a kind of "literacy," since it would appear to be gained to a greater or lesser extent at the expense of linguistic literacy.

The whole human notion on which literacy and our literate culture is based is in danger. The term "literacy" has been co-opted, transforming linguistic knowledge into procedural knowledge, privileging "smart skills" over self-reflective wisdom, emphasizing the "how" rather than the "why," and celebrating manipulation rather than contemplation. Rather than aiming to instill an appreciation of the beauty and truth of a literary text, what is taught as "literacy skills" aims to ensure effective use of mechanical and electronic devices for retrieval and development of information. Computer skills and contexts, and especially video games, are not only celebrating the skills of manipulation, but are almost always based on power – winning at any cost – and so setting up a situation where human connection is undercut. To win is to be skilled at this "literacy" – which runs counter to our belief that language and literature (our counterculture) bring human beings together and deepen their understanding of self and other. Human beings become the means to an end rather than an end in themselves – and empathy and compassion are reduced in favor of power and control.

We are worried about this future that our digital devices seem to be propelling us into. We are uncomfortable with some aspects of such acceptance and promotion of the status quo. Education should not only be for gaining practical skills but also for gaining knowledge. It should therefore be, as Newman (2008/1852) argued, not just "useful," a means to an end, but also an end in itself. Reading great literature is however not "useless" or impractical in this sense: it is not merely or only an end in itself, simply for the satisfaction knowing brings. It is in fact a very useful *human* way to know, especially to know the self and others – what it really means to be human. In *How to Read and Why*, Bloom (2000) observes, "Ultimately we read ... in order to strengthen the self, and to learn its authentic interests. ... The pleasures of reading indeed are selfish rather than social" (p. 22). While agreeing that knowing the self is a worthy goal in reading, we would take issue with this being entirely selfish, as knowing the self is also a way to get to know, and to understand, others.

Literary reading is therefore a powerful tool for education and human development that can impact people at a deep level, creating new understandings and opening them up to change. It is thus a part of a broader education that does not privilege science and technology to the exclusion of other subjects but includes a full measure of humanities. Wieseltier (2015, p. 14) argues that it is precisely their "nonutilitarian character" that makes the humanities worthwhile, "so that individuals can know more than how things work." We agree with him that the humanities teach more important things that prepare people "for the choices and the crucibles of private and public life" (ibid.). Reading literature within a humanities curriculum that includes analysis and discussion of the language and content of those texts is a means to the "nonutilitarian" – albeit extremely worthwhile and usable – ends which Wieseltier (2015) enumerates, of fostering discernment, judgment, and competence in matters of truth, goodness, and beauty. In this way, literature-based activity nurtures important elements of the foundation in human skills and human arts needed to make good choices in private and public life.

Yet young people are exposed less and less to literature within their educational contexts, which include less print text and written text in general, and more "born-digital" (Strickland, 2009) and digitally influenced texts. Texts produced in and for an online environment may include attention-grabbing features such as animation and multimodality as well as the attributes of webtext that contrast it with "born-print" text, such as short words, short sentences, and short paragraphs. We are worried about the amount of time that people, especially children and young adults, who together will determine the future of human literacy, culture, and humanity itself, are spending not reading literary works. We worry about what they are reading or doing instead.

What Students Are Reading: Written Genre Changes in the Era of Mass Media and the Internet

Written genres of all kinds are becoming increasingly "visualized" and "computerized" in the sense of being influenced by visual media and computers to become flashier, to have less print, and to have less complex or dense print. Another effect that is enhanced by the nature of the digital medium is the blurring of the distinction between written and spoken language. New registers combining the characteristics of spoken and written language are evolving in the "micro-texts" of the Web, as shown by the research of Maria Grazia Sindoni, reported in *Spoken and Written Discourse in Online Interactions: A Multimodal Approach* (Sindoni, 2013, p. 172). Social media are greatly influencing what students are spending their time reading, which are messages and other kinds of texts which are far different from those with literary characteristics. Such reading is far easier and less consequential than reading literary works, which touch people to their core.

David Shields, in *Reality Hunger* (Shields, 2010), argues that the essay and other forms of nonfiction such as the memoir and various types of pastiche are on the rise, along with hybrid forms that blur the distinction between fiction and nonfiction, while the literary form of the novel, which intentionally distances itself from living characters, eye witness accounts of events, and the author's personal experience, is falling out of favor. Although the figures we cited earlier would seem to suggest that the novel is still a popular literary genre, it is possible that it is starting to lose ground to other genres, both the shorter and the newer ones. The pricing structure of some online book publishers such as Kindle Unlimited encourages the production of short works. As noted by David Streitfeld, "Since the payment is the same whether the book is long or short, writers are taking the hint. Serial novels and short stories are increasing" (Streitfeld, 2014, p. 4).

With online publication, popular fiction genres such as romance, detective stories, and science fiction are doing well, with many new authors gaining a fan base online. There is however a glut of this type of work, especially by unknown authors. Writers may seek to gain a following by selling their works on their own websites at a low price or even allowing people to download them for free. This increases the amount of written work available online but not necessarily the supply of good-reads, much less of significant literary works. If students are not being assigned literature as part of their formal education, it is likely they are reading – if anything – books like the Harry Potter series or Hunger Games trilogy that may help to bring young people into reading but that pander to popular taste and are increasingly modeled on a mass-media aesthetic, or the shorter types of fiction and nonfiction that are being produced within a new-media, "short-and-sweet" flash aesthetic and that are flooding the online environment. Whether compatible with or inspired by mass media or new media, these works tend to reflect the values and aesthetics of screen culture. Even though students may be in some sense reading – and possibly also writing – more, we cannot cheer an effect which in many ways represents a downward trend in literacy in the sense of making them not good but at best middle-of-the-road and at worst weak readers and writers. Should we be satisfied with students' mediocre or poor performance and skills in literacy? Should we not aim for a higher standard and level of skill for their language and for written language in general?

The washback from the values and properties of screen media that seem to be weakening print text and diminishing its influence and, as a consequence, also weakening language and literacy skills can be described as a weakening – a "dumbing down" or "mediocritization" – of culture that is infiltrating education and also weakening (dumbing down or mediocritizing) it. Beyond its weakening in this sense, culture is weakened in another sense as works of fiction are increasingly influenced by Hollywood values, meaning that their plots reflect those of television and movies, which are sexualized, made to be violent and shocking, and constantly recycled and bowdlerized. The length, the structure, and the complexity of written forms is starting to be a reflection of what can be made into a television show or a movie. This is the celebrity culture, the image-saturated consciousness, the visual trumping of art by entertainment, and the uprooting of the linguistic self. When married to the constraints and values of mass communication by electronic means with digitalized information, fiction is transformed in ways that move it from the literature of the print era and towards sensationalized, made-to-be-viewed, pay-per-view scripts.

In these different ways, the culture of print is being increasingly influenced by the culture of mass media and the Internet, and giving way to it in many respects. Considering the changes in written genres, we might even say that the culture of print is being absorbed or transformed into a new form of mass-audience, quick-capture culture. Should we mind? While we have benefited in our own work and daily lives from electronic technologies and while we have enjoyed and admired some innovations of modern writing, we maintain that there is something special and worth preserving in the print culture, which is the focus on language and especially the complex forms of written language that have been the heart of organized knowledge and education and that have made possible the linguistic masterpieces of literature. At the very least, we should be skeptical that the new digitally influenced genres will have similarly profound and divers effects on the reader as those produced in a print context geared to a centrally linguistic aesthetic and recognized to be great works of literature.

New Born-Digital Works and the Digital Experiences Replacing Traditional Reading

A whole new group of digital creative writers has emerged in the last ten years, exploiting electronic and digital technologies to make types of poetry and fiction that are not possible other than on the Internet, while other kinds of digital poetry or fiction enhance works that appear in print form. Erik Loyer's *Strange*

Rain (Loyer, 2010), which has a continuous effect of rain hitting the screen that is integral to the poetry presented there, is an example of the first type, and his *Ruben and Lullaby* (Loyer, 2009), which transports the graphic novel to the digital environment, is an example of the second type. Both are powerfully effective and might be classified as works of digital art or literature. An earlier award-winning work by Loyer (2001), the digital serial novel *Chroma*, is included in Jessica Pressman's new canon of contemporary digital literature, which she argues in *Digital Modernism: Making It New in New Media* (Pressman, 2014) is a continuation of the 20th-century modernist trend of literature to engage with media. This new digital canon includes some important works that combine the values and effects of art and literature within technological affordances that cannot be duplicated by print alone.

With digital texts, reading becomes a much less linear and pre-sequenced activity and incorporates time spent listening and viewing – that is, on activities that are not reading per se but are meant to enhance the reading experience by digitally linking the text to supplementary or complementary information and nontextual media. Digital texts such as poetry or fiction may also provide ways for the audience to change the text or to add or subtract text or other media:

> Typical of digital creative texts is that they are not simply read but rather are interactively *played*, as in playing a game in which choices are offered that require decision-making and actions on the part of the audience. Digital texts may, for instance, offer different branches or orders in which to go through the parts of a text, along with optional paths and links to pictures, music, video, and supplementary information.
>
> *(Pennington, 2017, p. 269)*

Many poets are experimenting with poetry that can be digitally enhanced or altered, as in the work of the prize-winning poet Jena Osman. A digitally enhanced revision (Osman, 2011; http://jenaosman.com/zhivago/) of Osman's early digital poem "The Periodic Table as Assembled by Dr. Zhivago, Oculist" has poems linked to each of the elements of a periodic table that appears on the screen. Short poems, abstract and lyrical in character, are revealed by clicking on each element of the table. The periodic table interface is linked to various kinds of operations, analogous to chemical reactions, which deform and combine text so that the poems can be transformed in a number of ways. A person who interacts with these poems gains some control over them and is able to produce new forms of text from them, becoming in a sense a "player" of Osman's poems by creating different "textual reactions" on them. Much of digital poetry plays with similar built-in alteration, auto-deletion, and randomizing effects. The question is the extent to which poetry – or other print literary works – remain such when they are textually altered or deformed automatically by machine or by someone other than the author with the aid of a machine.

A common characteristic of digital creations is that they break up, or *fragment*, text or are constructed of pieces of text taken from larger works. The animated fragmentation effects which Osman incorporates into her poetry are one type of example. Other digital works break up continuous text with links to other text or digital objects such as sound files or video clips, or combine small pieces of text with other digital objects. For example, Maris Kreizman, a manager at Kickstarter, a funding platform for creative projects, created a blog in 2008 called Slaughterhouse 90210 (http://slaughterhouse90210.tumblr.com/), which she describes as "juxtapos[ing] images from TV shows with quotes from literature to comment on both and to create something that's entirely new" (Kreizman, 2015). The "bells and whistles" described by Biersdorfer (2015) contribute to this textual fragmentation effect in digital works, which in turn affects the reading process, making it fragmented as well. In an article entitled "Fragmentary: Writing in a Digital Age," Guy Patrick Cunningham reflects on the experience of reading such fragmentary texts:

> More and more, I read in pieces. So do you. … Even the longest stretches of text online are broken up with hyperlinks or other interactive elements (or even ads). This is neither a good nor bad thing, necessarily – it is simply a part of modern reading.
>
> *(Cunningham, 2012)*

Cunningham's perspective is that of a digital native, one whose world incorporates digital culture as the unmarked, natural baseline. For others of us who straddle the digital world and the ante-digital world, his easy acceptance of fragmented reading and writing as merely a form of "modern" reading and writing is a clear example of naturalizing the digital context and its artifacts. But this is not the only way to read the situation we find ourselves in. Even though it is true that this kind of fragmented interaction with text is a part, a very big part, of contemporary literacy, it may not be true that reading and writing in this disarticulated way is neutral, neither a good or a bad thing, nor that, as the term *modern* tends to imply, it represents progress. For the type of reading and writing that does not form a continuous and cumulative train of thought both models and contributes to the hyperactivity and shortened attention spans of digital natives that makes them read and write less, or at a less challenging and deep level, than is required for reading and writing in longer, more involved and involving, chains of thought.

From the early days of computer-based writing using word processing, it has been understood that reading on the screen is not as efficient or effective as reading from a printed page (see, e.g., the discussion in Haas, 1989). However, this fact seems to have been conveniently buried or forgotten for some years now in relation to the Internet – that is, until people like Wolf (2007) and Carr (2011/2008, 2010) started making a big noise about how onscreen reading might be rewiring people's brains in worrying ways, making it harder for them to concentrate and to learn. As Carr (2010) reviews from the research, "people who read linear text comprehend more, remember more, and learn more than those who read text peppered with links" (p. 127).

Yet the reading of books in general and of literary works in particular is on the decline, being steadily replaced by activities that employ other media. In addition to the "writing-lite" activity of texting, the reading-lite activities of screen viewing, and the pull of television, films, and other video modes, digital natives as well as digital immigrants may prefer to listen rather than read, through forms such as audiobooks, online broadcasts, and podcasts that make it possible to be enmeshed in an audio world while doing something else significant with the body and the eyes, such as shopping, exercising, even driving. In the Pew study of Americans' interactions with books, 14 percent reported listening to at least one audiobook in 2013 (Zickuhr & Rainie, 2014). James Atlas extols the virtues of literary listening rather than reading, as some writers are creating audio dramas which have no parallel book form as well as literary podcasts, which he believes are "evolving into a new literary form" (Atlas, 2015). Atlas is attracted to these new literary forms, especially the literary podcast, which to him combines the experiences of many media: "Listening to a podcast is like watching a movie, listening to music and reading a book all at once."

In the view of Atlas (2015), "there is something about the act of listening that invigorates the mind." We point out that exactly the same sort of comment is often made about reading a book, especially literary fiction. Atlas also comments on the efficiency and directness of listening as compared to reading, and notes the benefit of listening as allowing multitasking such as "driving to work or walking the dog." While this is obviously true, since reading a book requires sitting in one place and committing to it, mind and body, to a degree beyond doing anything else simultaneously – whether it be physical activity requiring movement or the online activities of reading emails, browsing, or surfing the Net – there are many benefits to sitting still and making such a whole-mind-and-body commitment in order to focus on the experience at hand. In fact, we suggest that part of the significance of literary reading (rather than listening to an audio recording) is that the reader can begin to hear his/her internal voice entering into dialogue with the imagination of the writer: the quietness of the text helps evoke such an experience.

Notes

1 Lists of best-selling books vary; see, e.g., www.listchallenges.com/101-best-selling-books-of-all-time; www.theguardian.com/news/datablog/2012/aug/09/best-selling-books-all-time-fifty-shades-grey-compare.
2 Bowker's figures for 2013 show juvenile books commanding second place (after fiction), with nearly 33,000 new ISBNs – though this figure represents a slight decline from 2012 (www.bowker.com/news/2014/Traditional-Print-Book-Production-Dipped-Slightly-in-2013.html).

References

American Academy of Pediatrics (2016a). Media and young minds. Council on Communications and Media Policy Statement. *Pediatrics*, *138*(5), 1–6. doi:10.1542/peds.2016–2591.

American Academy of Pediatrics (2016b). Media use in school-aged children and adolescents. Council on Communications and Media Policy Statement. *Pediatrics*, *138*(5), 1–6. doi:10.1542/peds.2016–2592.

Atlas, James (2015). Hearing is believing. *The New York Times*, Sunday Review. January 11, 2015, p. 8.

Biersdorfer, J. D. (2015). Through a touch-screen looking glass. *The New York Times*, Book Review. April 12, 2015, p. 29.

Bloom, Harold (2000). *How to read and why*. London: Fourth Estate.

Carr, Nicholas (2010). *The shallows: What the Internet is doing to our brains*. New York: W. W. Norton & Co.

Carr, Nicholas (2011/2008). Is Google making us stupid? In Mark Bauerlein (ed.), *The digital divide: Arguments for and against Facebook, Google, texting, and the age of social networking* (pp. 63–75). New York: Jeremy P. Tarcher/Penguin. Originally appeared in *The Atlantic*, July/August 2008.

Collins, Suzanne (2008). *The hunger games*. New York: Scholastic.

Collins, Suzanne (2009). *Catching fire*. New York: Scholastic.

Collins, Suzanne (2010). *Mockingjay*. New York: Scholastic.

Cunningham, Guy Patrick (2012). Fragmentary: Writing in a digital age. *The Millions* website. January 24, 2012. Retrieved on February 25, 2012 from www.themillions. com/2012/01/fragmentary-writing-in-a-digital-age.html.

Davidson, Cathy N. (2011). *Now you see it: How the brain science of attention will transform the way we live, work, and learn*. New York: Viking Press.

Debczak, Michele (2016). Kids' books have gotten longer thanks to the 'Harry Potter effect.' *Mental Floss* website. March 3, 2016. Retrieved on August 9, 2016 from http://mentalfloss.com/article/76466/kids-books-have-gotten-longer-thanks-to-harry-potter-effect.

Díaz-Vera, Javier E. (2012). *Left to my own devices: Learner autonomy and mobile-assisted language learning*. Leiden and Boston: Brill.

Greenfield, Patricia M. (2009). Technology and informal education: What is taught, what is learned. *Science*, *323*(5910), 69–71. doi: 10.1126/science.1167190.

Haas, Christina (1989). Seeing it on the screen isn't really seeing it: Computer writers' reading problems. In Gail E. Hawisher & Cynthia L. Selfe (eds.), *Critical perspectives on computers and composition instruction* (pp. 16–29). New York: Teachers College Press.

Kirby, Alan (2009). *Digimodernism: How new technologies dismantle the postmodern and reconfigure our culture*. New York: Continuum.

Kozlowska, Hannah (2014). Can 'Harry Potter' change the world? *New York Times* website. September 17, 2014. Retrieved on August 10, 2016 from http://op-talk.blogs.nytimes. com/2014/09/17/can-harry-potter-change-the-world/?_r=2.

Kreizman, Maris (2015). Don't reboot the recent past. *The New York Times*, Sunday Review. July 12, 2015, p. 8.

Kutz, Eleanor, & Roskelly, Hephzib (1991). *An unquiet pedagogy: Transforming practice in the English classroom*. Portsmouth, NH: Boynton/Cook.

Loyer, Erik (2001). Chroma. *Erik Loyer* website. Retrieved on October 25, 2015 from http://erikloyer.com/index.php/projects/detail/chroma/.

Loyer, Erik (2009). Ruben and lullaby. *Opertoon* website. Retrieved on September 1, 2013 from http://opertoon.com/2009/05/ruben-lullaby/.

Loyer, Erik (2010). Strange rain. *Opertoon* website. Retrieved on August 10, 2013 from http://opertoon.com/2010/11/strange-rain-for-ipad-iphone-ipod-touch/.

Maloney, Jennifer (2016). 'Harry Potter and the Cursed Child' book sales keep the magic alive. *The Wall Street Journal* website. August 3, 2016. Retrieved on August 9, 2016 from http://blogs.wsj.com/speakeasy/2016/08/03/harry-potter-and-the-cursed-child-book-sales-keep-the-magic-alive/.

McLuhan, Marshall (1964). *Understanding media: Extensions of man.* New York: Mentor.

Mills, M. Anthony (with Mills, Phil) (2014). The Harry Potter Paradox. *Real Clear Religion* website. January 24, 2014. Retrieved on August 9, 2016 from www.realclearreligion. org/articles/2014/01/24/the_harry_potter_paradox.html.

Newman, John Henry (2008/1852). *The idea of a university, defined and illustrated in nine discourses delivered to the Catholics of Dublin.* Published as an e-book by Project Gutenberg, February 5, 2008. Retrieved on July 24, 2015 from www.gutenberg.org/files/24526/24526-pdf.pdf.

Obesity Prevention Source (2016). Television watching and "sit time." *T. H. Chan School of Public Health* (Harvard University) website. Retrieved on March 10, 2016 from www.hsph.harvard.edu/obesity-prevention-source/obesity-causes/television-and-sedentary-behavior-and-obesity/.

Osman, Jena (2011). The periodic table as assembled by Dr. Zhivago, oculist (revised). *Digital Earthenware* website. Available at http://jenaosman.com/zhivago/.

Pennington, Martha C. (2001). Writing minds and talking fingers: Doing literacy in an electronic age. In P. Brett (ed.), *CALL in the 21st century* (CD-ROM). Barcelona: ESADE Institute (Idiomas) and Hove, U.K.: IATEFL. Papers from a conference sponsored jointly by ESADE Institute (Idiomas), Barcelona, and IATEFL CALL SIG, June 30–July 2, 2000.

Pennington, Martha C. (2011). Teaching writing: Managing the tension between freedom and control. *Writing & Pedagogy, 3*(1), 1–16. doi:10.1558.wap.v3i1.1.

Pennington, Martha C. (2013). Trends in writing and technology. *Writing & Pedagogy, 5*(2), 155–179. doi:10.1558/wap.v5i2.155.

Pennington, Martha C. (2017). Literacy, culture, and creativity in a digital era. *Pedagogy, 17*(2), 259–287. doi: 10.1215/15314200-3770149.

Poe, Marshall T. (2011). *A history of communications: Media and society from the evolution of speech to the Internet.* New York: Cambridge University Press.

Postman, Neil (1985). *Amusing ourselves to death: Public discourse in the age of show business.* New York: Penguin.

Prensky, Marc (2011/2001). Digital natives, digital immigrants. In Mark Bauerlein (ed.), *The digital divide: Arguments for and against Facebook, Google, texting, and the age of social networking* (pp. 3–11). New York: Jeremy P. Tarcher/Penguin. Originally appeared in *On the Horizon 9* (October 2001), 1–6.

Pressman, Jessica (2014). *Digital modernism: Making it new in new media.* Oxford: Oxford University Press.

Remley, Dirk (2013). Templated pedagogy: Factors affecting standardized writing pedagogy with Blackboard Vista. *Writing & Pedagogy, 5*(1), 105–120. doi: 10/1558/wap.v4i5.1.

Rogers, Bob (2005). When will they learn? *University Business.* November 2005, pp. 25–26.

Rowling, J. K. (1997). *Harry Potter and the philosopher's stone.* London: Bloomsbury.

Rowling, J. K. (1998). *Harry Potter and the sorcerer's stone.* New York: Scholastic.

Rowling, J. K. (2007). *Harry Potter and the deathly hallows.* New York: Scholastic.

Rowling, J. K., Tiffany, John, & Thorne, Jack (2016). *Harry Potter and the cursed child, parts one and two.* New York: Scholastic.

Shields, David (2010). *Reality hunger.* New York: Alfred A. Knopf.

Sindoni, Maria Grazia (2013). *Spoken and written discourse in online interactions: A multimodal approach.* New York and London: Routledge.

Slouka, Mark (2009). Dehumanized: When math and science rule the school. *Harper's Magazine.* September 2009, pp. 32–40.

Streitfeld, David (2014). Amazon offers all-you-can-eat books. Authors turn up noses. *The New York Times.* December 28, 2014, pp. 1, 4.

Strickland, Stephanie (2009). Born digital. *The Poetry Foundation* website. Retrieved on December 15, 2012 from www.poetryfoundation.org.

Tolkien, J. R. R. (1937). *The Hobbit.* London: George Allen & Unwin.

Tolkien, J. R. R. (1954–1955). *The lord of the rings.* London: George Allen & Unwin.

Waxler, Robert P., & Hall, Maureen P. (2011). *Transforming literacy: Changing lives through reading and writing.* Leiden and Boston: Brill.

Wieseltier, Leon (2015). Among the disrupted. *The New York Times,* Book Review. January 18, 2015, pp. 1, 14–15.

Wolf, Maryanne (2007). *Proust and the squid: The story and science of the reading brain.* New York: HarperCollins.

Wolf, Maryanne, & Barzillai, Mirit (2009). The importance of deep reading. *Educational Leadership,* *66*(6), 32–37. Available at www.ascd.org/publications/educational-leadership/mar09/vol66/num06/The-Importance-of-Deep-Reading.aspx.

Word Counter Blog (2016). How many words are there in the Harry Potter book series? November 25, 2015. Retrieved on August 9, 2016 from https://wordcounter.net/blog/2015/11/23/10922_how-many-words-harry-potter.html.

Zickuhr, Kathryn, & Rainie, Lee (2014). A snapshot of reading in America in 2013. *Pew Research Center* website. January 16, 2014. Retrieved on February 13, 2015 from www.pewinternet.org/2014/01/16/a-snapshot-of-reading-in-america-in-2013/.

7

HOW FICTION AND POETRY WORK THEIR MAGIC

Literature is the most exact expression of feelings, while science is the most exact kind of reporting. Poetry, which condenses the affective resources of language into patterns of infinite rhythmical subtlety, may be said to be *the language of expression at its highest degree of efficiency.*
– *S. I. Hayakawa,* Language in Thought and Action *(Hayakawa, 1990/1939, p. 158, original emphasis)*

Language and Story in Human Life

It is commonly said that language is the defining feature which sets humans above all other creatures and gives *H. sapiens* a competitive edge over other species. Beyond language per se, a number of linguists and scholars in related fields such as anthropology and sociology have argued that narrative or story is the core of human reality or a defining feature of human nature. As narrative researchers Michael F. Connelly and Jean D. Clandinin put it: "Humans are story-telling organisms who, individually and collectively, lead storied lives" (Connelly & Clandinin, 1990, p. 2). Catherine Kohler Riessman classified narrative as "a universal human activity" (Riessman, 1993, p. 3), and Nancy Huston, in *The Tale-Tellers: A Short Study of Humankind*, writes that "[n]arrative gives [human] life a dimension of meaning utterly unknown to animals" (Huston, 2008, p. 15) – just as language does.

It is a central thesis of this book that human language and story are a primary connective tissue of human nature. As human beings, we all construct our relationships, our world, our culture, and our civilization to a great extent by and through language, with story playing a crucial role in helping us both create and interpret our experience. Given the centrality of language in creating and maintaining human existence, it is also a central thesis of this book that if we, as a human community, do not continue to keep language, rather than the images and consumerism of mass media, at the center of our lives and culture, then we will no longer be able to create our own stories, our own narrative selves. When that happens – and more and more people seem to be walking around these days without a story – then an emptiness will remain to be filled, if at all, with cynicism, insecurity, even fear.

Human beings are predisposed (some believe pre-wired) for language and for story. Language and story are a key aspect of language users' cognitive and emotional architecture, and of their psychological and social selves as individuals and also as part of a community of others. Children learn and then create language and stories in a community of others. Through the process, they construct their identity and become members of that community. Language and stories both define a person as an individual and tie each individual to others and to the entire culture of human life events and meaning. People naturally live in and through language and stories: human beings are compelled to articulate their experience in language and to create autobiographical and narrative selves. One's identity and sense of personal history and coherence is based in a life story, unique yet connected to the stories of others.

A person's life journey is created and told through language and story: each human being has language in common with other human beings, and everyone has a personal history and a life story that overlaps the histories and life stories of others. Language in general and narrative in particular, the telling of stories, connect us all in a human chain of being. As Waxler (2007) maintains:

> We all have our stories and we all have the opportunity to make a story from the raw experience of our life. ... Story evokes story, builds community, because it offers us the opportunity to locate ourselves in the world, among other stories.
>
> (p. 128)

Our language and our stories define us, so much so that we could say it is impossible to lead a fully *human* life in the absence of language or story. For human beings, a life without language and a life without story – a life unarticulated and unnarrated – is a life of isolation, hardly worth living.

Language and story are also important vehicles through which people perform actions in the physical and social world, thus establishing their agency. Language and story are moreover a way to higher understanding, to abstraction and generalization, providing important pathways to human purpose and meaning. Much more than a means of communication, language and story are a means of fulfillment, a primary way to a rich and fully realized human existence. Language and story are the human means for not only describing but also creating our uniquely human reality: through our words and the concepts and narratives built around them, we articulate a world defined and comprehended in human terms – one interpreted through a human sense of meaning and meaningfulness.

We are drawn to Mark Turner's ideas as expressed in *The Literary Mind: The Origins of Thought and Language* (Turner, 1996) about parable and story being the historical and logical heart of language, and his account strengthens arguments that stories and the reading of fiction should have a central place in human life and the education of children. However, his evolutionary scenario, in which grammar originates in story, is not crucial to our argument. Whether story begat grammar or the other way around, narratives are an important way that humans organize experience through language and recreate that experience in the mind. There is evidence that the mind is organized in part in narrative structures (sometimes called scripts or schemas). Narrative is a main means that humans have to organize sensory information and build knowledge as a human-embodied sense of history relevant to their individual life stories. As linguist Mark Johnson maintains, "Narrative supplies and reveals the themes by which we seek to unify the temporal, historical dimension of our existence, and without which our lives would be a meaningless jumble of disconnected events" (Johnson, 1987, p. 170).

We would add that story is the emotional heart of language. Narrative language plays an important role in the experiencer's engagement in and connection to what is conveyed through that language. Narrative provides, through its richly textured language and its symbolic representations and evocation of experience, both sensuous pleasure and the interpretation of that sensuous experience in a meaningful way. It also can be considered as providing an ethical or moral structuring of human experience, as Anthony J. Cascardi, writing in *The Cambridge Introduction to Literature and Philosophy*, maintains:

> Narrative is not just a form that is laid over neutral content, but it is itself both an epistemological category and an ethical/moral one. It orders knowledge and values according to the elements of time and action that are basic to experience itself. Proponents of [this] strong view of narrative would say that narrative is basic to questions of truth and value because cognition and morality are themselves narratively structured.
>
> *(Cascardi, 2014, p. 155)*

From this perspective, narrative or story can perhaps be seen as embodying the moral heart of language.

In providing narrative structures and themes involving human purposes, stories or narratives are an essential means for creating coherence in life. As a consequence, according to the Italian philosopher and psychoanalyst Gemma C. Fiumara, stories or narratives have an essential function in ensuring psychological health:

> As developing humans absorb narratives they get ideas about how they may create links within potentially chaotic situations. Meaningful stories contribute

to maturing persons' attempts to engage with interactive life and to perceive some order in the disparate attachments they create.

(Fiumara, 1995, p. 90)

Donald E. Polkinghorne sees narrative as "the primary form by which human experience is made meaningful" (Polkinghorne, 1988, p. 3). Narrative and story are crucial binding agents in humans' abilities to make connections between disparate events and time periods, and so to establish cause-and-effect relations, continuity, and coherence. Narrative and story moreover offer ways of organizing and framing experience, and so of perceiving and understanding what is experienced, in human terms, that is, in relation to human meaning. Relating experience in a narrative or story structure makes that experience especially comprehensible, relevant, and memorable both to the storyteller and to others.

A considerable body of research with children and adults dating from the 1970s (e.g., Kintsch, 1977; Thorndyke, 1977) has demonstrated that information framed in a narrative structure is more comprehensible and memorable than information presented outside of a story frame. Later research (reviewed in Chapter 9) has shown how stories establish relevance and psychological ties to other human beings, by helping readers imagine their own responses in relation to the events and characters portrayed. The particular appeal of stories is that people can relate them to their own lives and so participate in them. This is because stories construct experience in ways that resemble, and so remind people of, their own lived experience. This personal relevance and opportunity to participate sets stories apart from other genres or ways of representing experience in language, such as a factual description or logical presentation of ideas. Framing events or ideas in a narrative structure, as a story, gives them a uniquely human cast which brings them alive in a way that a logical presentation or factual description devoid of narrative elements or story cannot. More than other ways of presenting information or ideas, a narrative engages not just the intellect, but also the emotions and the senses, one's very personhood, making for a more involved and memorable – sometimes even a life-changing – experience. Stories are more essentially human than information stripped bare of the complexity of feelings. They are in this sense more authentic or true to life than facts, or history, or science: they are a better representation of life and the world as humans experience it.

Stories are central to many aspects of our lives, as Gottschall (2012) observes. He notes that "[s]torytelling is the spine of televised sports" (p. 14), from the Olympics, to boxing, to pro wrestling, which "exaggerates what we find in legitimate sports broadcasting, where an announcer – a skilled narrative shaper – tries to elevate a game to the level of high drama" (p. 13). He comments on the prevalence of story in television programs and commercials, in other forms of advertising and in business more generally, as well as in politics. The connection of storytelling to pro wrestling, television, advertising, and politics reminds us of the "slippery slope" leading to deception and illusion that Boorstin (1961),

Hedges (2009), and Bruni (2015) have warned of, as a story can be the same thing as a lie. A literary story, though fictional, is not a lie but a realistic narrative in the sense that it captures something essentially true, and essentially human, by analogy to everyday experience. Rather than seeking to deceive or to "pull the wool over one's eyes," literary fiction seeks to remove any wool – or "curtain," as Milan Kundera puts it (Kundera, 2006) – which people have in front of their eyes that obscures their clear vision and keeps them from seeing things as they really are.

Writing about stories in organizations, Yiannis Gabriel defines stories as

> narratives with plots and characters, generating emotion in narrator and audience, through a poetic elaboration of symbolic material. This material may be a product of fantasy or experience, including an experience of earlier narratives. Story plots entail conflicts, predicaments, trials and crises which call for choices, decisions, actions and interactions, whose actual outcomes are often at odds with the characters' intentions and purposes.
>
> *(Gabriel, 2000, p. 239)*

Fiction moves us through the "poetic elaboration of symbolic material" in literary language, the words which the writer selects, and through plots and characters which the writer creates to symbolize the dilemmas and themes of human existence. It is in the nature of stories that they involve central characters and through them paint pictures of human nature, of courage and ideals that we would like to aim for, as well as human shortcomings, frailty, and their consequences. We see in those who populate our stories our heroes and our tragic failures, and most particularly we see people who are, in different ways, like ourselves. Skilled literary writers know how to create characters that remind us of ourselves and others we know – characters with whom we can empathize. The story works its magic through creating this empathic response in the reader. Brian Boyd, writing in *On the Origin of Stories: Evolution, Cognition, and Fiction*, maintains that narrative or story "develops our capacity to see from different perspectives, and this capacity in turn arises from and aids the evolution of cooperation and the growth of human flexibility" (Boyd, 2009, p. 176).

Reading literature is a main way humans can experience stories and through them gain perspectives on truth and the human condition as reflected in the lives of others and the reader's own life. As Denis Dutton observes in *The Art Instinct: Beauty, Pleasure, and Human Evolution*, "The teller of a story has, in the nature of the story-telling art, direct access to the inner mental experience of the story's characters. This access is impossible to develop in other arts – music, dance, painting, and sculpture" (Dutton, 2009, p. 118).

The reader of a story gains this same access to the story characters' mental experience. By portraying the "mundane imaginative structures of memory, immediate perception, planning, calculation, and decision-making, both as we experience them ourselves and as we understand others to be experiencing them" (Dutton, 2009, p. 119), literary narrative pulls the reader into the reading experience and so into the story itself.

The Nature of Fiction

Fiction is a category of linguistic genre, typically written, whose purpose is to move people into their imaginations and then to take them on an enjoyable – and, in the best case, enriching – psychological journey in that imaginary space created through language. A fiction writer succeeds in doing this by presenting a simulation of human life and experience in the form of a story that stimulates a reader's imagination and guides the reader's psychological journey. An effective simulation in a work of fiction takes readers on a mental journey that is both enjoyable and memorable as it traverses a "storyscape" which, while it has familiar resonances, offers much that is new and beckons to be explored. This is a journey leading from the beginning point of the story to its ending point via the new terrain created from the writer's mind and experience, as linked to the vast territory of the reader's own mind and experience.

Fiction builds a model world within the text that has resemblances to the nontextual "real world," that is, it has *verisimilitude*. In the view of Uffe Seilman and Steen Larsen, "verisimilitude seems to be a decisive feature of 'good' literature" (Seilman & Larsen, 1989, p. 166) that gives it "personal resonance" (p. 167) for the reader and helps distinguish literary reading from "ordinary text comprehension" (p. 166). James Wood, writing in *How Fiction Works* (Wood, 2008), stresses that verisimilitude is only one of two essential qualities of fiction – the other being *artifice*. Fiction is thus meaningful yet fantastical, balancing two deep psychological needs – one for understanding and the other for release (Pennington, forthcoming). It is the author's imaginative modeling of setting, characters, and events that are relatable to those of the "real world," combined with linguistic and narrative elements crafted to take the reader into a mental space of make-believe, which together give fiction its special power to engage human beings to exercise the mind and allow their feelings to flow freely in a safe context. Fictional texts also seem to invoke readers' memories of experiences in which they have actively participated, which Seilman and Larsen (1989) describe as the reader "recruiting previous, specific knowledge in order to understand the text" (p. 174). Their experiments with psychology students suggest that this process of recruitment of previous knowledge in comprehending a text is a more involved and personal one for readers of fiction than for readers of expository text, whose "remindings" of past experiences while reading are less likely to be ones in which they played an active part. These characteristics can all be considered ways in which fiction, like other literature and art more generally, is both imaginative and true to life – or, to put it in Wood's (2008) terms, realizes the combined features of artifice and verisimilitude.

A successful work of fiction can therefore be described as creating a hypothetical or imagined "parallel universe" that simulates the "real world" as human beings experience it within a compelling structure of language and narrative that stimulates readers to journey there in their minds and that moves them, figuratively and literally, through the story. The make-believe realm of a work of fiction must have enough resemblance to real life to be interpretable in terms of everyday experience, yet must diverge from it sufficiently to be recognized as fictional. These two features together create the characteristic of verisimilitude that is an essential feature of fiction. The effectiveness of a work of fiction depends on both its verisimilitude and its novelty as qualities that attract and hold readers' attention, maintain them in its story world, and stimulate their psychological journey there through the characteristics of its language and narrative elements. A well-crafted fictional work produces an interplay of verisimilitude – or "familiarization" – and novelty – or "defamiliarization" (Miall & Kuiken, 1994) – of content and language that works the imagination and gives pleasure. Experiencing this interplay of familiarization and defamiliarization produces feelings and understandings that connect to the reader's prior knowledge and memories and so reinforce those, as what can be called *aah* effects (Pennington, forthcoming), while also imprinting new knowledge and memories, as *aha!* effects of sudden insight.[1]

A work of fiction will be judged as literature based on the quality of the experience which it both simulates and stimulates, through the verisimilitude and the novelty of its language and its story. For that experience to stimulate a reader beyond escapist pleasure and to attain the aesthetic proportions of art, it must be an especially powerful and enduring one – an experience perceived as both universal and of particular relevance to everyone who enters the writer's imaginative world. The *aah* effect of connection to what is known and familiar and the *aha!* effect of new discovery must be especially striking in their combined quality and quantity and their staying power, resonating for readers in ways that make the fictional journey a major event. A reader's journey in literary fiction is neither the shortest and most direct path from point A to point B nor a mere escape from everyday life, but something high in uniqueness and significance, as in the experience of journeying to view a specific must-see sight or the accumulation of diverse experiences and impressions on an extended trip.

Fiction is psychological in nature, working mind-to-mind, as a reader channels the thoughts and feelings of a writer through the writer's words. A characteristic of novels which is shared with short stories is that both paint imaginative pictures of life through the reflections of another person – who may be a character in the story or novel, a narrator, or the author separate from these. Although every character or a narrator, if present, is a representative of the voice of the author behind the work, the author's voice or perspective may not be embodied in the onstage voice or thoughts of one or more characters or in the offstage observations of a narrator. Rather than being put into the mouths, thoughts, or perspectives of any person, the author's viewpoint may be indirectly incorporated into the warp and woof of the language and structure of the piece, in how something is expressed, what is said and unsaid, and, in general, what is included in and excluded from the work. Readers who share the same language and much of the same experience of being human with the writer are able to understand the writer's intention, including much that is implicit, and to read themselves into the work. Wood's (2008) discussion suggests that fiction has progressed by increasingly developing in its psychological dimension through expansion and refinement of ways to express the workings of the human mind explicitly and implicitly through language.

Creating a Story World in the Opening of the Tale of Rip Van Winkle

Washington Irving's story of Rip Van Winkle (Irving, 1864/1819), the man who fell asleep for 20 years, is a prime example of the combined properties of artifice and verisimilitude, and how they can be crafted by a writer to create an enchanting story world which readers willingly enter and dwell in for a time in their imaginations. The opening to this story shows how carefully crafted language and narrative establishes a frame for the reader to enter a new and different world, a story world that requires the reader to grapple with the writer's intention and to figure out what he is up to. The interpretive task set for the reader is apparent from the very beginning of the work, in the complexity and mystery of its framing, which lays the groundwork for the mystery in the story itself. In addition, for the modern reader, it requires grappling not only with the twists and turns of the story's framing and plot, but also with the unfamiliarity of some of its language.

"Rip Van Winkle, a Posthumous Writing of Diedrich Knickerbocker" is one of the earliest short stories of the modern type by an American author. It appeared in 1819 in the first installment of the serialized story collection *The Sketch Book of Geoffrey Crayon, Gent* (Irving, 1864/1819); another of Irving's best-known stories, "The Legend of Sleepy Hollow," appeared in the sixth installment, published the next year. Both of these stories are attributed to a fictional Dutch historian, Diedrich Knickerbocker, and are written in a way that builds a pretense of being true tales while reflecting both make-believe and verisimilitude. What might be considered the folktale of Rip Van Winkle, as set within and near a village in the Catskill Mountains, is widely known, though most people would not have read the original story. In it, Irving sets the central tale of Rip Van Winkle within a larger story context that portrays it as one of the historical writings of Diedrich Knickerbocker and relates it as well to some historical events. The setting of the story is pictured in considerable detail and in a realistic and highly evocative portrait of the Catskill Mountains. In this way, Irving adds further layers of complexity and storytelling to make this a substantial work of literary quality.

"Rip Van Winkle" is a story that transports the reader into the land of the imagination and creates enchantment – a literary fiction that delights us in its many layers of highly skilled and artistic storytelling. The beginning of the story sets it in a fictitious context that activates the reader's imagination and creates both an *aha!* effect of novelty and an *aah* effect of familiarity, as the reader catches on to what the writer is doing and, through his sensuous language and vivid description, is able to visualize the place and time described and the characters inhabiting that story world. Here is how the original story begins:

> By Woden, God of Saxons,
> From whence comes Wensday, that is Wodensday,
> Truth is a thing that ever I will keep
> Unto thylke day in which I creep into
> My sepulchre——
>
> > *CARTWRIGHT.*

In beginning the story with an oath to truth that is also an invocation to the legendary Norse god Woden, Irving suggests that the story he is about to tell is in the realm of legend. He further builds the artifice of the story in introductory commentary on its background, saying that the tale he is about to pass on to us "was found among the papers of the late Diedrich Knickerbocker," apparently an old gentleman of New York who was very curious about Dutch history, and verified by Knickerbocker, in a note appended to the story that was included in the revised edition, as "beyond the possibility of doubt" since he had himself interviewed Rip Van Winkle and "seen a certificate on the subject taken before a country justice and signed with a cross, in the justice's own handwriting." The introductory commentary also interjects notes of humor, as the narrator-author pokes fun at the story in saying, "There have been various opinions as to the literary character of his work," and "Its chief merit is its scrupulous accuracy."

Irving then skillfully leads the reader into the story by means of his carefully crafted, aesthetically pleasing language, which establishes a mood and setting for the tale. First, we are introduced to the Catskill Mountains, their sublime summit "swelling up to a noble height and lording it over the surrounding country." These mountains give over a kind of royal magic and illumination, "clothed in blue and purple" and radiant like the "setting sun" that lights up "like a crown of glory." They also represent the flux of time and change: "Every change of season, every change of weather, indeed, every hour of the day, produces some change in the magical hues and shapes of these mountains," the word "change" emphasized through a repetitive pattern and rhythm reminiscent of temporal movement and natural seasons. This is the world that Irving wants readers to first experience as they move down the mountain into the Dutch village: a world of romance and wonder, a mood infused with the sublime, a kind of awe that lends itself to the magic of fictional authority.

"At the foot of these mountains," readers are told in the next paragraph, nearer to human scale, the Dutch village is set. It is a place with its own mystery and romance, a village "of great antiquity," close to the first days of the colonists of New Netherland, which later became the state of New York. The author here reinforces the pretense of the truth of the story by connecting its origins to the historical figure of Peter Stuyvesant, who served as the last Dutch governor of the colony into the mid-1600s, and by saying that the village contained "some of the houses of the original settlers." These he goes on to describe as being built in the old style of "lattice windows, gable fronts surmounted with weathercocks, and built of small yellow bricks brought from Holland." The reader can visualize these houses from the details of the village as a place where "the shingle roofs gleam" and "where the blue tints of the upland" melt into "the fresh green of the nearer landscape," while taking in the conceit that the writer is describing a real, historical place. It is within such a setting that Rip Van Winkle will finally emerge, an imaginary but relatable character set in this imaginary but well-imagined (by the writer) and imaginable (by the reader) place.

Thus is the reader led into a world of fantasy and humor – a world where a person can go bowling with little men in the hills of the Catskill Mountains of upstate New York, drink too much, and fall asleep for 20 years. Rip Van Winkle is the center of a story which is humorous on more than one level – not only in the figure of Rip but its overall satirical purpose, which is to poke fun at the Dutch "country folk," who, as it were, "slept" through the American Revolution. The folktale and the fictional character that is at the heart of the Rip Van Winkle story have endured for nearly two centuries as part of our shared culture.[2]

The Nature of Poetry

A poem is an aesthetic object which engages the ear and often the eye as well, the emotions, and the intellect. A poem does not have any specific utility in the sense in which that is usually meant today, as something which is a means to a pragmatic end. Rather, as noted by Adam Kirsch, "A poem stands at the opposite end of the spectrum from a stop sign, in that it demands attention for itself, its specific verbal weight and nuance, rather than immediately directing us to take an action" (Kirsch, 2014). The key feature of a poem is its language, both the specific words selected and the pattern in which those words are arranged. The language of a poem functions as an aesthetic object and experience also through embodying the creative vision and style of its author, the poet's imagination and passion, and transmitting these to the reader. Absorbing the emotions underlying a poem through its language is an important aspect of the participatory experience of reading or hearing a poem that leads to both pleasure and understanding. When encountering these lines of Keats, for example, a reader can imagine the poet exclaiming these words and so hear, in the "mind's ear," his emotions and, through empathic connection and sensation, feel his passion:

> More happy love! more happy, happy love!
>> For ever warm and still to be enjoy'd,
>>> For ever panting, and for ever young;
>>>> *John Keats, "Ode on a Grecian*
>>>> *Urn" (Keats, 1820)*

In classic poems like those of Blake or Keats, even though the language is not modern – and even because it is not modern – the poet's words, so carefully selected and arranged, create a symphony of language in the ear and a landscape of meaning in the imagination, building to a passionate crescendo that makes the heart sing. This is poetry at its best.

Poets choose and arrange words carefully for their sound qualities and their associated images and meanings. That is, they choose and arrange words for their associations in terms of what they make a person remember or think of and feel, such as the word "panting" in Keats' poem, which might elicit impressions or memories to do with the sound or feel of panting, and of experiences associated with panting. A poet's choice of words and their arrangement is an artistic creation, forming aesthetically pleasing combinations, such as the following lines, written in 1929 but published posthumously, from D. H. Lawrence's "Bavarian Gentians":

> Reach me a gentian, give me a torch!
> let me guide myself with the blue, forked torch of this flower
> down the darker and darker stairs, where blue is darkened on blueness…
> *(Lawrence, 1933; to see the entire poem and commentary on it, visit the Poetry*
> *by Heart website www.poetrybyheart.org.uk/poems/bavarian-gentians/)*

Even if you have never heard of or seen a gentian, and even if you do not fully understand what this poem is saying, you can take pleasure in the poet's orchestration of language, the flow of words as these are arranged on the page and as they sound when read aloud. You can enjoy reading lines like these, which demand attention for themselves, for their "specific verbal weight and nuance" (Kirsch, 2014), as well as for the passion and sentiments which they convey. You may also take pleasure in the images created by Lawrence's stress on the blue color of this flower and his noting of its "forked torch" shape and likeness to an actual torch that might serve as a guide into darkness.

Unlike a philosopher, according to Mark Forsyth, "A poet is not somebody who has great thoughts" (Forsyth, 2013, p. 5). Rather, as Forsyth puts it in the preface to *The Elements of Eloquence: Secrets of the Perfect Turn of Phrase*: "A poet is somebody who expresses his thoughts, however commonplace they may be, exquisitely. This is the one and only difference between the poet and everybody else" (ibid.). This is a very big difference indeed, as poets are able to use language in ways that tap directly into human emotions, sensations, and imaginative abilities. A poem is designed to engage a reader or listener by the poet's ability to select and craft the elements of language into pleasing sounds and shapes that create images, scenes, and mood in the mind and feelings of the reader (or listener) and that connect to further meanings and things the reader knows and is interested in. In so doing, the poet aims to first stimulate and sharpen the senses, so that the person reading or hearing the poem is inspired to pay close attention and to both sense and think about what the poem means. The poet's *exquisite language* acts as a portal which those who encounter it are invited to go through in order to participate in the poem, to journey inside it, traveling ever more deeply to unlock its secrets.

Poems are highly compact forms of aesthetically patterned language that say much in few words. A poem is a sort of linguistic snapshot, made memorable by its linguistic patterning and pregnant with meaning. A poem may be lyrical in nature, focused on sound, mood, and feeling; it may play with language; it may incorporate a story or narrative. The meaning of a poem may be conveyed in indirect, suggestive ways, through its patterns of text – literally, its *texture* – and through implicit messages which must be discovered by the reader. The poet creates the meaning and effect of a poem through words and expressions carefully selected to have certain connotations and associations and carefully arranged in patterns which stand out and which, if read deeply, allow multiple layers of interpretation, leading to a sort of epiphany. In the words of David Morley in *The Cambridge Introduction to Creative Writing*, "Poetry is a form of creating ... epiphanies through making lines of language, the internal arrangement of which ... carries the poem into memory" (Morley, 2007, p. 196) and, we would add, into deep feeling and interpretive consciousness.

Poetry, like other forms of literature and art, is characterized by its originality and imaginative use of its medium of expression to create unusual verbal effects through defamiliarization and what the Czech linguist and literary theorist Jan Mukařovský described as "foregrounding" of expression to "[achieve] maximum intensity" (Mukařovský, 1964/1932, p. 44). As linguists and literary scholars have noted, poetry is characterized by novel or deviant language, such as original words, word combinations, and uses of words, and original structure – the linguistic grammar and rhetoric as well as the visual grammar or structure and rhetoric. Vendler (2015) characterizes "the import of poetry" as "the power of idiosyncratic style," which she goes on to classify as "linguistic and structural idiosyncrasy" (p. 2). Bloom, like Vendler a respected critic and scholar of poetry, describes it thus in *The Art of Reading Poetry*: "Poetry essentially is figurative language, concentrated so that its form is both expressive and evocative. Figuration is a turning from the literal, and the form of a great poem itself can be a trope ('turning') or figure" (Bloom, 2004, p. 1). Figuration comprises literary means to produce effects of defamiliarization and foregrounding. Bloom (p. 3) speaks of the "excess or overflow" and "newness" of meaning created by the poet's use of figurative language, including irony, synecdoche, metonymy, and metaphor.

In a poem, the individual words, collocations, and larger patterns of words on the page – by the very fact of having been so carefully selected and crafted in linguistic and visual patterns – speak volumes: by embodying tropes, by being typical or atypical, by what is said as well as what is not said, by suggesting certain images and associations, by making comparisons and contrasts. For every word that occurs in a poem, a great deal is implied. Part of the allure of a poem is the compactness and at the same time the fullness of its language – a kind of *verbal minimalism* that co-occurs with *semantic maximalism*, saying much in few words. According to Hayakawa (1990/1939), "Poetry … may be said to be *the language of expression at its highest degree of efficiency*" (p. 158, original emphasis). Or, as Michael Toolan, in his entry in *The Routledge Handbook of Language and Creativity* on "Poetry and Poetics," cites as a distinctive characteristic of poetry, "it aims to generate more new thoughts and imaginings (more surprises, or unforeseen ideas) in more recipients (in more times, and more places), while itself taking up less time and less space than all other verbal genres" (Toolan, 2016, p. 235).

As compared to other forms of writing, a poem is both compact and highly designed. A feature of poetry is its prosody, its meter or rhythm, and the phonetic properties and patterns in its words, such as rhyming, alliteration (repetition of consonant sounds in neighboring words), or assonance (repetition of vowel sounds in neighboring words). Rhythm and rhyming, along with other aspects of sound patterning in the words and lines of a poem, help to build a "soundscape" (Morley, 2007) that provides structure for the grammar and rhetoric of the poem (its langscape more generally) and also helps to construct the specific meaning of the words, how they will be received in terms of the images and associations a reader will be encouraged to make. The prosodic features of a poem are primary in capturing a reader's attention, focusing that attention, and moving the reader through the poem in a certain way and at a certain speed.

An Example of a Literary Poem about Trees

A literary poem is an aesthetic object, an object of beauty which, like other beautiful things, produces an emotional effect in those who absorb its language. A poem is also a linguistic object, which, like other linguistic objects, makes sense but generally means in a way that may not be entirely transparent at first. A poem therefore engages the intellect, making the person who engages with it think about its meaning. A poem can lead people deep within themselves, to the exercise of their mental reflective abilities that result in understanding and new insights. Poems can cause readers to reflect on things already known, giving them *aah* moments, and to discover new things, giving them *aha!* moments. As thinking creatures, humans take pleasure in contemplation, of both familiar and unfamiliar things, and especially in things which are partly familiar and partly novel. The combination of familiar resonance (*aah* moments) with novelty (*aha!* moments), which is a driving force in life and language

(Pennington, forthcoming), is a main reason people find poetry and literature more generally enjoyable to read.

We have selected "Winter Trees," by William Carlos Williams (1883–1963), as an example of a literary poem of lyrical or imagistic type by a writer recognized as a great poet. This poem, which appeared in his 1921 collection, *Sour Grapes: A Book of Poems* (Williams, 1921; www.poetryfoundation.org/poem/174773), illustrates how even a short literary work, such as a short poem, through the poet's skillful use of language and the building of image and story, can be a pleasurable sensual and intellectual experience, pulling readers into an imagined world that may connect them in a vivid way to themes of human existence – all marks of a literary poem. Such poems draw us to and into them, affect us, and stay with us in ways that other kinds of nonliterary writing simply cannot and do not.

"Winter Trees"

By William Carlos Williams

All the complicated details
of the attiring and
the disattiring are completed!

A liquid moon
moves gently among
the long branches.

Thus having prepared their buds
against a sure winter
the wise trees
stand sleeping in the cold.

In this poem, William Carlos Williams creates pleasure in the sound of language coupled with a sense of mystery and wonder in the words he uses and the images he creates, which amount to a story about trees that connects to the experience of human beings. As a short poem of lyrical or imagistic type, it creates mood, feeling, and images that lead the reader to process the poem as a sensual object, through a series of brief phrases arranged in stanzas, which together make up its soundscape and storyscape.

The poem's storyscape centers on the winter trees, personified metaphorically in the first and third stanza as "attiring," "disattiring," "wise," and "sleeping." They are implicitly compared to human beings also in being said to "stand," and they are brought alive in the reader's imagination through being described as active agents that have "completed" a "complicated" series of "details" and "prepared their buds / against a sure winter." Considering the extensive use of personification in this poem, a reader may be led to make different kinds of comparisons to human life, such as to wise parents having prepared their children against the cold and then also for bed, and perhaps for life beyond.

The poem's soundscape and lyrical quality is most apparent in the second stanza, which contains a flowing metaphor for the moon as being "liquid" and a considerable amount of alliterative language, in the repetition of "l"'s ("liquid," "gently," "long") and "m"'s ("moon," "moves," "among"). The repetition of the /l/ sound, which is sometimes classified by linguists as liquid in articulation, reinforces the sense of liquidity and flowing, while the carryover of the "mooing" sound of "moon" at the end of the first line to that of "moves" at the start of the second line reinforces the mysterious or dreamlike quality of the poem by calling up the calming sound of cattle lowing. The slow-moving, gentle qualities of the poem are reinforced in the second stanza by the presence of some *trochaic* words in each of its three-word lines ("liquid," "gently," "branches"). This type of rhythm, which starts strong and ends weak, softens the force of the language, simulating a rocking rhythm, almost like a lullaby. The second stanza can be seen as providing a moment's respite and reflection after the trees' completion of their work in the first stanza and before the third stanza's description of their disposition for the future.

Contemplation of this small poem about trees, its soundscape and its story-scape, and how much meaning is conveyed in its spare but exquisite language, makes clear that it is a work of art, a poem of literary stature.[3] It is an example of how a literary work can lead into mental images and emotions, can remind readers of stories that relate to their own lives and experiences, and can pull them into those stories, replaying them in their mind's eye as they read, think, and draw in memories and images from their own lives.

Entering the World of Poetic Language and Feeling

A poet describing the world is not simply mirroring the visible qualities of that world, but summoning before us aspects of the world that we can imagine and then help to elaborate or create further. As linguistic beings, humans know things and understand things through the sensory effects that words have, through the ability of language to fuel the imagination and create a "felt sense" of what something is or represents. People know the truth through what language makes them sense and feel: in the case of poetry, the truth is revealed in the poetic utterance. It is not that the poet finds words for objects but rather that the poet knows, as Cascardi (2014) reminds us, that the objects in the world are the words themselves, which make it possible for linguistic creatures to know not only those objects but also themselves.

Graham Harman, referring to a reading by Heidegger of a poem by the Austrian poet Georg Trakl (Harman, 2007, pp. 144–145), makes a similar point about the evocative quality of poetry as key to how it means. Trakl's (1915) poem, "Ein Winterabend," in the English version, "A Winter Evening," talks about snow, bells, threshold, pain, and a table set for many guests, among other things. But the poem does not simply express ready-made meanings, as Harman (2007) says, or give "titles to things that are already found present-at-hand" (p. 145). Rather, it triggers readers' (or listeners') senses and imagination, as if they are there experiencing the moment. Through the imaginative language, readers help create the moment and also have an opportunity to contemplate that moment as it relates to their own life and experience. Literary language shapes the world for human beings, makes it accessible for our species by revealing what is in the world, and in the process helps to make sense of events and ourselves.

One of the many benefits of the richly textured language of poetry is that it allows for the voice of the writer to be heard by the reader, creating a sense of connection and intimacy that invokes their shared experience and imagination as human beings and that activates the reader's emotions. The voice of the poet calls to the reader as an invitation to enter the world of the poem and "let the magic begin" – an invitation to start the "poetic event" and let the sensations and meanings that inhere in its language unfold. The connection and intimacy sensed in hearing the poet's voice forms a bond between writer and reader through the medium of language that opens the reader to fresh perspectives and insights gained through sharing the poet's experience and imagination as captured in the space of the poem and as linked to the reader's own experience and imagination. In this way, every reader recreates the emotional and imaginative experience of the poet, yet is led into new and unique imaginative and emotional experiences of a personal nature. Herein lies the universality and the particularity of the meaning and the aesthetic experience which a poem, in common with other forms of art, has for each person. Sensing the "universality-within-subjectivity" of the aesthetic experience is what the philosopher Immanuel Kant argued in his *Critique of Judgement* (Kant, 1914/1892) confirms the work as art.

An Illustration from a Literary Poem of the Past

We now move from these 20th-century poems to a classical poem of the early 19th century, "Ode on a Grecian Urn" (Keats, 1820; www.poetryfoundation. org/ poem/173742) by John Keats (1795–1821). This is a lyrical poem of the Romantic movement, which gave priority to emotion, imagination, and originality expressing themes of beauty in love and in nature over rationalism, materialism, and realism. This poem by Keats, one of six odes that he composed in 1819, is considered by many to be one of the greatest poems written in the English language, and it provides an opportunity to understand what a great poem offers if we are willing to devote time and focused energy to reading and reflecting on it. A great many people have in fact reflected on this poem, which has had more said about it in English classes and more written on it by literary scholars than almost any other.[4] The poem has attracted so much interest not only for the themes it addresses but also for the ability of its language to move readers to go deep within it and their own imagination, to discover and also to create its many layers of meaning. Keats' language carries with it a particularly rich and sensuous beauty. The intensity and the beauty of the poet's words incorporate the knowledge of his own mortality – as one who contracted tuberculosis in his early 20s and died from it at age 25, just two years after this poem was written – and, by implication, the reader's mortality as well.

In "Ode on a Grecian Urn," Keats allows readers to share with him what it means to experience a moment of beauty and truth within a finite world which he knows is filled with pain and suffering, having lost his father at age 8, his mother at age 15, and his brother just months before he wrote this poem, the latter two from the same disease, tuberculosis, which he has himself contracted. Within the space of the poem, the poet encounters an ancient urn, a visible image that sets his imagination in motion as he contemplates the apparent timelessness of this artifact and its reminder of mortality. Readers do not observe the "Grecian urn" themselves but rather see it through their own consciousness, as pricked by this great poet:

> Thou still unravish'd bride of quietness,
>   Thou foster-child of silence and slow time …

The poet speaks to the urn, the personification drawing readers in and connecting the poet and those who experience his words to the urn, as if it were a person – a virginal "bride" to be greatly admired and put on a pedestal. Being "still unravish'd," the urn/girl would not have experienced the fullness of a flesh-and-blood, mortal human life but rather stand at some remove from it, as a lovely but at the same time not fully alive and so not fully realized model of human existence. Keats also speaks to the urn as a thing of "quietness," "of silence and slow time," suggesting that it is a thing which is eternal and lives through time, though it is not alive. The ancient urn remains perpetually young, and is thus not a real child of nature but rather an eternally silent and pure "foster-child" that cannot literally speak but nonetheless communicates with human beings from the poet's vantage point and through his words. Readers of the poem are positioned within a kind of tension between the world of immortality and perfection and the world of mortality and imperfection – in essence, the world of art versus the "real" world of everyday life – a theme which is threaded through this poem.

The mood of the poem vacillates between the poet's excited imagination in contemplating the urn and feelings of joy mixed with longing and sadness that may mirror his own attempts to stay positive, as a young man stricken with tuberculosis yet filled with hopes and desires. In the third stanza, referring to the images on the urn, the "boughs" are exclaimed to be happy because they "cannot shed" their leaves "nor ever bid the Spring adieu," and the musician ("melodist") is described as happy because he is "unwearied, / For ever piping songs for ever new." The poet seems to be saying: How could they not be happy in this eternally perfect state? And then there is, topping these other reasons for eternal happiness, the joy of love "for ever young":

> More happy love! more happy, happy love!
>> For ever warm and still to be enjoy'd,
>>> For ever panting, and for ever young;

Oh, to be this happy, the poet seems to be saying, to be "All breathing human passion far above," like being in heaven.

And yet this is a love which is "more happy" when "still to be enjoy'd" – one which is most enjoyed in imagining it rather than in the reality of passion which leaves "a heart" sad ("high-sorrowful") and weary from too much happiness ("cloy'd") – even with signs of sickness ("A burning forehead, and a parching tongue."). Thus, do the poet's darker thoughts reassert themselves, bringing him, and readers, back down to earth and ending this stanza on a more realistic note suggesting that he cannot sustain his optimism and idealism. Readers understand the downside which Keats portrays by way of contrast with the ideal of the urn – the fading of love and beauty over time, the "sickness" of love and passion – even as they understand the "bliss" of human love and passion which is intensified precisely because it also carries with it an expectation of fulfillment, a sense of both a beginning and an ending.

The urn, being eternal, has a wisdom that can perhaps calm Keats' passions and fears: in the end, it offers a kind of insight and comfort in pronouncing, "Beauty is truth, truth beauty, – that is all / Ye know on earth, and all ye need to know." The urn seems to be saying that Keats should stay calm, not worry about the ups and downs of human existence but just rest in this wisdom given from an eternal source. Yet the urn and its images are only cold and lifeless marble. The urn knows beauty and truth in an ideal sense, but that is all it knows, separate as it is from the passionate desire and changing reality of human experience. Human beings know more than the urn knows: they understand that both beauty and truth, and art and life, exist in the tension between the unchanging ideal and the mutable real. Both are true; both are beautiful.

The idea of constructing deep reflections as arising from contemplation of an ancient urn, a lovely piece of art capturing scenes of human life on its surface, is part of what makes this poem a great work of art and an object of great value, just as priceless as a Greek vase from antiquity – in fact, even more priceless in showcasing the exquisite gift of language.

Through the authentic voice of the poet, expressed in the richly sensuous and finely orchestrated language of the poem, people can experience Keats' ode as what literary scholar Derek Attridge, writing in *The Singularity of Literature*, describes as an event which mobilizes meanings so that readers can experience the "singularity" of the writer's creation within themselves (Attridge, 2004), connecting to their own personal meanings and experiences. Through the shared experience of poetic language, readers are reminded of what it means to be human, to experience art and language through the work of another human being. Shaped by the rich and sensuous complexity of poetic language, Keats' urn takes on life, the life of the mind and emotions of the poet and the reader in ongoing movement, unfolding through time, offering inspiration, insight, and deepened human understanding and feeling. It is just this kind of personal knowledge, gained through the rich texture of literary language, which Keats offers. And it is just this kind of experience which we believe can work as a countercultural hope, a contrary to the mainstream values of the digital culture, and in general, to the superficiality and triviality of a life lived for "pop" and "bling."

The Importance of Literary Poetry and Fiction

As writers of this book, we are concerned that the Digital Age cannot provide people with the kind of engagement and enchantment that they can discover in the poetry of writers like John Keats and William Carlos Williams. As Rita Felski has argued in *Uses of Literature*, "Enchantment matters because one reason people turn to works of art is to be taken out of themselves, to be pulled into an altered state of consciousness" (Felski, 2008, p. 76). Great poems provide a linguistic and emotional space that readers can enter and experience as a way of reinvigorating their senses and their imagination, as we showed in the experience of reading poets' reflections on Bavarian gentians, winter trees, or love forever young. In like manner, the fiction of writers like Washington Irving, Kate Chopin, Junot Díaz, and Gary Shteyngart opens mental spaces where readers' emotions and imagination lead into deep contemplation, new insights, and enlightenment. Such an experience is never mere entertainment. In each encounter with literature, something is revealed that readers did not know before about themselves or the depth of the world that they are part of. Like other kinds of art, literature creates new meaning, new perspectives that the one who experiences it was not previously aware of, and it does so in ways that make the singular event of one person reading one specific poem or story resonate in both its particularity – its meaning for the individual – and its universality – its meaning for all.

In leading people to reflect on themselves and others, and on the world they inhabit, literature raises questions of not just an intellectual but also an ethical nature. As Attridge (2004) maintains, literature in its transformative power falls into the realms of both aesthetics and ethics. Literature has the power to arouse human beings in both mind and heart. The digital culture has not enhanced our ability to access the human heart – "the passion, piety or affections," as William Butler Yeats, in his poem, "Among School Children" (Yeats, 1933), put it. Instead, it continues to draw people away from the kind of language that opens them to their own emotional depths and powers of envisioning what cannot be measured or defined even with sophisticated databases. We have observed in our own classrooms today more and more students who shy away from deep engagement with what they are learning and who have lost the ability to grapple with poetic language and make it their own. They have increasingly grown accustomed to the fragmented images racing across their screens and cannot create for themselves the sensuous experience that the richly textured, aesthetic language of great poetry offers them. Humans are first and foremost linguistic beings given the gifts of imagination and language, as connected to their physical bodies and sensing mechanisms, to shape their interior and exterior experiences into moments of coherence and meaning, of purpose and direction – which are in the best case fueled and strengthened by sensory connections provided through affect.

The speed and the "bells and whistles" of digital technology seem to work against such imaginatively and linguistically focused and affectively charged possibilities, as they encourage readers to race through a text, jumping through it and finishing with it as quickly as possible, rather than absorbing it slowly and in full, to holistically visualize or "play" it rather than actually read it. We predict that most people now would be more drawn to the textual operations that can be performed digitally on Osman's (2011) poetry in "The Periodic Table as Assembled by Dr. Zhivago, Oculist" that we referenced in the last chapter than would read and reflect on her poems one by one. And while some digital works, such as Loyer's (2001, 2009, 2010) digital poetry and graphic novels, exhibit the characteristics of works of art and literature, some features of the digital environment encourage works of a different, more transient and accessible, popular or vernacular type (Pennington, 2017) that makes them less artistic and less literary in quality.

A Review of What Literature Does That Makes It Different and Important: Revisiting Our Literary Examples

The examples of "How to Date a Browngirl (Blackgirl, Whitegirl, or Halfie)" (Díaz, 1996/1995) and "The Story of an Hour" (Chopin, 1895/1894) demonstrate the power of literature to enlarge readers' consciousness and sympathies, as it takes them out of themselves. The example of "Rip Van Winkle, a Posthumous Writing of Diedrich Knickerbocker" (Irving, 1864/1819) shows how literature leads into the imagination and makes it possible to experience other places, times, and circumstances. Not only stories but also poems can have these effects, as we sought to illustrate in Keats' (1820) "Ode on a Grecian Urn," a poem which exercises the imagination and expands the consciousness of those who dwell in it and find the voice of the poet there, baring his soul and connecting to readers on a deep, emotional and empathic level. Keats' poem and Díaz's and Chopin's stories illustrate well the exceptional linguistic skill of the literary artists behind those works that connect so strongly to readers. Williams' (1921) poem "Winter Trees" likewise demonstrates the exceptional ability of a great writer to create a work of art in language.

All of these works illustrate the complexity of an artistic story or poem, the depth of emotion and meaning, and the layers of interpretation and understanding that one who reads deeply and stays with the work can be led to experience. These are effects that are unique to literary art, which works through the medium of language to communicate powerful messages affectively. In communicating affectively about the human condition, literature touches the reader on a deep, person-to-person level that inspires empathy. As illustrated by Díaz's (1996/1995) "How to Date a Browngirl (Blackgirl, Whitegirl, or Halfie)," by Chopin's (1895/ 1894) "The Story of an Hour," and by Shteyngart's (2010) *Super Sad True Love Story: A Novel*, a writer's ability to create powerful messages through affective communication can be a way to make social commentary which is more eye-opening than statements of fact and more persuasive than logical argument. In affectively communicating about people's struggles as representatives of those in similar conditions, literary narratives also function to effectively communicate ethical and political messages. In these ways, the reading of literary works can spark change.

Works of literary fiction and poetry have rhetorical and structural characteristics that differentiate them from a range of nonliterary genres as well as from literary essays, creative nonfiction, and memoir. Yet other forms of writing may have some of the same effects on readers as poetry or literary fiction. Nonfictional essays of a literary type, such as those of George Eliot, George Orwell, Susan Sontag, or Jonathan Franzen, are written in a way that makes them both intellectual and aesthetic texts and that may trigger some of the same emotive effects as other forms of literary or artistic text. Indeed, any text that has aesthetic qualities, as seen in its language and rhetoric, or that has some of the same features (e.g., of storytelling or poetry) which call to readers in literary works, may affect them in ways that go beyond (mere) comprehension or intellectual response and towards affective response. Such affective response may include appreciation of the author and feelings of awe or excitement at the new understandings and discoveries that can come through the act of reading. Sky Marsen notes that many of the same creative devices (e.g., metaphor and unusual language) are used in both literary and nonliterary writing (Marsen, 2012), and Pennington (2016a, 2016b) illustrates the psychological effects which scholars can build into academic texts, in part by use of literary devices.

Yet it is clear that the genres of literary prose and poetry deal with topics differently than these other genres, representing things in a deeper and often less explicit way. They are not designed to lead all readers to draw the same conclusions, nor to be clear and unambiguous – rather the opposite. In being designed to engage the imagination and to work through the senses, they take a different pathway to the mind than other kinds of writing. As compared to other kinds of writing, literature allows the reader to contribute more to its meaning, to exercise human inferencing abilities. As Frank B. Farrell, in *Why Does Literature Matter?*, observes:

> [I]n our fundamental orientation to the world we are sophisticated pattern-recognizers, adept filters of patterns from the world's noise. ... If this is our

typical mode of operation, works of literature may stand out as letting us see patterns that are only faintly emergent, that cut across different semantic registers in unexpected ways, and that are not visible elsewhere or otherwise.

(Farrell, 2004, p. 11)

The analogical relationship of literature to real-world facts and events exercises human cognitive abilities of pattern recognition and interpretation that were developed in our biological evolution in prehistoric time and then further elaborated during historical time as part of our ongoing linguistic and cultural evolution. The cognitive workout provided by literary language and narrative structure within fiction is of an especially strenuous and valuable kind, leading readers to gain insights and discover abstract patterns that go beyond aiding survival in the immediate environment to preparing humans for survival in whatever new environments can be imagined. The mental workouts provided by literary encounters thus not only build and strengthen brain circuitry, but also, as we will see in Chapter 9, keep the mind of the deep reader open to new experiences that can prompt significant change. These are powerful reasons to make a significant place for literature in education and society.

Notes

1 Pennington (forthcoming) describes the workings of language and humor (and human cognition more generally) as involving the interplay of *aah* and *aha!* effects.
2 See Pennington (forthcoming) for further discussion.
3 A number of awards are evidence of William Carlos Williams' stature, including the first National Book Award for Poetry in 1950 as well as a Pulitzer Prize for poetry and the Gold Medal for Poetry from the National Institute of Arts and Letters, both post-humously in 1963. There is also a prestigious poetry prize named after him by the Poetry Society of America. To learn more about this poet and his poems, you may wish to visit the Poetry Foundation website: www.poetryfoundation.org/bio/william-carlos-williams.
4 To get a sense of this, see the collection of essays edited by James O'Rourke, available at the Romantic Circles website (O'Rourke, 2003).

References

Attridge, Derek (2004). *The singularity of literature.* New York: Routledge.

Bloom, Harold (2004). *The art of reading poetry.* New York: HarperCollins.

Boorstin, Daniel J. (1961). *The image: Or what happened to the American dream.* New York: Atheneum.

Boyd, Brian (2009). *On the origin of stories: Evolution, cognition, and fiction.* Cambridge, MA: Harvard University Press.

Bruni, Frank (2015). We invited Donald Trump to town. *The New York Times*, Sunday Review. August 2, 2015, p. 3.

Cascardi, Anthony J. (2014). *The Cambridge introduction to literature and philosophy.* New York: Cambridge University Press.

Chopin, Kate (1895/1894). The story of an hour. *St. Louis Life*, January 5, 1895. Originally published in *Vogue*, December 6, 1894, under the title "The dream of an hour." Retrieved on August 4, 2015 from http://my.hrw.com/support/hos/hostpdf/host_text_219.pdf.

Connelly, F. Michael, & Clandinin, D. Jean (1990). Stories of experience and narrative inquiry. *Educational Researcher*, *19*(5), 2–14. doi: 10.3102/0013189X019005002.

Díaz, Junot (1996/1995). How to date a browngirl (blackgirl, whitegirl, or halfie). In *Drown* (pp. 143–149). New York: Riverhead Books. Originally appeared in *The New Yorker*. December 25, 1995, pp. 83–85.

Dutton, Denis (2009). *The art instinct: Beauty, pleasure, and human evolution*. London: Bloomsbury.

Farrell, Frank B. (2004). *Why does literature matter?* Ithaca, NY: Cornell University Press.

Felski, Rita (2008). *Uses of literature*. Malden, MA: Blackwell.

Fiumara, Gemma C. (1995). *The metaphoric process: Connections between language and life*. New York: Routledge.

Forsyth, Mark (2013). *The elements of eloquence: Secrets of the perfect turn of phrase*. London: Icon Books Ltd.

Gabriel, Yiannis (2000). *Storytelling in organizations: Facts, fictions, fantasies*. Oxford: Oxford University Press.

Gottschall, Jonathan (2012). *The storytelling animal: How stories make us human*. Boston, New York: Houghton Mifflin Harcourt.

Harman, Graham (2007). *Heidegger explained: From phenomenon to thing*. Chicago and La Salle, IL: Open Court.

Hayakawa, S. I. (1990/1939). *Language in thought and action* (5th edition). New York: Harcourt Brace & Company.

Hedges, Chris (2009). *Empire of illusion: The end of literacy and the triumph of spectacle*. New York: Nation Books.

Huston, Nancy (2008). *The tale-tellers: A short study of humankind*. Toronto: McArthur & Company.

Irving, Washington (1864/1819). Rip Van Winkle, a posthumous writing of Diedrich Knickerbocker. In *The sketch book of Geoffrey Crayon, Gent*. First installment. New York: C. S. Van Winkle. Revised and expanded "Artist's Version" published in 1864 by G. P. Putnam, New York. Retrieved on October 31, 2016 from www.gutenberg.org/files/2048/2048-h/2048-h.htm#link2H_4_0008.

Johnson, Mark (1987). *The body in the mind: The bodily basis of meaning, imagination, and reason*. Chicago: University of Chicago Press.

Kant, Immanuel (1914/1892). *Kant's critique of judgement* (2nd revised edition, trans. with introduction and notes by J. H. Bernard). London: Macmillan. http://oll.libertyfund.org/titles/1217.

Keats, John (1820). Ode on a Grecian urn. *Annals of the Fine Arts*, *15*, January 20, 1820, published anonymously. Retrieved on May 3, 2015 from www.poetryfoundation.org/poem/173742.

Kintsch, Walter (1977). On comprehending stories. In M. A. Just and P. A. Carpenter (eds.), *Cognitive processes in comprehension* (pp. 33–62). Hillsdale, NJ: Erlbaum Associates.

Kirsch, Adam (2014). Bookends. *The New York Times*, Book Review. September 7, 2014, p. 31.

Kundera, Milan (2006). *The curtain: An essay in seven parts* (trans. Laura Asher). London: Faber and Faber.

Lawrence, D. H. (1933). Bavarian gentians. In *Last poems*. London: Heinemann / New York: Viking Press.

Loyer, Erik (2001). Chroma. *Erik Loyer* website. Accessed on October 25, 2015 from http://erikloyer.com/index.php/projects/detail/chroma/.

Loyer, Erik (2009). Ruben and lullaby. *Opertoon* website. Accessed on September 1, 2013 from http://opertoon.com/2009/05/ruben-lullaby/.

Loyer, Erik (2010). Strange rain. *Opertoon* website. Accessed on August 10, 2013 from http://opertoon.com/2010/11/strange-rain-for-ipad-iphone-ipod-touch/.

Marsen, Sky (2012). Detecting the creative in written discourse. *Writing & Pedagogy*, 4(2), 209–231. doi: 10.1558/wap.v4i2.209.

Miall, David S., & Kuiken, Don (1994). Foregrounding, defamiliarization, and affect: Response to literary stories. *Poetics*, 22(5), 389–407. doi: 10.1016/0304-422X(94)00011-5.

Morley, David (2007). *The Cambridge introduction to creative writing*. Cambridge: Cambridge University Press.

Mukařovskỳ, Jan (1964/1932). Standard language and poetic language. In P. Garvin (ed.), *A Prague school reader on esthetics, literary structure and style* (pp. 41–54). Washington, DC: Georgetown University Press. Retrieved on November 3, 2012 from http://digilib.phil. muni.cz/bitstream/handle/11222.digilib/131565/Books_2010_2019_071-2014-1_7.pdf.

O'Rourke, James (ed.). (2003). Ode on a Grecian urn: Hypercanonicity and pedagogy. *Romantic Circles* Praxis Series. Retrieved on September 15, 2015 from https://www.rc. umd.edu/praxis/grecianurn/index.html.

Osman, Jena (2011). The periodic table as assembled by Dr. Zhivago, oculist (revised). *Digital Earthenware* website. Available at http://jenaosman.com/zhivago/.

Pennington, Martha C. (2016a). A 3-D approach to discovering and creating the features of written text. *Writing & Pedagogy*, 8(1), 161–191. doi:10.1558/wap.v8i1.29525.

Pennington, Martha C. (2016b). *Writing at the creative edge: Tracing the evolution of a new idea in language*. Invitational talk. School for Oriental and African Studies, University of London. November 29, 2016 Video available at www.youtube.com/watch? v=vW5FZxFwgvA&t=6s.

Pennington, Martha C. (2017). Literacy, culture, and creativity in a digital era. *Pedagogy*, 17(2), 259–287. doi: 10.1215/15314200-3770149.

Pennington, Martha C. (forthcoming). *Humor and language: Two things that make us human*. Sheffield, U.K. and Bristol, CT: Equinox.

Polkinghorne, Donald E. (1988). *Narrative knowing and the human sciences*. Albany, NY: State University of New York Press.

Riessman, Catherine Kohler (1993). *Narrative analysis*. Newbury Park, CA: Sage.

Seilman, Uffe, & Larsen, Steen (1989). Personal resonance to literature. *Poetics*, 18 (1–2), 165–177. doi: 10.1016/0304-422X(89)90027-2.

Shteyngart, Gary (2010). *Super sad true love story: A novel*. New York: Random House.

Thorndyke, Perry W. (1977). Cognitive structures in memory and comprehension of narrative. *Cognitive Psychology*, 9(1), 77–110. doi:10.1016/0010-0285(77).90005-6.

Toolan, Michael (2016). Poetry and poetics. In Rodney H. Jones (ed.), *The Routledge handbook of language and creativity* (pp. 231–247). London and New York: Routledge.

Trakl, Georg (1915). Ein Winterabend ("A winter evening"). Leipzig: Kurt Wolff Verlag. Retrieved on December 23, 2015 from www.literaturnische.de/Trakl/english/seb-e. htm#awinterevening.

Turner, Mark (1996). *The literary mind: The origins of thought and language*. New York: Oxford University Press.

Vendler, Helen (2015). *The ocean, the bird, and the scholar: Essays on poets and poetry*. Cambridge, MA: Harvard University Press.

Waxler, Robert P. (2007). In honor of Rassias: What literature and language mean to me. In Mel B. Yoken (ed.), *Breakthrough: Essays and vignettes in honor of John A. Rassias* (pp. 125–130). New York: Peter Lang.

Williams, William Carlos (1921). *Sour grapes: A book of poems* (p. 36). Boston: The Four Seas Company. Retrieved on October 31, 2016 from www.gutenberg.org/ebooks/35667.

Wood, James (2008). *How fiction works*. New York: Farrar, Straus and Giroux.

Yeats, William Butler (1933). *The poems of W. B. Yeats: A new edition* (ed. Richard J. Finneran). New York: Macmillan Publishing Company. Retrieved on July 25, 2015 from www.poetryfoundation.org/poem/172065.

8

A CLOSER LOOK AT READING

What reading does, ultimately, is keep alive the dangerous and exhilarating idea that a life is not a sequence of lived moments, but a destiny. ... [T]he time of reading, the time defined by the author's language resonating in the self, is not the world's time, but the soul's.

– *Sven Birkerts,* The Gutenberg Elegies: The Fate of Reading in an Electronic Age *(Birkerts, 1994, p. 75)*

Children Beginning to Read

When we think of reading, we think of individual, silent reading as the primary type, though this was not always the case. At first reading was performed aloud with an audience and only later became an individual, private, and silent activity. When performed aloud, reading had a close connection to spoken language that emphasized the sound of words. And, as a communal activity, reading had a strong performance aspect, like performing a play, and so was connected to a whole array of bodily activity, including facial expression, gesturing, physical movement, pausing, and rhythmicality. Even as a personal and silent activity, reading has a significant physical component: the sounds of words and the physical activities surrounding reading and the actions portrayed are still present as the echoes of past voices and the memory traces of past reading events.

Children's early experiences of reading are often within this kind of performative context, in which stories are, to different degrees, dramatically recounted to them from memory or read to them aloud, acted out both for and with them, and elicited from them in a question-and-answer or call-and-response format within a larger interaction with a reading parent or other person. It is very likely that the child's first interest in and attraction to reading is because of the connection to a valued other, to the physical closeness to the other's body and to the sound of the caregiver's voice, and also because of the interaction with that other through the activities surrounding reading and storytelling. Children who are read to get a taste for pleasure reading as they experience the world of the imagination and storytelling mediated through human connection in the context of books.

The child who is read to on a regular basis soon learns the opportunities the reading process offers for interaction with the book, such as turning pages, and with the reader, such as being smiled at and smiling back, or being asked to point at a picture and doing so. As the child is learning to understand speech and then soon afterwards learning to talk, the reader may give encouragement to repeat words that are illustrated in the book, or may ask questions about pictures or about the plot to encourage the child to imagine, to make inferences, or to recall information from memory:

MOTHER WITH OPEN BOOK:	Are Hansel and Gretel going to go into the witch's candy house?
CHILD LOOKING AT PICTURE:	Yeah!
MOTHER POINTING:	What's that?
CHILD LOOKING AT PICTURE:	Candy house.
MOTHER LOOKING AT CHILD:	That's right. The witch's house is made of candy.
CHILD LOOKING AT MOTHER:	Witch house – candy!
MOTHER WITH BOOK:	What do you think the witch is going to do?
CHILD LOOKING AT MOTHER:	Shrugs shoulders indicating "I don't know."

Children who are read to are highly motivated to learn to read, and begin to learn to read through being partnered by a reading companion, such as a parent or older child, entering what Lev Vygotsky called the "zone of proximal development" (Vygotsky, 1978). Within this collaborative zone and process, they gradually take on aspects of the reading process through at first mimicking and then, with increasing confidence, learning to control and self-direct their reading, so that they are gradually able to fully acquire the behaviors modeled in the actions of the other person.

Children are scaffolded and propelled into the world of storytelling through their early experiences of reading. In the ideal case, the beginnings of literacy, like all language use, is a pleasurable social experience. A child's experience of reading is connected to the physical closeness and psychological connection to the mother or other caregivers and home. There is no echo of this experience in an electronic environment. It seems doubtful that readers of e-books or other kinds of screen pages will be as involved in the reading process. It is doubtful that their more mechanical, less embodied experience of reading will be able to trigger the holistic, fully engaged mind-and-body experience of reading nor the intended pleasurable sense of being transported to another world that has been up to now so central to literary reading. In fact, using an electronic device for reading can focus a child's attention on the device – its "bells and whistles" and the mechanics of its operation – as much as on the content or language of the story. Even if an electronic device is employed with a young child for reading a book together with a parent or other reading person, the interaction may not be the same as that which typically occurs between a child and a parent or other person and which promotes and aids language development. In this connection, Douglas Quenqua reports on a 2013 study showing lower reading comprehension among children aged 3–5 whose parents read to them from an e-book: "Part of the reason ... was that parents and children using an electronic device spent more time focusing on the device itself than on the story (a conclusion shared by at least two other studies)" (Quenqua, 2014, pp. 1, 27). As we would predict, the machine changes the reading event and interferes with it in some ways, reducing the effectiveness of the reading process. Even though the humans outnumber the machine in this case 2 to 1, the machine has a powerful effect on the human-to-human interaction.

What Is Reading?

In the broadest sense of the word, reading can be seen as a basic human function involving pattern-detection, inferencing, and sense-making. Alberto Manguel, in *A History of Reading*, observes: "We all read ourselves and the world around us in order to glimpse what and where we are. We read to understand, or to begin to understand. Reading, almost as much as breathing, is our essential function" (Manguel, 1997, p. 7). Reading in this broad sense is the most basic human ability to decipher, to interpret, and to understand. It is thus an ability that underlies humans' meaning-making capabilities to connect pieces of information in ways that make sense to us, such as to connect disparate events and perceptions into coherent scenarios of cause and effect, and thus into stories. In the words of Elena Semino, "We make sense of new situations – and of texts in particular – by relating the current input to pre-existing mental representations of similar entities, situations and events" (Semino, 1997, p. 123). We understand a new situation by relating it to things we already know, fitting it into what Roger C. Schank calls a "scene," by which he means an event within a larger chain that relates to our prior experiences and expectations of how things happen in the world (Schank, 1999, p. 79). Like other scholars, Schank maintains that stories are a main way that information is organized in memory (pp. 90–91).

Reading as we usually think of it, involving written text, is a cultural invention that piggybacks on the prior inventions of language and of writing, and that utilizes many different types of human abilities. The decoding and comprehension of written text – first in the form of Egyptian hieroglyphics (pictographs) and later in the form of Chinese characters (logographs), cuneiform logosyllabic script combining logographs with signs for syllables, and Phoenician sound-based scripts that were the basis of the Greek and Roman alphabets – involved co-opting the parts of the brain used for visual recognition and forming complex networks of connections to words and their meanings. The decoding and comprehension of cuneiform tablets, for instance, like the decoding and comprehension of any form of written language, from simple road signs to complex poetry, requires discovering the meaning within the marks or characters used to write them. This involves, first, recalling or figuring out what the marks or characters stand for and then coming to understand the larger meaning of the combinations of marks/characters. Reading links perception and memory in an increasing activity of recognition and comprehension through a process of "connecting the dots," where the dots are the written marks or characters and the connections are supplied by memory and inferencing, often aided by the creative imagination. Learning to read requires constructing a sort of internal mapping system for finding one's way through a text so that those dots can be connected, that is, for being able to connect signs into a meaningful map or schema that can guide comprehension.

Reading as a Cognitive Process

Both Poe (2011) and Wolf (2007) have commented that reading required humans to adapt visual and other capabilities to new kinds of tasks. Wolf, Director of the Center for Reading and Language Research at Tufts University, emphasizes the dynamic plasticity of the brain in relation to reading, remarking on its "astonishing ability to rearrange itself ... its protean capacity to make new connections among structures and circuits originally devoted to other more basic brain processes ... such as vision and spoken language" (Wolf, 2007, p. 4). The brain is especially malleable in the period from early infancy into early adulthood, when its mapping systems are most active and its initial cognitive maps, or networks of connections, are made and then expanded and complexified with experience.

Learning anything involves changes in the strength of the brain's wired connections, its *synapses*, in gray matter (the cortex); and time spent doing anything also causes structural changes in the brain's underlying layer of white matter (Fields, 2008, 2010). The functioning of the brain is improved through the bundling of nerve fibers, or *axons*, "that connect neurons in different brain regions into functional circuits" (Fields, 2010, p. 768). The connectivity of different parts of the brain into functional circuits is facilitated through a process of *myelinization*, in which axons become coated with myelin, a type of electrical insulation that "is essential for high-speed transmission of electrical impulses" (ibid.) across different parts of the brain. Learning to read increases the volume and connectivity of white matter tracts linking those regions of the cortex that must work together for all the processes of reading to take place and to proceed smoothly and quickly. We might say that the map of the brain used for reading is increasingly filled in and becomes increasingly well-traveled and well-trained as the various activities of reading become increasingly coordinated. Many kinds of cognitive impairment seem related to abnormalities in white matter (Fields, 2008), including dyslexia, which "results from disrupted timing of information transmission in circuits required for reading; brain imaging has revealed reduced white matter in these tracts, which could cause such disruption" (Fields, 2008, p. 59). It appears, then, that dyslexia may involve problems in coordination of the component tasks of reading.

The development of the brain – the vast cognitive mapping system that guides understanding and action – takes place from two directions, from physiology (nature) and from social experience (nurture). The brain becomes wired based on innate predispositions, perceptions of the world, and specific experiences. Learning to read requires a repurposing of brain circuitry, which Stanislas Dehaene terms "neuronal recycling" (Dehaene, 2009, p. 147), to "[connect] two sets of brain regions that are already present in infancy: the object recognition system and the language circuit" (p. 195). Wolf (2007) describes the changes in human brain circuitry made necessary by the development of writing away from a pictographic form and towards abstract marks in the form of cuneiform script and later forms of writing connected to spoken words. For reading to be possible:

> First, considerably more pathways in the visual and visual association regions would be necessary in order to decode what would eventually become hundreds of cuneiform characters. … Second, the conceptual demands of a logosyllabary would inevitably involve more cognitive systems, which, in turn, would require more connections to visual areas in the occipital lobes, to language areas in the temporal lobes, and to the frontal lobes.
>
> *(Wolf, 2007, p. 32)*

Wolf and Barzillai (2009) further comment on the differences in brain circuitry that have developed for reading different writing systems.

To delve a little more deeply into the process, reading in the usual sense involves perceptual deciphering of marks representing words, the cognitive comprehension of words in the context of other words, and the holistic understanding of patterns of meaning as represented by words and their connection to other things which the reader knows and has experienced. The skills that are needed for reading are built on the human abilities to perceive patterns and to draw inferences from things present in the immediate environment – centrally, the visual field – to things not present, by relating perceivable "clues" to knowledge housed in long-term memory. Specifically, reading requires making logical and creative connections of visible words and larger linguistic patterns to words and linguistic patterns stored in memory, including their denotation, or dictionary meaning, as well as their connotations based on past usage and associations in the reader's experience of language, both oral and written. Identifying and interpreting words and larger structures of connected language will typically activate different kinds of memory – such as visual, auditory, olfactory memory; memory for motion and for other kinds of bodily sensation – all of which are part of the reading experience and the meaning of what is read for a particular reader. The potential activation of so many areas of memory and the diverse mental connections that might be made among these means that reading is highly variable depending on the reader's current mental state, vocabulary knowledge and experience of specific words and word combinations, and general knowledge and experience. Although all readers will have a considerable amount of overlap in their cognitive (or mapping) systems for reading and in their specific conceptual maps and experiential networks, these will differ to a greater or lesser degree depending on such factors as their language and their culture, their life experience, and their areas of knowledge.

Even when two readers might know and understand all of the words in a text, they are unlikely to have identical knowledge and experience of those words stored in memory. Based on their past experience with the words, they may interpret what they read in somewhat different, or largely different, ways. Add to this the fact that what a reader recalls about the words in a text at the moment of reading might not be the same as what is recalled by a different reader or even by the same reader when reading the same passage at a different time. In reading, the brain can connect the words and larger linguistic patterns of the text to any area of the reader's knowledge and experience that seems relevant or, simply, that occurs to a reader while reading: a feature of the reading brain's internal GPS system is that it can take readers not only on the most obvious route from point A to point B but on many less obvious and more circuitous routes through the territories of memory both near and far. The reading process can therefore be described as both orderly and, as Grate (2014) observes, serendipitous – in part a predictable one for all readers but in part unpredictable and different for every individual, so that no two people will make the same connections to a given text nor remember it in just the same way. And in some cases, their responses to a text may be diametrically opposed, even when they agree on its content. The larger and more individual aspects of reading response make clear that reading as a cultural invention is more than a connect-the-dots puzzle or guessing game, as we have been stressing all along: It is an imaginative process in which individual readers understand a text by making connections to their specific knowledge and experience.

Reading and Memory

The activity of the brain in reading texts involves short-term or working memory to decode and connect pieces of information that are perceived in the written marks and other pieces of information that are recalled from long-term memory to interpret these. In this sense, reading is, in the characterization of Michael Burke in *Literary Reading, Cognition and Emotion: An Exploration of the Oceanic Mind*, both "sign-fed" – print-based and bottom-up – and "mind-fed" – memory-based and top-down (Burke, 2011). The function of working memory in reading is to piece together a representation of the text, which may include images as well as concepts and schemas or scripts, in the mind of the reader. For beginning readers, much of the capacity of working memory is used to piece together representations of individual words, whereas for more experienced readers, it can be used for more creative interpretive processes of envisioning and understanding the characters, scenes, and events portrayed, with much greater involvement of large structures in long-term memory.

It requires effort on the part of the brain to retrieve stored memories as well as to encode new ones, and to manage information in working memory. Working memory has a limited capacity and is constantly changing as information is being processed. Long-term memory has far more stable content, existing in the form of an extensive network of informational nodes organized by commonalities and differences. When some part of the network is triggered by working memory in response to some thought, perception, or bodily sensation, this will activate other parts of the network. The brain is thereby flooded with relevant information to interpret the triggering event. Long-term storage contains memory of different types, particularly, word-based memory for the sounds and meanings of words, and *episodic memory* for events and experiences, including memory for stories. James E. Zull locates much of memory in the integrative cortex which sits between the three sensory regions: visual, auditory, and somatic (Zull, 2002, p. 155). There is therefore a close connection between bodily sensations and episodic memory. Indeed, all cognitive processing takes place, as observed by Walter Kintsch, "not ... in a disembodied mind but in a perceiving, feeling, acting body" (Kintsch, 1998, p. 410).

> Perception is not only a cognitive process but also an emotional process. We react to the world not only with our sense organs but also with gut-level feelings. The things that excite us, please us, scare us are most closely linked to the somatic level. Our most central memories are the ones most intimately linked to our body.
>
> *(Kintsch, 1998, p. 412)*

Elaborating on this notion, Burke (2011) maintains, "Cognitive mnemonic images that are activated and processed during all acts of perception, including reading, appear to be saturated with affective-embodied input" (p. 33).

This insight has been developed in a theory termed *embodied semantics*, according to which, in the words of Lisa Aziz-Zadeh and Antonio Damasio,

> concepts are represented in the brain within the same sensory-motor circuitry in which the enactment of that concept relies. For example, the concept of "grasping" would be represented in sensory-motor areas that represent grasping actions; the concept of "kicking" would be represented by sensory-motor areas that control kicking actions.
>
> *(Aziz-Zadeh & Damasio, 2008, p. 35)*

It is relatively well-accepted among psychologists (see, e.g., Barsalou, 1999, 2008; Ritchie, 2010, pp. 62–66) that the deep processing of language triggers partial simulations of the sensory information and actions associated with specific words and word combinations that have been stored in memory from previous experiences connected to those words and to the actions, concepts, or qualities that they signify. Thus, the smell, feel, or taste of an onion, as well as some specific events or contextual associations of onions, may be triggered when encountering the word "onion," and various mental pictures, feelings, and memories of experiences related to poisonous snakes may be triggered by hearing or reading the words "poisonous snake." Such simulations, comprising elements of external as well as internal perception and involving bodily states, emotions, and introspection, can be activated by highly expressive language, including metaphor, narrative, or playful language (Ritchie, 2006). What have generally been referred to by literary scholars as the "images" evoked by hearing or reading specific words are, as René Wellek and Austin Warren put it in their classic *Theory of Literature*, "the vestigial representatives of sensations" (Wellek & Warren, 1949, p. 191): "In psychology, the word 'image' means a mental reproduction, a memory, of a past sensational or perceptual experience, not necessarily visual" (ibid.) but also olfactory, gustatory, and kinaesthetic.

Sensory simulation involving bodily states, emotions, and introspection seems to occur in processing not only words and phrases but also the larger structures made from language. When hearing a person tell about something that person has witnessed or experienced, other people, if they are paying attention and really listening, tend to imagine and therefore mirror to an extent, or partially simulate, their own performance and response to what is being described. They might, for example, not only project visual images in their "mind's eye" of how they would look or act in that situation but also experience to some degree the kinds of sensations or feelings that they might have if in the same situation, and even involuntarily activate relevant movements or facial expressions. In like manner, we can assume that people reading a narrative, if they are fully engaged and reading deeply, enter the narrative, as it were, to a certain extent, imagining the things described as happening to and around themselves, and partially simulating these imagined happenings. This is a reason that reading fiction can increase openness and empathy, as we will see in the next chapter.

Peter Stockwell, a linguist working in an area of research and theory termed "cognitive stylistics," observes that reading literature produces not only imagined experiences but also real sensory responses: "Literary reading generates a range of emotions, moods, and other effects that are actual emotions and moods: we do not feel *fictional* sadness, or *imaginary* melancholy, or *pretend* laughter during literary experiences" (Stockwell, 2016, p. 224, original emphasis). These real sensory responses connect the reading of literature to other experiences of art that move us, such as the experience of viewing a great painting or sculpture, hearing a great piece of music, or watching a great dramatic performance in a play. The reading of literature also activates episodic memory. Episodic memory tends to be imprecise, not a perfect rendering of events and scenes but a more abstract and less detailed version that incorporates images and feelings – both emotion and bodily sensation – as Marcel Proust (in Á la Recherche du Temps Perdu, or In Search of Lost Time; Proust, 1913–1927) represented in his famous account of olfactory memory (the smell of freshly baked madeleine cookies) being a window into many other kinds of memory. Auditory and visual memory are more vivid but generally rapidly decaying, involving mental "echoes" of sounds perceived through the auditory system (echoic memory) and mental "photos" of sights perceived through the visual system (iconic memory).

Literary reading may activate a type of episodic memory, autobiographical memory, which helps to create a sense of one's core identity. In the depiction of Antonio Damasio,

> the autobiographical self depends on systematized memories of situations in which core consciousness was involved in the knowing of the most invariant characteristics of an organism's life – who you were born to, where, when, your likes and dislikes, the way you usually react to a problem or a conflict, your name and so on.
>
> (Damasio, 1999, p. 17)

Recalling the insight of Kintsch (1998) that "[o]ur most central memories are the ones most intimately linked to our body" (p. 412), we can note that our auto-biographical memories, in being connected to things that excite, please, and scare us and in being some of our most central memories, are highly embodied.[1]

In general, it can be said that all memory, once removed from the immediate context of experience rapidly "fades" in relation to the original experience and, when recalled later, becomes subject to distortion (Kandel, Kupfermann, & Iverson, 2000). Memory is generally not replicative but rather somewhat vague and imperfect, and varies from person to person. This is the reason that different people remember different things about an event that both attended at the same time, whether together or separately. This fact is the basis of the great Akira Kurosawa film Rashomon (Kurosawa, 1950) as well as a feature of plots in numerous stories and films. When retrieved from memory, previously stored information is given a personalized reconstruction with new features which connect it to other information that is also activated at the time of recall. In addition, we may retrieve memories not as wholes, but as memory fragments or components, which we then place into scenes and schemas to create new memories.

Deep, Connected Reading

Birkerts (1994) noted that in being an activity which readers control and can adapt to their "needs and rhythms," reading can be a deeply involving, meditative activity in which "[w]e are free to indulge our subjective associative impulse; the term I coin for this is 'deep reading': the slow and meditative possession of a book. We don't just read the words, we dream our lives in their vicinity" (p. 146). In sharp contrast to deep reading, which involves a large part of the map of the brain and its two hemispheres (Wolf & Barzillai, 2009, p. 34), reading online is a form of surface reading that engages the brain much less, and in a different way. The brain is thereby reconfigured for this quicker and more superficial form of reading-lite. The circuitry for deep reading is either never developed, as can happen in digital natives, or loses functionality or strength of connectivity as a result of disuse, that is, inactivity causes the weakening or pruning of synaptic connections, as can happen in digital immigrants.

Deep reading not only engages complex intellectual skills and cognitive processes, but is also a highly involved emotive and personal experience. Unlike one reading a computer screen or watching television, deep readers – specifically, of print literature, since reading deeply implies a kind of deep engagement not generally attained from engaging with other media – constantly move from the story being read to their own deeper self, discovering unknown dimensions of the self and then creating from that unfamiliar territory new connections with the surrounding world, new meaning and interpretative possibilities. In the words of Waxler and Hall (2011),

> the dynamic of deep reading ... is a dialectic of the self and the other, of the familiar and the unfamiliar. ... The reader shuttles between his or her own identity and the identity of the other found in the narrative, making comparisons and contrasts, and, in so doing, moves beyond the familiar, the stereotypes, and so learns more about the self and the world.
>
> *(p. 33)*

This is parallel to the broad sense of reading as the meaning-making, interpretive process connecting the experience of the here and now, of one particular context, with other contexts which readers can connect to themselves and to the world as they know it, in order to make sense of it and to understand it fully.

The meaning-making process is a whole-person dialogic, dialectic process of a human being in interaction with other human beings and the world at large. As the Russian literary theorist Mikhail Bakhtin (Bakhtin, 1984/1929) put it:

> Life by its very nature is dialogic. To live means to participate in dialogue: to ask questions, to heed, to respond, to agree, and so forth. In this dialogue, a person participates wholly and throughout his whole life, with his eyes, lips, hands, soul, spirit, and with his whole body and deeds.
>
> *(p. 293)*

Bakhtin discussed the idea of people's internal voices, or perspectives, coming from external ones, those of other people, that they internalize (Bakhtin, 1984/ 1929). Philip Lewin elaborates on Bakhtin's dialogic view as follows:

> [A]t first I speak myself though the voices of others. The process of forming a coherent self becomes a process of sorting through … this multiplicity of voices that co-exists first around me and then within me, until discourses that are "internally persuasive" emerge.
>
> *(Lewin, 1997, p. 4)*

Reading, like conversation, is about making connections in dialogic ways. It is intimately related not just to interpretation but to all kinds of thinking and knowing.

The degree of contribution by the recipient marks a big difference between reading a book and watching television:

> Unlike watching television or engaging in other illusions of entertainment, deep reading is not an *escape*, but a *discovery*, an encounter with the truth of our own feelings and emotions. Deep reading provides a way of discovering how we are all connected to the world and to our evolving stories. Reading deeply, we find our own plots and stories unfolding through the language and voice of others.
>
> *(Waxler & Hall, 2011, p. 35, original emphasis)*

Given the ways in which readers project themselves into story contexts, there is a much deeper personal involvement and investment in reading a story than in watching a television program. The recipient is far less involved and far less imaginatively engaged in the latter activity. As to reading on a screen, it is in another sense far less active and involved than reading a book, as it is more surface than deep, as we argue throughout this book.

Deep reading provides a means to concentrate the mind; it gives a person added focus, purpose, and direction – in opposition to the distraction and chaotic experience of electronic daily life. It also offers one the possibility of becoming lost in space and time, and of having a sort of "out of body" experience, as "reading transcends space: it takes you away. You don't think about where you are because, your consciousness being the most important part of you, you aren't *there* in the most important sense" (Cohen, 2011, p. 237, original emphasis). Deep reading transports readers to a dream space: it takes readers out of the body (a sublime and dreamlike effect) but then also calls to them to return with this experience to the ordinary world – perhaps seeing new beauty in it or appreciating something they had not dared to confront before. Reading in this sense is quite different from the skimming and scanning of images and texts that young people think they are "reading" on the Internet. It is a much deeper engagement with what they are perceiving, enough to become curious and engaged so that they wish to try to understand its meaning and relevance for their own thinking and their own lives. It is far more involved than the reading-lite which is performed these days within so-called "multitasking," which takes place largely within short-term memory and hardly involves long-term memory – or any great effort or commitment of any kind. This reading-lite also involves minimal risk of challenging long-held notions or beliefs – about the world, about others, and about the self. Reading-lite therefore avoids the sort of encounter with the unknown, with unexplored psychological territory and depths of the self, and with ethical and moral questions, that is unique to the experience of reading literary fiction.

Although readers may find themselves absorbed in deep reading without trying and sometimes even against their will, almost as soon as they sit down with an engaging book or other piece of writing, these days deep reading sometimes has to be willfully and deliberately planned and sustained. There are so many distractions, and the potential for merely skimming and scanning, flitting across the page, is there, on the computer screen and on the Internet. As David L. Ulin remarks in *The Lost Art of Reading: Why Books Matter in a Distracted Time*:

> Reading, after all, is an act of resistance in a landscape of distraction, a matter of engagement in a society that seems to want nothing more than for us to disengage. It connects us at the deepest levels; it is slow, rather than fast. That is its beauty and its challenge: in a culture of instant information, it requires us to pace ourselves. … Even more, we are reminded of all we need to savor – this instant, this scene, this line. We regain the world by withdrawing from it just a little, by stepping back from the noise, the tumult, to discover our reflections in another mind. As we do, we join a broader conversation, by which we both transcend ourselves and are enlarged.
>
> (*Ulin, 2010, pp. 150–151*)

The Nature of Literary Reading

Why is it that, even in this age of science and the Internet, people are still drawn to fiction, the core genre of literature? The preface to *Transforming Literacy: Changing Lives through Reading and Writing* gives a sense of what the reading of literature entails:

> [W]hen we talk about literature, we are … talking about … something alive, something that calls to the reader, something that can excite the imagination and something that, once actively engaged, can stir the human heart. … That kind of reading experience does not end when the book ends. It continues to call to you, inviting you to read the narrative again, to discuss it with others, to move deeper into yourself, to extend yourself out to others.

For us, that is the activity of reading as we understand it, and it is also the activity of learning, the adventure of education.

(Waxler & Hall, 2011, p. xi)

As Michael Wood maintains in "A World Without Literature?":

Literature is embodiment, a mode of action; it works over time on the hearts and minds of its readers or hearers. Its result in us, when we are receptive or lucky, is the activation of a knowledge ... so intimate and so immediate that ... it feels like something we have always known.

(Wood, 2009, p. 62)

For such an involved reading process to be possible, the reader must be highly engaged in reading and thinking about the text. Literary reading, much more than simply functioning for the reader to "imbibe" literary language, is a highly engaged, imaginative, and sensuous experience. Christopher A. Dustin and Joanna E. Ziegler characterize reading as an embodied process in the following way: "We engage things in our bodies, senses, and memories, and that in and of itself puts us in touch with the deepest layer of meaning" (Dustin & Ziegler, 2005, p. 157).

Literature both mirrors and expands the reader's context. By reflecting familiar themes and human characteristics blended with new and unfamiliar ones, it offers the reader a view of human experience and "the workings of the human mind" (Turner, 1987, p. 9). It engages the intellect and the emotions, stimulates the imagination, and exposes the reader to new worlds, ideas, and values that lead to deep contemplation – of the nature and meaning of life, and of the self in relation to others. A story is like a snapshot of life, providing but a partial picture, which the reader must fill in. A literary story creates a partial picture with sufficient vividness that it stimulates the reader's imagination, so s/he can bridge any gaps and fill in any holes in the story to make it cohere. This the reader does by projecting her/himself into the story, activating autobiographical memory, and simulating involvement in the actions or scenes portrayed. James Wood discusses this sort of projection (Wood, 2008, pp. 238–239) in relation to what he calls "truthful texts" (p. 85): those which allow the reader to have the sense of being in the narrative, of having the experience the character has, of feeling like the character feels.

As compared to other kinds of reading, literary reading has more "personal resonance" (Seilman & Larsen, 1989, p. 167) for the reader, who connects the events of the story to past events in which s/he participated, that is, the reader's autobiographical memories. Seilman and Larsen (1989) described "the experience of personal resonance to a text when pieces of this self-knowledge are mobilized during reading" (p. 169). They found that when two groups of psychology student readers were given different kinds of texts, either expository or literary, the readers of the literary text were much more likely than those who read expository texts to experience mental imagery while reading as personal experiences in which they actively participated. The authors also found that most of this personally involved mental imagery was invoked in the mind of the reader at the start of the story. The literary text seemed to "require more intense mobilization of knowledge in the beginning than an expository text" (p. 174). This seemed to be required for setting the scene or frame of the story, as "purely descriptive passages seemed to elicit relatively many remindings in the subjects, whereas passages concerning action and communication elicited almost none" (p. 176).

The sensuousness of the language is an important element that stimulates and simulates that involvement. Words on the page, and especially literary language, can trigger the reader's memory, emotion, and imagination: they can evoke mental pictures and connections to remembered scenes and events as well as newly created ones, making new mental connections and images, while also flooding the mind with emotions linked to those remembered events and imagined scenes. In the view of Waxler and Hall (2011), "Humans need sensuous language, the feel of a story, just as the sensuous body needs an environment in which to live and to learn" (p. 63). As Denis Donoghue, writing in *The Practice of Reading* (Donoghue, 2000), and Rosenblatt (1978) before him have argued, we need to read not merely for information but for pleasure, as a type of aesthetic experience.

In this context, it is worthwhile to consider the difference between reading literary texts and most other texts designed primarily to convey information. The latter type of texts, in being *literal* rather than literary, gain their coherence and interpretation not through a story construction but through other forms of logical or expository construction. Literary texts activate personal knowledge, whereas most nonliterary or expository texts, by contrast, activate knowledge of a more impersonal and abstract kind. Rosenblatt (1978) challenged the notion that there is some priority to literal reading, with artistic qualities merely "tacked" on in literary, or aesthetic, reading. In her view:

> In nonaesthetic reading, the reader's attention is focused primarily on what will remain as the residue after the reading – the information to be acquired, the logical solution to a problem, the actions to be carried out.
>
> [...] In aesthetic reading, in contrast, the reader's primary concern is with what happens during the actual reading event. Though, like the efferent reader of a law text, say, the reader of Frost's "Birches" must decipher the images or concepts or assertions that the words point to, he also pays attention to the associations, feelings, attitudes, and ideas that these words and their referents arouse within him. "Listening to" himself, he synthesizes these elements into a meaningful structure. *In aesthetic reading, the reader's attention is centered directly on what he is living through during his relationship with that particular text.*
>
> (Rosenblatt, 1978, pp. 23–25, original emphasis)

Giving oneself over to deep reading of literature would therefore appear to mean reading in an aesthetic way that involves the senses and the mind – the heart and the head – working together.

Rosenblatt (1981) later elaborated on this view of aesthetic reading as "a distinct kind of reading," describing it as "requiring an initially different stance, a different focus of attention, a concentration of lived-through experience, on the part of the reader" (p. 24). She argued that reading is or should be an essentially aesthetic experience combining a recognition of beauty and emotional response. For this to be possible, what is written needs to have certain literary – artistic or poetic – characteristics. Birkerts (2010) maintains that "a receptivity can be created" (p. 39) by the "rhythmic musicality" (ibid.) of words, which "bring sensation to life in the mind" (p. 43) and engage the imagination. The sensuality of language itself is important for that receptivity and engagement, and for sustaining the imagination once engaged, which he believes is not possible when reading onscreen digital artifacts.

Good literature and deep reading do not merely present meaning ready-made but pull meaning from the reader. The meaning of the work is not "sealed within a text," as Iser (1978) observed; rather, "the meaning brings out what had previously been sealed within us" (p. 157). A story, whether in the form of a novel or a short story, is only a partial representation of life and so is always incomplete: it raises questions but does not offer easy answers. The deep reading of literature stimulates a reader's thoughts and emotions and takes the reader deep within her/himself. Reading literature is therefore a way for humans to journey into new worlds and to develop a greater understanding of themselves as individuals and social beings. Literature pulls readers into the imaginative world created by the author, beckoning to them to become involved in a story, as if it were happening to them, and to become involved with its characters, as if they, or their own friends and relatives, were those characters – or could be. This following of the stories of others as if they are our own is what happens in deep reading of a literary kind.

The great literary writers know how to mesh language and story in myriad ways to engage readers at a deep level and entice them to take the first step in a journey that will intersect their own life story and life journey. Thus does Keats (1820), through his skillful use of poetic language and structure, paint pictures on a Grecian urn, turn them into a story, and draw the reader into that story in ways that reflect life far beyond the time or context of the urn, of Keats, or of any particular time, context, or poem. In a very different but equally skillful way, Ernest Hemingway creates a story in *The Old Man and the Sea* (Hemingway, 1952) through spare language which acts as "a taut line" that catches and "pulls us into the depth of ourselves" (Waxler, 2014, p. 87).

As the power of language and narrative pulls readers into a space where they journey into themselves through fictional characters who, in different ways, resonate with their own character and personhood, the reading of literature is, as

Waxler describes it in *The Risk of Reading: How Literature Helps Us to Understand Ourselves and the World* (Waxler, 2014), a "risky" activity in that it may reveal people's buried truths and secrets. Yet from the point of view of the value of deep, literary reading for increasing people's knowledge of self and others, their openness, and their empathy, what is revealed is buried treasure. Moreover, while literary reading may be risky, not reading puts people at much greater risk, as electronic media beckon.

Note

1 Lawrence W. Barsalou studied the organization of autobiographical memories, finding that they were organized first and foremost by event types (the types of events the person was participating in at the time); then by participants (the people involved in those events), activities, and location (the things people were doing and where the events remembered and activities were taking place); and finally by time (when the events and activities occurred), which was a weak component of the memories (Barsalou, 1988). It is interesting that time seems to play a relatively minor role in the organization of autobiographical memory, whereas the classification of types of events (e.g., a graduation ceremony, a wedding, a school performance) is a major organizing principle of how we remember the parts of our life story. What this suggests is that our autobiographical memories are organized not in terms of specific historical points but in terms of large structures – whole events – defined as significant in terms of human culture and life stories, representing major milestones in a life journey, and classified into types on this basis. It does not seem surprising that participants – who was involved – are a key organizing principle in memory nor that our autobiographical memories are organized in terms of activities – the things we were doing at the time the memory was formed – since both our language and our stories are organized with actors – people – as key focal points and with those people's actions as a central theme. It is also not surprising that our autobiographical memories are organized in terms of the place where we were, since humans have very good spatial memory and organize much of their experience spatially (Bachelard, 1964/1958).

References

Aziz-Zadeh, Lisa, & Damasio, Antonio (2008). Embodied semantics for actions: Findings from functional brain imaging. *Journal of Physiology – Paris, 102*, 35–39. doi:10.1016/j.jphysparis.2008.03.012.

Bachelard, Gaston (1964/1958). *The poetics of space.* Boston: Beacon Press.

Bakhtin, Mikhail M. (1984/1929). *Problems of Dostoevsky's poetics* (ed. and trans. Caryl Emerson). Minneapolis, MN: University of Minnesota Press.

Barsalou, Lawrence W. (1988). The content and organization of autobiographical memories. In Ulric Neisser and Eugene Winograd (eds.), *Remembering reconsidered: Ecological and traditional approaches to the study of memory* (pp. 193–243). Cambridge: Cambridge University Press.

Barsalou, Lawrence W. (1999). Perceptual symbol systems. *Behavioral and Brain Sciences, 22*(4), 577–609. PMID: 11301525.

Barsalou, Lawrence W. (2008). Grounded cognition. *Annual Review of Psychology, 59*, 617–645. doi:10.1146/annurev.psych.59.103006.093639.

Birkerts, Sven (1994). *The Gutenberg elegies: The fate of reading in an electronic age.* Boston: Faber and Faber.

Birkerts, Sven (2010). Reading in a digital age. *The American Scholar* website. Retrieved on December 20, 2010 from www.theamericanscholar.org/reading-in-a-digital-age/.

Burke, Michael (2011). *Literary reading, cognition and emotion: An exploration of the oceanic mind.* London: Routledge.

Cohen, Michael (2011). A place to read. *Southern Humanities Review, 45*(3), 236–249.

Damasio, Antonio R. (1999). *The feeling of what happens: Body and emotion in the making of consciousness.* Orlando, FL: Harcourt Inc.

Dehaene, Stanislas (2009). *Reading in the brain: The science and evolution of a human invention.* New York: Viking.

Donoghue, Denis (2000). *The practice of reading.* New Haven, CT: Yale University Press.

Dustin, Christopher A., & Ziegler, Joanna E. (2005). *Practicing mortality: Art, philosophy, and contemplative seeing.* New York: Palgrave Macmillan.

Fields, R. Douglas (2008). White matter. *Scientific American*, Brain Science, 54–61. Retrieved on October 20, 2015 from www.cs.unc.edu/~styner/public/DTI_tutorial/1%20Scientific%20American%202008%20Fields.pdf.

Fields, R. Douglas (2010). Change in the brain's white matter: The role of the brain's white matter in active learning and memory may be underestimated. *Science, 330*(6005), 768–769. doi:10.1126/science.1199139.

Grate, Rachel (2014). Science has great news for people who read actual books. *Mic* website. September 22, 2014. Retrieved from http://mic.com/articles/99408/scien ce-has-great-news-for-people-who-read-actual-books.

Hemingway, Ernest (1952). *The old man and the sea.* New York: Charles Scribner's Sons.

Iser, Wolfgang (1978). *The act of reading.* Baltimore, MD: Johns Hopkins University Press.

Kandel, Eric R., Kupfermann, Irving, & Iverson, Susan (2000). Learning and memory. In Erik R. Kandel, James H. Schwartz, & Thomas M. Jessel (eds.), *Principles of neural sciences* (4th edition, pp. 1225–1246). New York: McGraw-Hill.

Keats, John (1820). Ode on a Grecian urn. *Annals of the Fine Arts, 15*, January 20, 1820, published anonymously. Retrieved on May 3, 2015 from www.poetryfoundation.org/ poem/173742.

Kintsch, Walter (1998). *Comprehension: A paradigm for cognition.* Cambridge: Cambridge University Press.

Kurosawa, Akira (Director) (1950). *Rashomon* (film). Tokyo: Daiei Film.

Lewin, Philip (1997). *The ethical self in the play of affect and voice.* Presentation at the After Post Modernism conference. University of Chicago, November 14–16, 1997. Retrieved on May 20, 2012 from www.focusing.org/apm_papers/Lewin.html.

Manguel, Alberto (1997). *A history of reading.* New York: Penguin Group.

Poe, Marshall T. (2011). *A history of communications: Media and society from the evolution of speech to the Internet.* New York: Cambridge University Press.

Proust, Marcel (1913–1927). *Á la Recherche du Temps Perdu (In Search of Lost Time).* Paris: Grasset and Gallimard. Originally published in seven volumes.

Quenqua, Douglas (2014). Is e-reading to your toddler story time, or simply screen time? *The New York Times.* October 12, 2014, pp. 1, 27.

Ritchie, L. David (2006). *Context and connection in metaphor.* Basingstoke, U.K.: Palgrave Macmillan.

Ritchie, L. David (2010). Between mind and language: "A journey worth taking." In Lynne Cameron and Robert Maslen (eds.), *Metaphor analysis: Research practice in applied linguistics, social sciences and the humanities* (pp. 57–76). Sheffield, U.K. and Bristol, CT: Equinox.

Rosenblatt, Louise M. (1978). *The reader, the text, the poem: The transactional theory of the literary work.* Carbondale: Southern Illinois Press.

Rosenblatt, Louise M. (1981). Aesthetics as the basic model of the reading process. *Bucknell Review, 26*(1), 21–22; 24–25.

Schank, Roger C. (1999). *Dynamic memory revisited.* Cambridge: Cambridge University Press.

Seilman, Uffe, & Larsen, Steen (1989). Personal resonance to literature. *Poetics, 18*, 165–177.

Semino, Elena (1997). *Language and world creation in poems and other texts.* London and New York: Longman.

Stockwell, Peter (2016). Cognitive stylistics. In Rodney H. Jones (ed.), *The Routledge handbook of language and creativity* (pp. 218–230). London and New York: Routledge.

Turner, Mark (1987). *Death is the mother of beauty.* Chicago: University of Chicago Press.

Ulin, David L. (2010). *The lost art of reading: Why books matter in a distracted time.* Seattle, WA: Sasquatch Books.

Vygotsky, Lev S. (1978). *Mind in society: The development of higher psychological processes* (ed. Michael Cole, Vera John-Steiner, Sylvia Scribner, & Ellen Souberman). Cambridge, MA: Harvard University Press.

Waxler, Robert P. (2014). *The risk of reading: How literature helps us to understand ourselves and the world.* New York: Bloomsbury.

Waxler, Robert P., & Hall, Maureen P. (2011). *Transforming literacy: Changing lives through reading and writing.* Leiden and Boston: Brill.

Wellek, René, & Warren, Austin (1949). *Theory of literature.* New York: Harcourt Brace.

Wolf, Maryanne (2007). *Proust and the squid: The story and science of the reading brain.* New York: HarperCollins.

Wolf, Maryanne, & Barzillai, Mirit (2009). The importance of deep reading. *Educational Leadership, 66*(6), 32–37. Available at www.ascd.org/publications/educational-leadership/mar09/vol66/num06/The-Importance-of-Deep-Reading.aspx.

Wood, James (2008). *How fiction works.* New York: Farrar, Straus and Giroux.

Wood, Michael (2009). A world without literature? *Daedalus, 138*(1), 58–67. doi: 10.1162/daed.2009.138.1.58.

Zull, James E. (2002). *The art of changing the brain: Enriching the practice of teaching by exploring the biology of learning.* Sterling, VA: Stylus.

9

PSYCHOLOGICAL EFFECTS OF READING LITERATURE

Narrativization of information imbues a text with more dramatic impact and emotional effect as well as enabling readers to empathize with actions and events described and therefore to invest them with more meaning and value.
  — *Sky Marsen, "Detecting the Creative in Written Discourse"*
  (Marsen, 2012, p. 226)

The Many Benefits of Reading Fiction

It is widely accepted that reading a lot, and especially reading what are considered "good books," promotes intellectual and linguistic development. Reading has major value in scaffolding and developing language (Krashen, 2004), and reading good literature, as a type of well-crafted and challenging ("advanced") text, can help develop vocabulary, grammatical competence, and knowledge of genre and stylistic conventions, as well as knowledge of culture, human nature, and other areas of knowledge and wisdom which can be found between the covers of a book. People who read a lot generally excel in word knowledge as well as general or world knowledge.[1] Given the nature of reading as a process of comprehension that involves perceiving and deciphering cues and patterns in order to figure out what they mean, reading high-quality text such as literature also has major value in sharpening inferencing and interpreting capabilities that are useful in all kinds of learning and many other kinds of cognitive activity.

It seems that book reading also has a "protective effect" (Bavishi et al., 2016, p. 47) that helps maintain cognitive functioning and can extend life. A study on the reading habits and mortality rates of older American adults who participated in a national Health and Retirement study by Avni Bavishi, Martin D. Slade, and Becca R. Levy of the Yale University School of Public Health has shown that people who read books live longer than people who don't, "suggest[ing] that the benefits of reading books include a longer life in which to read them" (Bavishi et al., 2016, p. 44, Abstract). The researchers observed "[a] 20% reduction in mortality ... for those who read books, compared to those who did not read books. ... [A]ny level of book reading gave a significantly stronger survival advantage than reading periodicals" (p. 47). Based on their results, they suggest the value for survival of switching some or all of the time adults over 65 spend reading magazines and newspapers, which averaged just over 6 hours per week, to book reading, which averaged just under 4 hours per week, and of redirecting the time adults over age 65 spend watching television, reported to be an average of 4.4 hours a day, to reading books. They speculate that most of their book-reading participants would likely have been reading fiction.

Any artistic work has a complexity to it, embodying a range of elements (e.g., color and shape, harmonies and disharmonies) that can elicit different perspectives, lines of thought, and emotions in the audience. Literary works – where language can be unusual and nonliteral, where symbols and multiple meanings abound, where much is often implicit and requires interpretation, and where the everyday is mixed with enduring truths and universal themes – can attain an especially high degree of complexity. The reader will nonetheless be willing to expend significant time, energy, and effort to see the experience of the work through to completion because its high complexity helps to maintain a high level of stimulation and ultimately ensures an intense affective, aesthetic response to the work as a sort of psychological "explosion" (Vygotsky, 1971, p. 205). It is part of our evolutionary fitness and human nature that we crave the highly stimulating and complex aesthetic experiences that we can discover in the language of literature through reading and that may have survival value for individuals of our species.

As reviewed earlier, reading literature has psychological benefits in promoting feelings of pleasure and emotional well-being. In addition, reading literature has social benefits having to do with learning by way of apprenticeship with other human beings, in the "zone of proximal development" (Vygotsky, 1978), and connecting with other people *in* what is read (the characters of a story, the author of any text) and *through* what is read, such as through talking with others or writing for an audience about what is read. But the cognitive, psychological, and social benefits of reading, especially of fiction, go beyond these.

As an undergraduate at Bryn Mawr College, one of the authors (Martha) took a course at Haverford College called "Religion and Modern Man," in which students read and discussed philosophical books and essays, in addition to fictional stories and books having to do with the course topic. Although Martha was a philosophy major, she found that by far the most profound effect she experienced from the reading in the course was that of Graham Greene's fictional account, in *The Heart of the Matter* (Greene, 1948), of a man wrestling with difficult issues of faith in the modern world. In answer to a final examination question as to whether the philosophical or the fictional readings had had more of an effect in the course, and why, she argued that the emotional connection achievable in literature was more profound, occupied her thoughts much more, and stayed with her for a much longer time than the philosophical essays and books. Indeed, Graham Greene's book is with her to the present day, as a powerful *feeling*, though she can no longer remember any details. In this connection, Birkerts (2015) remarks on how after reading a book of fiction, "the details of plot fall away" and what is left is a sort of "residue ... of personal resonance" (p. 149).

The powerful effect of reading literature and the long-term residue of personal resonance and feeling which Martha experienced has been confirmed in much scientific research focused on the effects of reading fiction and of aesthetic reading more generally. A substantial amount of research carried out in the field of psychology has now demonstrated the different ways in which people are affected and become open to change through reading fiction as well as through reading other forms of literary text.

What Research in Psychology Shows about the Power of Literature and Aesthetic Reading to Effect Change

Reading Fiction Increases Empathy and the Ability to Read Others

A considerable body of empirical research led by university psychologists in Canada[2] suggests that reading fiction has significant beneficial cognitive, psychological, and social effects related to its ability to energize a reader's emotions and imagination. Frank (Jémeljan) Hakemulder of the Institute for Cultural Inquiry at the University of Utrecht explored the psychological effects of information read in the form of a story, finding that information framed as a story could change people's attitudes and beliefs by increasing their sense of empathy, as they were able to imagine what it was like to be someone else (Hakemulder, 2000). Hakemulder maintained that fiction could function as a "moral laboratory" for exploring and developing new and more empathic attitudes to others. A number of research studies by Keith Oatley, Professor Emeritus of Cognitive Psychology at the University of Toronto, and colleagues at Toronto and other universities point to the power of reading stories, of entering the imagined worlds created there, to increase readers' ability to empathize. A team led by Raymond A. Mar, Associate Professor of Psychology at York University in Canada, together with Oatley and collaborators Jacob Hirsch, Jennifer Dela Paz, and Jordan B. Peterson (Mar, Oatley, Hirsch, Dela Paz, & Peterson, 2006) revealed that heavy readers of fiction scored higher than heavy readers of nonfiction on measures of empathy and social ability, including the ability to read people's feelings in their eyes and the ability to read the meaning of people's interactions in social situations. Research by Maja Djikic, Director of the Self-Development Laboratory at University of Toronto, together with Oatley and Mihnea C. Moldoveanu (Djikic, Oatley, & Moldoveanu, 2013) confirmed the relationship of heavy reading of fiction to measures of empathy. Thus, it appears that readers of fiction become skilled in reading not only linguistic signs – that is, the language of literature – but also other communicative indicators of human feelings and motives. Other research by Mar, Oatley, and Peterson (2009) confirmed that readers of fiction are skilled in reading people's eyes, which is considered to be a test of affective theory-of-mind ability, and also showed that avid readers of fiction tended to enjoy more support in social networks than those who read nonfiction, who were likely to experience loneliness and low social support. The latter finding suggests that reading fiction is related to sociability and the making of connections to other human beings, whereas reading nonfiction can have negative effects in terms of low sociability and lack of connection to others.

Oatley (2011a, 2011b) reports on studies in which an experimental group read a literary, fictional story and a control group a nonfictional account which was otherwise parallel to the story, maintaining that readers' responses to the people in the two versions were different: only in the literary, fictional version were readers led to feel empathy with the people whose stories were told. Even though the same information was given about the events and the people depicted, when not framed within a literary, fictional narrative, readers did not relate to those people. This result is fascinating, as it suggests that the language and structure of literary fiction enhances the human tendency or ability to feel connected to other people. Oatley (2011b) observes that "writers and readers … use fictional characters to think about people in the social world" (p. 63) and concludes that this focus is key to the effects which fiction has: "Reading fiction trains people in [the social] domain, just as reading nonfiction books about, say, genetics or history builds expertise in those subject areas" (p. 66). Since people tend to learn whatever they are taught and exposed to, and often model their behavior accordingly, it is perhaps not surprising that those who have the most exposure to the type of reading that emphasizes human nature and themes – especially human relationships and feelings – are more tuned in to those features and more affected by them than people who read other things.

Drawing on the work of Jerome Bruner (Bruner, 1990), Oatley (2011b) maintains that the modeling of human actions in narrative form gives stories a particular importance in human life, functioning as simulations of human interactions that "can hone your social brain" (p. 64). In the characterization of Djikic et al. (2013), fiction is a simulation in the senses of helping people to "imagine possible worlds and possible outcomes" and to empathize through "coming to understand emotions of others by feeling them in oneself" and through "understand[ing] what others are thinking, … known as theory of mind" (p. 32).

The relationship of empathy and the ability to read others to the reading of literary fiction specifically has been confirmed in other research. A study by David Comer Kidd and Emanuele Castano compared people who read literary fiction versus popular fiction and nonfiction texts, as well as those who did not read anything, under experimental conditions (Kidd & Castano, 2013), finding that the former improved significantly as compared to the other groups in both cognitive and affective theory-of-mind tasks, based on a test administered before and after they read the texts.[3] The researchers interpret this finding as showing that reading literary fiction temporarily enhances theory of mind. There seems to be some unique triggering mechanism in literary fiction and the experience of reading it that heightens the human ability to connect mentally and emotionally with other people.

Eva Maria Koopman and Hakemulder explore the effects of reading literary works in terms of the characteristics of *narrativity, fictionality,* and *literariness* that might together account for the effects which reading literature can have. Narrativity is that characteristic of literature which expands readers' perspectives to include those of other people. This effect is not surprising since (as discussed in Chapter 7) narratives structure information in terms relevant to, and usually focused on, human actors and their experience of events. Koopman and Hakemulder describe fictionality in relation to the notion of fiction as providing a "moral laboratory":

> Fictionality might stimulate readers to consider the narrative they read as a thought experiment, creating distance between them and the events, allowing them to experiment more freely with taking the position of a character different from themselves, also in moral respects.
>
> *(Koopman & Hakemulder, 2015, p. 79, Abstract)*

The idea of fiction offering readers a way to carry out "thought experiments" is similar to our idea of the "mental journey" which readers of fiction go on that may give them new perspectives and change them, including in moral aspects. Their multifunctional model suggests that empathy results from the role-taking which literary reading encourages, as first noted by Oatley (1994, 1999). Role-taking involves a reader's projection into the imagined roles and circumstances depicted in story characters and events. As explored by Kuiken, Miall, and Sikora (2004), readers' personal identification with story characters and story events which they could link to their own personal memories promotes feelings that can open the self to modification.

Koopman and Hakemulder (2015) also stress reflectivity as an effect of reading literature which can train readers' theory-of-mind and inferencing abilities. They maintain that reflection results from the defamiliarization produced by the characteristics of literary language and text, as previously discussed by Miall and Kuiken (1994, 1999). Inexplicit and ambiguous text and unusual and aesthetic language are features of literature which can be considered to characterize its literariness. Based on interviews with readers, Miall and Kuiken (1999) had proposed that literariness involves "foregrounded textual or narrative features, readers' defamiliarizing responses to them, and the consequent modification of personal meanings" (p. 121, Abstract). Koopman and Hakemulder's (2015) model of literariness combines the foregrounding and defamiliarization characteristics of literature with the role-taking and identification with characters and events, and the "aesthetic distance" or "stillness" invoked by deep reading, which together seem to encourage deep contemplation, personal reflection, and emotive and empathic response. Other research has explored the potential of reading literature to change personality and other aspects of the self.

Reading Fiction Opens One's Personality and Behavior to Change

A considerable body of research confirms the fact that reading fiction promotes positive psychological change that can cause social change as well. A number of studies led by Djikic (e.g., Djikic, Oatley, & Carland, 2012; Djikic et al., 2013; Djikic, Oatley, Zoeterman, & Peterson, 2009) have demonstrated effects on personality traits as measured before and after reading literature. In one of the studies led by Djikic (Djikic et al., 2009), undergraduate participants were asked to read a story by Anton Chekhov, "The Lady with the Dog," while a control group read a specially written alternative version that was documentary in form. Care was taken to make the two versions exactly the same length and difficulty level, and to ensure that readers found the versions equally interesting. Both before and after their reading, participants responded to questionnaire items assessing them on what are known as the "Big Five" personality dimensions (Extraversion, Conscientiousness, Agreeableness, Emotional stability/neuroticism, Openness) and also responded to an emotion checklist assessing them in terms of the intensity of ten emotions (sadness, anxiety, happiness, boredom, anger, fearfulness, contentment, excitement, unsettledness, and awe).[4]

After reading the texts, both groups scored higher on the combined Big Five personality traits and in the combined emotions, but participants' change in Big Five personality traits and in intensity of emotions in response to their reading was greater for those who had read the Chekhov story. The amount of emotion change was also moderately correlated with the amount of change in personality traits. In discussing the findings of their research, Djikic et al. (2009) comment on the "somewhat surprising" (p. 27) fact that this Russian story could change the personality traits of a group of 21st-century undergraduates. They note "that human psyche appears to respond to the artistic form through subtle shifts in the vision of itself" (p. 28), and further note the observed mediating effect of emotion. Because the reading of the Chekhov story affected participants' entire personality trait profile, they suggest that "the quality of art-induced emotions – their complexity, depth, range, and intensity – [may] facilitate the process of trait change" (Djikic et al., 2009, p. 28). Again, we note the relevance and potential of these findings for education and social change.

As another important finding, Djikic et al. (2013) discovered that those who were low in the Big Five personality trait of "Openness to new experiences" exhibited an increase in empathy, as measured by a psychological perspective-taking scale, when they read a fictional story randomly selected from a literary anthology, whereas those who read a randomly selected nonfictional essay from the same literary anthology did not. Oatley (2011b) cites a series of research studies suggesting that those who read fiction are better able than those who do not read fiction to read social cues and are also more likely to develop the Big Five personality trait of Openness.

Dan R. Johnson carried out a series of studies on the effects of reading fiction on people's attitudes and behaviors. In one study (Johnson, 2012), he found that after reading a fictional story, participants who showed great engagement with the story – those who read deeply and were more "transported into the story" – had greater empathy for the protagonist and were more likely to engage in "prosocial" helping behavior towards a stranger. These findings suggest that high engagement with a story increases the alignment of the reader with a principal story character and opens the reader's mind to others outside the story context. Johnson (2012) also found that those with higher empathy after reading fiction were more attuned to subtle indications of fear in facial expressions, suggesting that their perception of facial cues, an important feature of human communication related to empathic response and a recognized indicator of affective theory of mind, was enhanced. Yet they were less accurate in judging the meaning of different facial expressions, suggesting that their enhanced perception of facial features perhaps made them less sure about how to interpret the enhanced detail. On a positive interpretation, this can be seen as opening the minds of deep readers of fiction to new possibilities in interpreting people's communicative behaviors.

That this may be the right sort of interpretation is supported by the findings of a further investigation by Johnson together with Brandie L. Huffman and Danny M. Jasper, in which participants read a fictional story about an "atypical" Arab-Muslim woman and then were asked to carry out racial categorizations based on pictures. Johnson, Huffman, and Jasper (2014) report that participants who were asked to determine the race of "ambiguous-race Arab-Caucasian faces" after reading the story of the Muslim woman were less likely to perceive a clear racial boundary between Arabs and Caucasians than were those exposed to the same content but not in story form. In other words, they were less sure they could perceive distinguishing racial features and boundaries. The researchers also found that those who read the story were less likely to show perceptual bias by classifying angry faces among the pictured ambiguous Arab-Caucasian faces as Arab.

The value of fiction to affect people's racial biases was confirmed in a related study by Johnson (2013), in which he reports that after reading, those who had been more transported into the story rated Arab-Muslims more positively than those who had been less transported, and they showed greater empathy for Arab-Muslims and also had higher intrinsic motivation to reduce prejudice than they had before reading the story. It therefore appears that deep reading of appropriate fictional material has value in reducing prejudice. If so, it is a powerful tool for changing people's minds and improving social relationships. As Johnson (2013) concludes, "Narrative fiction offers a safe and rich context in which exposure and understanding of an out-group can occur and can easily be incorporated in educational and applied settings" (p. 77, Abstract). This is a very important effect of reading fiction, as it can potentially aid the process of harmonizing races that can take generations to accomplish, if ever.

Of interest in this context is a group of findings about the influence of the Harry Potter books on children and young adults suggesting their potential to encourage open-mindedness and tolerance of others. Research by Italian educational researcher Loris Vezzali and colleagues Sofia Stathi, Dino Giovannini, Dora Capozza, and Elena Trifiletti investigated whether exposure to the Harry Potter books might foster tolerant attitudes among young people to stigmatized groups, specifically, immigrants, refugees, and homosexuals (Vezzali, Stathi, Giovannini, Capozza, & Trifiletti, 2014). In an experimental intervention with two groups of Italian elementary schoolchildren, one group read and discussed passages from Harry Potter books that included statements showing prejudice (e.g., the negative stereotyping of Harry's friend Hermione as a "filthy little Mud-blood" by the blond, pure-blood wizard Draco Malfoy), while the other group read and discussed passages where there were no such prejudicial statements.[5] Before beginning the reading sessions and then again a week after completing them, the children responded to a questionnaire examining their attitudes to immigrants, who are often subject to prejudice in Italy. The intervention was effective in improving attitudes to immigrants among those children who identified with Harry Potter and had attended the group that read and discussed the prejudicial passages, whereas those who read the neutral Harry Potter passages showed no change in their attitudes towards immigrants. This research suggests the potential value of highlighting prejudice in a school context through reading and discussion of books whose characters children can relate to (e.g., Harry and Hermione) as models for positive behavior and/or people they might sympathize and empathize with.

In another study reported by Vezzali et al. (2014), the researchers found more positive attitudes towards homosexuals among Italian high school students who were Harry Potter readers than those who were not. Those readers tended to identify with the character of Harry Potter, suggesting that identification with this main character, who is both an underdog and a hero, was a key aspect of their more tolerant attitudes. In a third study which they report in the same article, Vezzali et al. (2014) discovered that British university students who were Harry Potter readers had more positive attitudes towards refugees than those who were not. In this case, lesser prejudice among the Harry Potter readers was associated with disidentification with the negative character Voldemort. This perhaps reveals a difference between younger and older readers, as the former may be more likely than the latter to be influenced by their reading through identification with a character as an idealized role model whom they might aspire to be like, whereas readers in late adolescence and early adulthood may be less likely to identify with Harry, a character younger than they are, or with anyone, as they begin to experience life as independent adults. At this point, they may define themselves significantly through contrast with those whom they do not wish to be like and through empathy or sympathy with others whom they see as possessing some positive human characteristics.

The influence of the Harry Potter books, and the films and other related activities spun off from those books, on today's children and those just leaving childhood (i.e., the Millennials) cannot easily be dismissed. A political science professor at the University of Vermont, Anthony Gierzynski, published a book with Kathryn Eddy, *Harry Potter and the Millennials: Research Methods and the Politics of the Muggle Generation* (Gierzynski, 2013), based on a study of over 1,100 university students in the United States examining the characteristics of Harry Potter fans in the Millennial Generation. Gierzynski found correlational relationships between being a fan of the Harry Potter series and being more tolerant and accepting of diversity, more in favor of equality, more politically liberal, less authoritarian and more strongly opposed to use of deadly force or torture, more active politically, and less cynical – even after controlling for other factors such as parental influence.[6] It is of course difficult to determine how representative these results are for the Millennial Generation, since it is unclear how representative an all-American sample of university students who responded to Gierzynski's survey might be of that whole generation. It is moreover difficult to determine cause and effect here, whether J. K. Rowling helped to shape the characteristics of a generation or rather became rich and famous by tapping into the spirit of an age.[7]

At any rate, the findings of this group of studies highlight the significance of the Harry Potter books and the larger Harry Potter phenomenon – and by implication the Tolkien books and related larger Hobbit and Lord of the Rings phenomena that preceded Harry Potter and are still continuing, as well as the later Hunger Games books and other Hunger Games media. Since we know that reading literary fiction can influence people's empathic responses, openness, and perception of others, it can be speculated that deep engagement with the J. K. Rowling books, and perhaps other books of the popular fiction genres geared for children and young adults, may have some similar effects in the younger generation that can be usefully exploited in education. Further experimentation with specific interventions geared to increasing students' tolerance and empathy, such as those of Vezzali et al. (2014) with elementary schoolchildren using the Harry Potter books or similarly targeted interventions using other children's books, juvenile or young adult fiction, or indeed adult literary fiction suitable for adolescents, would increase our understanding of the potentials of reading fiction of all kinds for encouraging positive social attitudes and social change.

Narrative Transportation

A study by Melanie Green and Timothy Brock (Green & Brock, 2000) investigated the effect of what the authors defined as "narrative transportation" (p. 701), a unique mental state integrating attention, imagery, and feelings while reading a narrative. The researchers found that when readers experienced this state, becoming deeply absorbed in terms of their attention and deeply involved in terms of their affective and imaginative responses to what they were reading, their minds were changed both in the sense that their ideas became more congruent with those expressed through the story and in the sense that they read in an open-minded way. Commenting on this research, Gottschall (2012) makes the following point: "When we read nonfiction, we read with our shields up. We are critical and skeptical. But when we are absorbed in a story, we drop our intellectual guard. We are moved emotionally, and this seems to leave us defenceless" (pp. 151–152). In Green and Brock's research, however, these effects of deeply engaged, transported reading appear to have been based on the nature of the narrative itself, since they were seen whether or not the narrative was labeled fact or fiction. Green and Brock (2002, 2005) reviewed the research on the persuasive power of narratives to change people's minds, finding that this emotional lowering of readers' defensive shields is specifically an effect not of fiction per se (in contrast to nonfiction), but of *narrative* (in contrast to logical argument, or rhetoric). They reached this conclusion after finding little difference between the effects of true and fictional narratives on changing people's beliefs, as long as certain factors were present.

Reviewing their own and others' research, Green and Brock (2002) proposed a Transportation-Imagery Model specifying the factors making narratives persuasive so that they can change people's beliefs. As summarized by Green and Brock (2005), to effect change in thinking, narratives must, first of all, involve content that implicates people's beliefs. Story worlds often put beliefs into play, such as when readers must suspend rationality or their previous beliefs in order to dwell for a time in the pretend world of make-believe or to open themselves to a new idea. Beliefs are also connected to stories in another way, in being themselves essentially stories – about what happens, why, and how people and which people influence what happens. Is it any wonder, then, that stories influence people's beliefs?

To be effective in changing beliefs, narratives must also, according to the model of Green and Brock (2002, 2005), evoke images. Based on the evidence of many studies, they suggest that the more the evoked images cause "readers [to] become absorbed in the narrative world" (Green & Brock, 2005, p. 125) through narrative transportation, the more effective the narrative is in persuading people to change their ideas. Green and Brock (2005) note that emotion can strongly affect the persuasiveness of a message and speculate that "images are more likely to evoke strong emotions than are arguments" (p. 136). As they conclude: "When people become transported into a narrative world, their emotional responses and their creation of vivid mental images of characters and settings influence their beliefs and behaviors after people have left the narrative world" (p. 138).

According to Green and Brock (2005), certain attributes of a text make it more likely to result in narrative transportation, including its "artistic craftsmanship and the extent of adherence to narrative format" (p. 125). They especially note the narrative device of suspense that makes readers care about what happens next and literary devices such as alliteration, irony, and metaphor used in defamiliarization or foregrounding to "lead [readers] to see some aspect of the human experience with fresh eyes" (p. 131). Individual differences in imagery skill, transportability, and propensity to be transported by a specific narrative medium (e.g., television vs. book) were also proposed as affecting the persuasive outcome of a narrative. In sum, the work of these scholars and of other researchers whose research they reviewed demonstrates the power of narratives – in any form, including fiction and nonfiction, print and audiovisual such as television shows or advertisements – to move people, especially when they are well-crafted in terms of their overall design and language. Literary fiction, which comprises distinguished examples of narrative genre and artistic language, thus stands out in its ability to effect psychological change.

We should probably not be surprised that spending time with one's guard down, in a transported state of high cognitive and emotional engagement absorbing images through narrative structure and language, produces results that train the brain to notice patterns analogous to those which have been experienced in reading while also training the psyche to respond outside the fictional context in ways similar to those experienced during a state of narrative transportation. It would be of considerable interest for empirical researchers to systematically investigate what nonfiction readers are learning from their reading and what models for behavior that reading is providing. There are obviously important implications from this work for the education of children and the formation or alteration of people's beliefs.

The Effects of Reading Poetry

The effects of poetry, though they may not be identical to those of literary prose, can be equally dramatic in terms of being transported to a different world or space by language and imagery, being powerfully affected on an emotional level, and developing new perspectives. A study by Adam Zeman, Professor of Cognitive and Behavioural Neurology at the University of Exeter, and colleagues (Zeman, Milton, Smith, & Rylance, 2013) compared activation of areas of the brain while reading fiction or poetry. Reading either one activated certain areas of the brain which had previously been associated with reading, though reading self-selected poetry that was well-known to the reader activated these brain areas only weakly, whereas reading unfamiliar poetry activated brain regions associated with introspection. Stylistically compact prose and poetry (e.g., that of Keats) activated left-brain areas having to do with memory as well as right-brain areas that are also activated in emotional response to music. These are the kinds of texts that are "pregnant with meaning," existing in multiple layers which the reader discovers in the ongoing process of comprehension and interpretation, and which make use of novel language that creates an emotional response in the reader and also requires extra effort in cognitive processing, thereby triggering the activities of deep and creative reading.

Reading Mind to Mind

There is increasing evidence from brain scans that people understand others' actions and feelings by connecting to the parts of their brains where they would themselves perform those actions or experience those feelings. This is the ability of "mind-reading," or theory of mind, in the cognitive sense of understanding people's intentions and recognizing their perspectives, and the interconnected emotion-reading ability – the affective side of theory of mind, which Dennett (1987) described as underlying empathy. Theory of mind, which may operate in terms of a set of brain cells called "mirror neurons" (Rizzolatti, Fogassi, & Gallese, 2001), allows speakers and writers, on the one side, to gear messages to their audience, and hearers and readers, on the other side, to interpret those messages communicated from another human mind. The ability to mind-read in this sense appears to engage a large part of the brain's map or network of connections.[8]

The evidence from brain scans is that comprehending and relating to a story involves the internal simulation of the actions and feelings of the story characters. In reading fiction, people mirror a character's experiences in themselves: functional magnetic resonance imaging (fMRI) shows activity in those areas of the reader's brain which would be stimulated when the person performs the same action as that of the story character (Oatley, 2011b, p. 66). As Oatley (2011a) observes: "Recognition of an action in the imagination when we hear or read about it involves brain systems responsible for initiating that action" (p. 20). When people read stories, projecting themselves mentally into the story context and characters, it is as if they were actually there and the things happening to the characters were happening to them. Literature can then be described as "a cognitive and emotional simulation" that "[runs] on our mind" (Djikic et al., 2009, p. 25). In the words of Djikic and Oatley (2014):

> Stories told orally were probably the very first simulations, with subject matter based on the closest interests of our ultrasocial species. These simulations are of what we and others are up to with each other, and of how to understand such matters.
>
> (p. 500)

Theory of mind is perhaps a misnomer since this reflective or "mirroring" ability, presumably enabled by mirror neurons, involves getting not only into another person's head but also into the person's heart. Perhaps the term "simulation" can cover both aspects of putting oneself into another's shoes. In this connection we can draw on Barsalou's (1999, 2008) view that long-term memory is organized in terms of simulators of experiences, based on the original events that created the memories, which are then run as simulations in working memory based on some triggering event. As defined in this context by L. David Ritchie, Professor of Communication at Portland State University,

> simulation refers to a neural process in which either the same neural groups that would be activated during direct experience (or parallel groups) are partially activated: in most cases the actual performance of simulated muscular actions and the interpretation of simulated perceptions as 'real' are inhibited.
>
> (Ritchie, 2010, pp. 62–63)

In humans, it seems that the triggering event can be sensory, cognitive, or linguistic, including:

- an experience felt in one or more sensory modalities (visual, auditory, etc.) to be similar to the original event (e.g., the smell or sight of fire, the sight and sound of a speeding fire engine);
- an experience perceived and judged to be similar (e.g., the sight and sound of a speeding police car, or another person's facial expression);
- a heard or read description of an experience judged to be similar (e.g., in a spoken or written narrative about a fire, or of the look on someone's face); or
- even just a word or phrase connected to the original event or descriptive of it (e.g., "fire," "emergency situation," or "I smell smoke").

It would seem, within this simulation view, that many different types of simulation may occur during reading, as working memory simulates: the sounds of words, projecting the reader into the role of one who hears, maybe also speaks, the words of the author or a character in the story; the events portrayed, thereby projecting the reader into the roles of the characters or into memories of past acts and events similar to those portrayed, and the bodily sensations and emotions associated with them; or the experience of prior reading events.

How Does Literary Reading Change People?

On the basis of their own and others' research showing that reading literary prose increases empathy and the ability to understand others, and so can cause change in personality traits, Djikic and Oatley (2014) propose three features of artistic literature that account for its psychological effects: its simulative nature, its potential to open personality to change, and its indirect and exploratory nature. All three of these attributes, in concert, give literary reading considerable potential to change people. The last of these, in their view, may be especially important in the capacity of literature to open people to change, making it different from direct persuasion in leading people to change in their own ways.

Artistic literature, literary fiction in particular, invites readers to enter an envisioned world that they can observe, reflect on, and participate in. That world is one based on the author's creation, the artistry of which is to produce one particular microscopic or telescopic representation of life – a picture or a sketch – that has sufficient interest and verisimilitude to attract readers and to propel them forward through their reading. Being a limited and particular instance of life, a fictional or poetic world is not fully determined but rather requires each individual reader to fill in details, which readers do based on their own experiences, memories, modes of thinking, and reflective powers. Electing to enter such a world offers readers the chance to go on a journey which has been stimulated by the author but which readers also participate in creating and propelling forward in their own ways. This is a journey which leads through the literary work, that is, from beginning to end of the text, but is a journey which also traverses the reader's world – whether running parallel to it or detouring into it from time to time. The reader's active participation and interaction in fleshing out the details of a story or poem forges pathways through the reader's own cognitive and emotional territory, as each reader reimagines and recreates the world imagined and created by the author as a reflection – a microcosm – of his/her own mind and experience.

Thus does reading a work of fiction, and to a greater or lesser extent also a poem, begin a journey through a story world that intersects a reader's own world and personal story – that is, the reader's physical and mental worlds, including those of fantasy, and that reader's own historical and imagined self. A fictional story or a poem which draws a reader in both cognitively and emotionally and which simulates aspects of the reader's own story therefore has a transformative power to impact that person's story going forward, as a stimulus and model for future thought and action. Djikic and Oatley (2014) propose that literature makes it possible to "[transcend] our current self" and also presents models of "potential future selves" (p. 503) – most directly, we note, as characters in fiction.

Other research has examined whether the effects of reading fiction have staying power. Research by a team at Emory University – Gregory S. Berns, Kristina Blaine, Michael J. Prietula, and Brandon E. Pye – looked at the effects on the brain of reading a novel consecutively every evening over nine days (Berns, Blaine, Prietula, & Pye, 2013). Comparing scans of undergraduate student participants' brains every morning before, during, and after the nine-day period of reading the novel, the researchers found significant increases in the amount of resting-state brain connectivity in areas of the brain known to involve perspective-taking – that is, being able to project oneself into another person's situation – and story comprehension, though these decayed rapidly after participants had finished reading the novel. These results can be interpreted as supporting the research findings of the Toronto psychologists while also suggesting the need for follow-up to reading, such as the group discussion recommended in the CLTL program, in order to have a chance to secure the changes observed over a longer time period.

A further finding was of some changes in connectivity that persisted for several days after the reading. These involved the part of the brain (the somatosensory cortex, in both hemispheres), representing physical sensation and movement. This lingering effect of enhanced connectivity in the areas of the brain having to do with actions can be interpreted as enhancement of the memory traces for the actions portrayed in the novel and of the concepts associated with those actions, thus making it more likely that they will be activated in the future. Assuming that the depicted actions and related concepts represent positive behaviors, this is good news for possible lasting effects in terms of responding in similar ways to similar situations in the future, which *Psychology Today* blogger Bergland (2014) connects to the kind of imaginative visualization and "muscle memory" which athletes make use of in sports and which he also connects to fiction readers' "ability to put themselves in another person's shoes." Thus, reading fiction could change behavior indirectly through modeling and imprinting certain ways of acting and thinking.

Fiction has a vividness and an emotional reality not found in factual recounting of events, as the writer Nadine Gordimer quipped in an interview: "If you want to understand Napoleon's retreat from Moscow, what it meant to the Russians and what it meant to his soldiers, to soldiers on both sides, you have to read Tolstoy, not a history book" (quoted in Harper, 2012, p. 131). The vivid world and the emotional reality that is created in a work of fiction is highly attracting. Citing work by Mar and Oatley (2008) showing that readers' attitudes tend to become aligned with those in a fictional narrative, Gottschall (2012) observes: "The emotions of fiction are highly contagious, and so are the ideas. ... In fact, fiction seems to be more effective at changing beliefs than nonfiction, which is *designed* to persuade through argument and evidence" (p. 150, original emphasis).[9] It is an aspect of human nature that people are more powerfully affected by fiction or story – and, in general, by literary writing – than by factual information or logical argument: "As the Greeks understood, communication can be focused in different ways in order to influence people: by focusing on (1) information and logic (*logos*), (2) strong feelings (*pathos*), (3) personal values and relationship (*ethos*), or (4) a combination of these" (Pennington, 2016, p. 165). Researchers and scholars from a number of disciplines are now writing about the power of story, and of literary or aesthetically crafted language, to both move and persuade people.

Brock, Strange, and Green (2002) report that narrative can change people's knowledge as well as their beliefs and memories and so have powerful effects in persuasion. From a practical perspective, the narrative characteristics of stories can be effective in persuasive writing, such as proposals of all kinds (Walwema, 2015). Green and Brock (2005) suggest that the subjective experience of "story consumers" (p. 123) is different from that of those who consume information in the form of rhetoric and makes for a different kind of persuasion. Djikic et al. (2012) argue that artistic (i.e., literary) texts, unlike other kinds of persuasive texts, do not attempt "to persuade in a way that a writer has chosen, but to enable people to change in their own way, should they be open to such change" (p. 33). They therefore label literary texts as "change-inviting" rather than "persuasive" (p. 33). This invitation to change, and the openness to change that it engenders in readers, is an essential and important feature of literature. This may result from the reader's identification with the characters and the "narrative voice" of the author (Djikic et al., 2012).

In addition to providing a model which readers can emulate, the plot or development of a story may provide models for actions or goals which readers can aspire to, thus influencing people's planned and future behaviors. In both of these cases in which literary works offer models for behavior, the content of a story may affect readers' images of themselves as well as their aspirations and ideals, thereby fueling change.

A further potential reading effect stems from the art or artistry of a text – not only what is written but how it is written. Djikic et al. (2012) report on an experiment which demonstrated increased variability in participants' scores on the Big Five Personality Inventory administered both before and after reading a work that participants judged to be artistic – either a literary essay or a literary short story. The researchers interpret this finding as evidence of fluctuations in personality resulting from participants' experience of literary reading. In particular, their experiment showed that certain personality traits which tend to be stable in young adults, Openness and Agreeableness, had the most variability as a result of reading a literary work. This finding suggests that reading artistic literature can be especially effective in opening up Millennials to change.

The researchers speculate that readers' subjective experience of the artistic qualities of a literary text makes them "more flexible in how they define themselves" (Djikic et al., 2012, pp. 26–27). This type of effect, which they believe is shared by other art forms, is labelled "non-directional" by the researchers, meaning that it is not aimed at any specific persuasive or other outcome, but rather can influence personality traits by "making one feel less like one's usual self" (p. 27). The implication is that the reading of literary text, as a form of artistic experience, is so deeply involving that it opens a person's core being to change. It is noteworthy that this capacity for participatory, emotional, mind-altering effects, which the Greeks recognized in the potential of a live dramatic performance to produce a cathartic outpouring of emotion and change of mental state, can also be an outcome of reading a highly involving written text.

Reading in a Different Way

The studies reviewed in this chapter support the fact that literary works are read in a different way than other kinds of written works: they evoke different modes of perception and processing for reading than other kinds of text do. Like other forms of art, literary works affect people in ways which nonartistic works do not – or do to a much lesser degree. Their artistic qualities engage the emotions and the imagination of the reader more than other forms of writing, and this emotional and imaginative engagement involves the reader more fully as a person – body as well as mind – than the experience of reading other kinds of text. Reading a literary work makes the reader both think and feel in a highly involved way. The combined emotional and imaginative involvement seems to stimulate deep aspects of the reader's being, reaching into the psyche and opening up the reader psychologically to new influences on the self, including identity and personality.

The reason may be that the author's use of aesthetic language and/or rhetorical devices such as storytelling, narrative structure, or personal experience triggers an especially direct mode of cognitive-affective processing, one suffused with images and sensations which relate to and simulate the reader's experiences. Such a direct, sensuous and imagistic, processing mode makes for a more involved and embodied reading process, meaning one that has both deeper and broader personal connections in memory and one that triggers physical sensations. As a different or additional effect of aesthetic language, it may be that the reader more directly experiences the voice of the author in the evocative or sensuous language of the text, triggering a socially engaged reading process that involves relating to another person (i.e., the author). Many forms of text would not engender these effects, being written in language that relies on abstract concepts and avoids anything personal or subjective, aiming for an impersonal, "objective" mode of communication which removes signs of the author behind the text. An additional effect of aesthetic language and rhetoric seen especially in fiction is to take people outside themselves, transporting them to a different place or space – another world or dimension of thinking, feeling, and understanding.

The sensuous, transporting, and transforming potential of language itself – and especially of artistic language – is an important part of the argument we are making about the powerful effects of literary or aesthetic reading. In the characterization of Farrell (2004), literature comprises "those [texts] in which the way particular words are arranged in a particular order matters greatly" (p. 152), as "features internal to the literary work, such as rhythm and style, are not mere ornaments but contribute essentially to constituting a heightened space of significance" (p. 18). The reader's sensation of the "heightened space of significance" that is created by the special language of an artistic text seems to be an important trigger for the openness to change which Djikic et al. (2012) recognize and for the kinds of effects which Green and Brock (2000) term "narrative transportation" and which Burke (2011) describes as "disportation."

From early childhood, humans have a natural appreciation for unusual language as found in literary or artistic writing. Such writing by its very nature gives joy and heightens alertness and sensation, as it moves the reader from the ordinary world of the familiar to a less ordinary and unfamiliar world – a new plane of meaning and perception. As an aspect of this effect, artistic language and content can transport a reader to a world of play and fantasy – a world in which, like the world of humor (Pennington, forthcoming), writers and readers can not only gain new insights, but also imagine new things and experiment with new ideas. The potential of literary or aesthetic reading seems to include imagining and experimenting with new characteristics and aspects of the self.

Christina Vischer Bruns, in *Why Literature? The Value of Literary Reading and What It Means for Teaching* (Bruns, 2011), describes this potential as making it possible for people to reimagine and re-form themselves without the danger of losing the self in the process, a potential which makes people develop a love of literature as providing opportunities for personal growth:

> Enchanting or disporting literary reading temporarily blurs the boundaries between fiction and reality, between self and other, between inner and outer experience, and so it calls for readers to enter a state that resembles that of early self-formation in which the boundaries of the self are more malleable. This temporary blurring or softening of these dividing lines allows us to rework our ways of relating across them, enabling us to take on stances more responsive to the world around us. ... I contend that this is what we seek out when we pursue experiences of other worlds and mind-sets through literary reading. ... This account of literature's significance can both explain and validate the importance of the love of literature that many people proclaim. ... In this conception pleasure is not the ultimate end of literary reading nor tangential to its use, but intrinsic to gaining benefit from reading. Here the delight of literature is tied to its capacity to instruct its readers or, more accurately, to provide its readers opportunities for their own growth.
>
> *(Bruns, 2011, pp. 25–26)*

In its capacity to give pleasure and to open readers to exploring different mind-sets and states of themselves, literature holds significant potential to change people, as Waxler and colleagues (Trounstine & Waxler, 2005; Waxler, 1997, 2008; Waxler & Hall, 2011; Waxler & Trounstine, 1999) have proven in their CLTL reading initiatives with prisoners, teachers, and students, to be explored further in Chapter 10.

Giving Pride of Place to Literature

As we have shown, the process and the content of reading is a very significant development of language and mind that functions as a primary resource for learning and living. What you read and how you read is a large determinant of who you are and what is contained in your brain, and may affect your overall cognitive fitness for survival. The research summarized in this chapter suggests the power of narrative versus nonnarrative, fictional versus nonfictional, and literary versus nonliterary texts to affect people's feelings and their ways of thinking and acting in relation to others. To summarize, artistic literature opens people to these sorts of change by stimulating their imaginations, their emotions, and their intellect, thereby giving them pleasure, reinforcing the messages and feelings connected to the text, and leading them to new understandings. Some kinds of literature, fiction in particular (and possibly drama), open people to change by also simulating real-life situations and modeling sympathetic characters that one might emulate or empathize with. In these different ways, artistic literature expands people as individuals, helping to ful-fill personal needs for mental and emotional stimulation, and as social creatures, enhancing their social fitness by increasing their empathy, tolerance, and flexibility.

In stimulating and simulating human feeling and connection with other people, literature – which incorporates the features of narrative, fictional, and literary text in the form of novels, short stories, poetry, and plays – would seem to be an important resource for opening people to new experiences and therefore an important resource for learning and teaching. However, literature has at best a peripheral place in much of education today. The tradition of nonliterary, nonfictional, nonnarrative – logical or argumentative – writing, which Olivia Archibald relates to the attempt to make essay writing "scientific" and "objective" (Archibald, 2009), has been to eradicate the presence of the human being, the author, and human feeling from academic texts and curriculum. Yet the value of so-called "logical" analysis and argumenta-tion, and of so-called "critical thinking," is not just determining the facts of the case but thinking like a person, a human being, weighing alternatives in connection with human outcomes, which inevitably involve others. As Hermans and Kempen (1993) noted, "It is only when an idea or thought is endowed with a voice and expressed as emanating from a personal position in relation to others that dialogical relations emerge" (p. 212). Removing the author removes the dialogue that is at the heart of human meaning and the making of meaning.

We can surmise that all of us schooled in the Western academic writing tradition would have learned to read nonfiction school texts in an impersonal, uninvolved way. If so, it is perhaps not surprising that we approach fiction in a different way, viewing a novel, a short story, a poem, or a play as a vehicle for a more subjective and hence fully engaged, fully human mode of reading in which we can give free rein to the imagination and get emotionally involved in a way not encouraged or allowed by other kinds of writing and academic curriculum. If literature has this capacity to energize the imagination and feelings for other human beings, it can be argued that it provides an important corrective or counterbalance to other kinds of texts and curriculum, which leave less room for imagination and human feelings.

Even those who insist on education privileging job skills and practical training might agree to the value of reading fiction in training openness to new experiences and ideas, which is connected to creativity and innovation, and in training the social skills needed to work with others. As we, like Harvard ethicist Zygmunt Bauman, would argue, in the new global village that is our world, "the skills we need more than any others are the skills of interactions with others – of conducting a dialogue, of negotiating, of gaining mutual understanding, and of managing or resolving the conflicts inevitable in every instance of shared life" (Bauman, 2008, p. 190). Along similar lines, Nussbaum (2010, pp. 45–46), in her goals for education to create good citizens and a healthy democracy, stresses empathy and concern for other human beings, and "the skill and courage [required] to raise a dissenting voice," as much as she stresses critical thinking, responsibility, and individuality.

Reading literature may then be a valuable complement to face-to-face human interactions. In his prior work, Waxler has shown the great value of reading literature to change lives, such as of prisoners and hard-core, disaffected or delinquent secondary school students (see Chapter 10). Maybe reading literature can be of particular value for people who are disenchanted or to a greater or lesser degree are antisocial or asocial, including school and societal dropouts and possibly autistics as well. In addition, the more people's "interactions" move online, into the restricted contexts of Facebook, Twitter, and texting, the more we can argue, as educators, about the need to supplement these with fictional interactions and other experiences of literature, in order to keep people thinking about and empathizing with others. Thus, the enduring culture of reading literature, which we maintain at present offers an alternative to the culture of screen media, may offer a critical corrective to the isolation and antisocial effects of screen media, including so-called "social" media.

Gottschall (2012) observes that story has a central role in society, as it

> continues to fulfill its ancient function of binding society by reinforcing a set of common values and strengthening the ties of common culture. Story enculturates the youth. It defines the people. It tells us what is laudable and what is contemptible. It subtly and constantly encourages us to be decent instead of decadent. Story is the grease and glue of society: by encouraging us to behave well, story reduces social friction while uniting people around common values. Story homogenizes us; it makes us one.
>
> [...] Story – sacred and profane – is perhaps *the* main cohering force in human life.
>
> *(pp. 137–138, original emphasis)*

An acceptance of the importance of story – and literature more generally – in human life and its communal value in enculturation and civilization is the starting point for the alternative future we discuss in the final chapters of this book.

Notes

1 Using a number of different measures and factoring out people's age, education level, general ability, and working memory, Stanovich, West, and Harrison (1995) determined that the number of author names which a person recognizes is highly correlated to the amount of reading the person does and is also a good predictor of that person's vocabulary and general knowledge.

2 This research has been reviewed by Keith Oatley in a *Scientific American* article (Oatley, 2011b) and more extensively in his book *Such Stuff as Dreams: The Psychology of Fiction* (Oatley, 2011a) as well as in an article by Maja Djikic and Oatley that appeared in the journal *Psychology of Aesthetics, Creativity, and the Arts* (Djikic & Oatley, 2014).

3 Oatley and Djikic (2017) question the significance of these results, which have not been replicated in other comparable studies of very short-term fiction reading effects, while

noting the robustness of medium- and long-term effects of reading fiction on measures of empathy and theory of mind. In another study, Katrina Fong and Justin B. Mullin teamed with Mar to investigate the relationship of reading different genres of fiction to the affective theory-of-mind task of reading people's eyes (Fong, Mullin, & Mar, 2013). They found the strongest relationship for the genre of Romance fiction when other variables (age, gender, personality, English fluency, and exposure to nonfiction) were factored out of the experiment. It can be suggested that fiction which implicates emotions connected to people's relationships with other humans focuses attention on feelings and the signals of those feelings, thereby training the ability to read those signals and increasing empathy.

4 As a check on the equivalency of the two different readings, participants also responded to the text they read using adjectives (e.g., "interesting," "artistic") on an intensity scale. The focus of the study was on the personality characteristics, with the emotions checked for potential mediating function, that is, to see if the results of the study would vary depending on how participants evaluated the readings. The ratings of participants who read the short story were higher than the control group's rating of their text for artistic content but not for interest.

5 Each group met once a week for six weeks to read and discuss the Harry Potter excerpts with a research assistant.

6 It is notable that these characteristics seem to overlap substantially the views of those who supported Vermont Senator Bernie Sanders for President in the 2016 election. The large numbers of university students and other young people among "Berners" may therefore also have been "Potters."

7 It is tempting to label the Millennial Generation the "Harry Potter Generation" (even though not all Millennials are Harry Potter fans).

8 Mar (2011) used meta-analysis techniques to review a large number of brain-scanning (neuroimaging) studies to try to identify the areas of the brain that are involved when experimental subjects carry out various types of cognitive theory-of-mind (ToM) tasks involving recognizing another's perspective in story-based and non-story-based studies. From his review, Mar identified a larger than previously recognized part of the brain, a "core mentalizing network," that was activated when test subjects in a large number of studies were asked to carry out both story-based and non-story-based ToM tasks. He then reviewed brain-imaging studies of narrative comprehension, finding that "[t]he core mentalizing network, defined as the overlap between story- and non-story-based studies, [overlapped the areas of the brain for] narrative comprehension" (p. 122). Mar concluded "that a shared network exists for ToM and narrative comprehension" (p. 124), "but the precise relation between these two processes remains to be elucidated" (p. 125), as does the resemblances of the network shared by ToM and narrative comprehension with one "associated with a great number of other processes (e.g., day-dreaming, future-thinking, and autobiographical memory)" (ibid.).

9 Again we note that Gottschall contrasts fiction and nonfiction whereas some researchers contrast narrative and rhetoric, or narrative and nonnarrative genres, especially those of logical argument which are taught in school as primary modes of writing.

References

Archibald, Olivia (2009). Representation, ideology, and the form of the essay. *Writing and Pedagogy* 1(1), 11–36. doi: 10.1558/wap.v1i1.11.

Barsalou, Lawrence W. (1999). Perceptual symbol systems. *Behavioral and Brain Sciences*, 22(4), 577–609. PMID: 11301525.

Barsalou, Lawrence W. (2008). Grounded cognition. *Annual Review of Psychology, 59*, 617–645. doi: 10.1146/annurev.psych.59.103006.093639.

Bauman, Zygmunt (2008). *Does ethics have a chance in a world of consumers?* Cambridge, MA: Harvard University Press.

Bavishi, Avni, Slade, Martin D., & Levy, Becca R. (2016). A chapter a day: Association of book reading with longevity. *Social Science and Medicine, 164*, 44–48. doi:10.1016/j.socscimed.2016.07.014.

Bergland, Christopher (2014). Reading fiction improves brain connectivity and function. *Psychology Today* website. January 4, 2014. Retrieved on October 15, 2015 from www.psychologytoday.com/blog/the-athletes-way/201401/reading-fiction-improves-brain-connectivity-and-function.

Berns, Gregory S., Blaine, Kristina, Prietula, Michael J., & Pye, Brandon E. (2013). Short- and long-term effects of a novel on connectivity in the brain. *Brain Connectivity 3*(6), 590–600. doi:10.1089/brain.2013.0166.

Birkerts, Sven (2015). *Changing the subject: Art and attention in the Internet age.* Minneapolis, MN: Graywolf Press.

Brock, Timothy C., Strange, Jeffrey J., & Green, Melanie C. (2002). Power beyond reckoning: An introduction to narrative impact. In Melanie C. Green, J. J. Strange, & Timothy C. Brock (eds.), *Narrative impact: Social and cognitive foundations* (pp. 1–15). Mahwah, NJ: Lawrence Erlbaum.

Bruner, Jerome S. (1990). *Acts of meaning.* Cambridge, MA: Harvard University Press.

Bruns, Christina Vischer (2011). *Why literature? The value of literary reading and what it means for teaching.* New York: Continuum.

Burke, Michael (2011). *Literary reading, cognition and emotion: An exploration of the oceanic mind.* London: Routledge.

Dennett, Daniel (1987). *The intentional stance.* Cambridge, MA: The MIT Press.

Djikic, Maja, & Oatley, Keith (2014). The art in fiction: From indirect communication to changes of the self. *Psychology of Aesthetics, Creativity, and the Arts 8*(4), 498–505. doi: 10.1037/a00037999.

Djikic, Maja, Oatley, Keith, & Carland, Matthew (2012). Genre or artistic merit? The effect of literature on personality. *Scientific Study of Literature 2*(1), 25–36. doi: 10.1075/ssol.2.1.02dji.

Djikic, Maja, Oatley, Keith, & Moldoveanu, Mihnea C. (2013). Reading other minds: Effects of literature on empathy. *Scientific Study of Literature 3*(1), 28–47. doi: 10.1075/ssol.3.1.06dji.

Djikic, Maja, Oatley, Keith, Zoeterman, Sara, & Peterson, Jordan (2009). On being moved by art: How reading fiction transforms the self. *Creativity Research Journal 21*(1), 24–29. doi: 10.1080/10400410802633392.

Farrell, Frank B. (2004). *Why does literature matter?* Ithaca, NY, and London: Cornell University Press.

Fong, Katrina, Mullin, Justin B., & Mar, Raymond (2013). What you read matters: The role of fiction genre in predicting interpersonal sensitivity. *Psychology of Aesthetics, Creativity, and the Arts 7*(4), 370–376. doi: 10.1037/a0034084.

Gierzynski, Anthony (with Eddy, Kathryn) (2013). *Harry Potter and the millennials: Research methods and the politics of the Muggle generation.* Baltimore, MD: Johns Hopkins University Press.

Gottschall, Jonathan (2012). *The storytelling animal: How stories make us human.* Boston, New York: Houghton Mifflin Harcourt.

Green, Melanie C., & Brock, Timothy C. (2000). The role of transportation in the persuasiveness of public narratives. *Journal of Personality and Social Psychology 79*(5), 701–721. doi: 10.1037/0022-3514.79.5.701.

Green, Melanie C., & Brock, Timothy C. (2002). Transportation-Imagery Model of narrative persuasion. In Melanie C. Green, Jeffrey J. Strange, & Timothy C. Brock (2005), *Narrative impact: Social and cognitive foundations* (pp. 315–342). Mahwah, NJ: Lawrence Erlbaum.

Green, Melanie C., & Brock, Timothy C. (2005). Persuasiveness of narratives. In Timothy C. Brock & Melanie C. Green (eds.), *Persuasion: Psychological insights and perspectives* (2nd edition, pp. 117–142). Thousand Oaks, CA: Sage.

Greene, Graham (1948). *The heart of the matter.* London: William Heinemann.

Hakemulder, Frank (Jémeljan) (2000). *The moral laboratory: Experiments examining the effects of reading literature on social perception and moral self-concept.* Amsterdam: John Benjamins.

Harper, Graeme (ed.). (2012). *Inside creative writing: Interviews with contemporary writers.* London: Palgrave.

Hermans, Hubert J. M., & Kempen, Harry J. G. (1993). *The dialogical self: Meaning as movement.* New York: Academic Press.

Johnson, Dan R. (2012). Transportation into a story increases empathy, prosocial behavior, and perceptual bias toward fearful expressions. *Personality and Individual Differences, 52*(2), 150–155. doi: 10.1016/j.paid.2011.10.005.

Johnson, Dan R. (2013). Transportation into literary fiction reduces prejudice against and increases empathy for Arab-Muslims. *The Scientific Study of Literature 3*(1), 77–92. doi: 10.1075/ssol.3.1.08joh.

Johnson, Dan R., Huffman, Brandie L., & Jasper, Danny M. (2014). Changing race boundary perception by reading narrative fiction. *Basic and Applied Social Psychology, 36*(1), 83–90. doi:10.1080/01973533.2013.856791.

Kidd, David Comer, & Castano, Emanuele (2013). Reading literary fiction improves theory of mind. *Science, 342*, 377–380. doi:10.1126/science.1239918.

Koopman, Eva Maria, & Hakemulder, Frank (2015). Effects of literature on empathy and self-reflection: A theoretical-empirical framework. *Journal of Literary Theory 9*(1), 79–111. Abstract available www.jltonline.de/index.php/articles/article/view/759/1779.

Krashen, Stephen (2004). *The power of reading: Insights from the research.* Portsmouth, NH: Heinemann.

Kuiken, Don, Miall, David S., & Sikora, Shelley (2004). Forms of self-implication in literary reading. *Poetics Today, 25*, 171–203. Project MUSE, muse.jhu.edu/article/169625.

Mar, Raymond A. (2011). The neural bases of social cognition and story comprehension. *Annual Review of Psychology, 62*, 103–134. doi: 10.1146/annurev-psych-120709-145406.

Mar, Raymond A., & Oatley, Keith (2008). The function of fiction is the abstraction and simulation of social experience. *Perspectives on Psychological Science, 3*(3), 173–192. doi: 10.1111/j.1745-6924.2008.00073.x.

Mar, Raymond A., Oatley, Keith, Hirsch, Jacob, Dela Paz, Jennifer, & Peterson, Jordan B. (2006). Bookworms versus nerds: Exposure to fiction versus non-fiction, divergent associations with social ability, and the simulation of fictional social worlds. *Journal of Research in Personality, 40*(5), 694–712. doi: 10.1016/j.jrp.2005.08.002.

Mar, Raymond A., Oatley, Keith, & Peterson, Jordan B. (2009). Exploring the link between reading fiction and empathy: Ruling out individual differences and examining outcomes. *Communications: The European Journal of Communication, 34*(4), 407–429. doi:10.1515/COMM.2009.025.

Marsen, Sky (2012). Detecting the creative in written discourse. *Writing & Pedagogy, 4*(2), 209–231. doi: 10.1558/wap.v4i2.209.

Miall, David S., & Kuiken, Don (1994). Foregrounding, defamiliarization, and affect: Response to literary stories. *Poetics, 22*(5), 389–407. doi: 10.1016/0304-422X(94)00011-5.

Miall, David S., & Kuiken, Don (1999). What is literariness? Three components of literary reading. *Discourse Processes, 28*(2), 121–138. doi:10.1080/01638539909545076.

Nussbaum, Martha C. (2010). *Not for profit: Why democracy needs the humanities*. Princeton, NJ: Princeton University Press.

Oatley, Keith (1994). A taxonomy of the emotions of literary response and a theory of identification in fictional narrative. *Poetics, 23*(1), 53–74. doi: 10.1016/0304-422X(94)P4296-S.

Oatley, Keith (1999). Meetings of minds: Dialogue, sympathy, and identification in reading fiction. *Poetics, 26*(5), 439–454. doi:10.1016/S0304–0422X(99).00011-X.

Oatley, Keith (2011a). *Such stuff as dreams: The psychology of fiction*. Chichester, West Sussex: Wiley-Blackwell.

Oatley, Keith (2011b). In the minds of others. *Scientific American Mind, 22*(5), 63–67. doi: 10.1038/scientificamericanmind1111-62.

Oatley, Keith, & Djikic, Maja (2017). Psychology of narrative art. *Review of General Psychology, 21*, in press.

Pennington, Martha C. (2016). A 3-D approach to discovering and creating the features of written text. *Writing & Pedagogy, 8*(1), 161–191. doi:10.1558/wap.v8i1.29525.

Pennington, Martha C. (forthcoming). *Humor and language: Two things that make us human*. Sheffield, U.K. and Bristol, CT: Equinox.

Ritchie, L. David (2010). Between mind and language: "A journey worth taking." In Lynne Cameron and Robert Maslen (eds.), *Metaphor analysis: Research practice in applied linguistics, social sciences and the humanities* (pp. 57–76). Sheffield, U.K. and Bristol, CT: Equinox.

Rizzolatti, Giacomo, Fogassi, Leonardo, & Gallese, Vittorio (2001). Neurophysiological mechanisms underlying the understanding and imitation of action. *Nature Neuroscience Reviews, 2*, 661–670. doi:10.1038/35090060.

Stanovich, Keith E., West, Richard F., & Harrison, Michele R. (1995). Knowledge growth and maintenance across the life span: The role of print exposure. *Developmental Psychology, 31*(5), 811–826. doi: 10.1037/0012-1649.31.5.811.

Trounstine, Jean, & Waxler, Robert P. (2005). *Finding a voice: The practice of changing lives through literature*. Ann Arbor: University of Michigan Press.

Vezzali, Loris, Stathi, Sofia, Giovannini, Dino, Capozza, Dora, & Trifiletti, Elena (2014). The greatest magic of Harry Potter: Reducing prejudice. *Journal of Applied Social Psychology, 45*(2), 105–121. doi:10.1111/jasp.12279.

Vygotsky, Lev S. (1971). *Psychology of art*. Cambridge, MA: MIT Press.

Vygotsky, Lev S. (1978). *Mind in society: The development of higher psychological processes* (eds. Michael Cole, Vera John-Steiner, Sylvia Scribner, & Ellen Souberman). Cambridge, MA: Harvard University Press.

Walwema, Josephine (2015). The art of storytelling: A pedagogy for proposal writing. *Writing & Pedagogy 7*(1), 15–38. doi: 10.1558/wap.v7i1.26246.

Waxler, Robert P. (1997). Why literature? The power of stories. In Megan McLaughlin, Jean Trounstine, & Robert P. Waxler (eds.), *Success stories: Life skills through literature* (pp. 2–5). Washington, DC: Office of Correctional Education, U.S. Department of Education.

Waxler, Robert P. (2008). Changing lives through literature. *Publications of the Modern Language Association (PMLA), 123*(3), 678–682. doi: 10.1632/pmla.2008.123.3.678.

Waxler, Robert P., & Hall, Maureen P. (2011). *Transforming literacy: Changing lives through reading and writing*. Leiden and Boston: Brill.

Waxler, Robert P., & Trounstine, Jean (eds.). (1999). *Changing lives through literature*. Notre Dame, IN: Notre Dame Press.

Zeman, Adam, Milton, F., Smith, A., & Rylance, R. (2013). By heart: An fMRI study of brain activation by poetry and prose. *Journal of Consciousness Studies, 20*(9–10), 132–158.

10

WE POINT THE WAY AND TAKE YOU HALFWAY THERE

The greatest benefit we owe to the artist, whether painter, poet, or novelist, is the extension of our sympathies. Appeals founded on generalizations and statistics require a sympathy ready-made, a moral sentiment already in activity; but a picture of human life such as a great artist can give, surprises even the trivial and the selfish into that attention to what is a part from themselves, which may be called the raw material of moral sentiment.

– George Eliot, "The Natural History of German Life" (Eliot, 1856, pp. 144–145)

Learning through Literature

Human beings are born with an innate desire to learn. Yet there are various orientations to what, how, and why people learn. There is clearly value in the acquisition of specific skills, the learning of task-oriented behavior through modeling and apprenticeship – the kind of learning that helps a person make a living. Less popular these days, not as directly practical in application as skill-based learning, is what the great philosopher Socrates claimed is the real goal of learning, the fundamental quest of human knowledge: to know the self. This ancient wise man was less interested in what a person could *do* and more concerned with who a person *is*. He was exploring something that cannot be measured by achievement or computation – something deeper and more holistic about the meaning of a human life; and it should not be a surprise to realize that Socrates came up with his ideas without any help from smartphones or the Internet. Those living in the present era are in need of just such a sense of learning, an educational journey to (re-)discover their humanity and their connection to others in the human community. It is troubling that it is just this way of thinking about learning that seems most in jeopardy today.

Throughout this book, we have been suggesting that encounters with great literature can provide this kind of learning. Attentively journeying into the depths of significant literary narratives and poetry is one of the best ways people have to learn about the unknown dimensions of themselves and the relationships which they have with others. Literature does not offer immediate solutions to problems or skills that might be means to some other practical ends. Instead it accomplishes something which is ultimately far more important: it puts people on a path to knowing themselves and improving themselves as thinking, feeling, and social beings. This it does through simulations of human life that run through a reader's mind and have the power to educate. Their power derives from the medium of language shared with authors who practice creative writing at the highest level, producing art-in-words that can initiate a full human response which unleashes the reader's own creative resources. Reading the works of these creative writer-artists triggers the emotions and the imagination and sets them on a creative journey, expanding a person's horizons beyond the immediate context and everyday world. The act of creative reading opens the mind and starts it wandering and wondering, at the same time as the simulation initiated by reading literature points to deep truths about the self and opens the heart to connecting with other human beings more fully and in more open and tolerant ways.

Reading great literature is a creative journey that incorporates a challenge: it is a quest to know that opens up endless questions about the complexity, the mystery, and the twists and turns of human life – that invites readers to contemplate the depth and value of human existence. When people go far into themselves in this way, they also go far out to the possibilities of the world before them (Waxler & Hall, 2011), journeying into what they might have feared and kept at a distance. This is what makes reading literature challenging and even risky (Waxler, 2014), but also rewarding and meaningful. Discovering something that was unknown before, something sensed only vaguely and not fully understood, something strange – readers suddenly realize that this undefined "something" is part of them, and that this something, which they apprehended only vaguely or not at all before, connects them to The Other, meaning the rest of humanity. Through reading deeply, they acknowledge this something in themselves that is also in others. They empathize with it and might even want to embrace it.

A Program That Works: Changing Lives Through Literature

In 1991, Waxler, together with Massachusetts judge Robert Kane and probation officer Wayne St. Pierre, started an alternative sentencing program for criminal offenders called Changing Lives Through Literature (CLTL), in which eight men, many of them not high school graduates and all of them with multiple convictions for serious crimes, were given probationary sentences on condition that they complete a seminar in Modern American Literature with Professor Waxler. The seminar involved discussing books such as James Dickey's *Deliverance* (Dickey,

1972) and Jack London's *Sea Wolf* (London, 1904) as a way to get the men to express their thoughts and feelings to their peers and people in authority "in a democratic classroom where all ideas were valid. Instead of seeing their world from one angle, they began opening up to new perspectives and started realizing that they had choices in life. Thus, **literature became a road to insight**" (http://cltl.umassd.edu/AboutHistory.cfm, original emphasis). Soon a woman's program was added, and later the program was adapted for use in education.

Waxler's idea was based on the notion that reading and discussing literature could make more of a difference in people's lives than sending them back to jail. As he pointed out in the early days of the CLTL program, "Reading and discussing good literature are closely connected activities that give power to each other, just as the power of literature is closely connected to the power of language itself" (Waxler, 1997, p. 5). He knew that many of the students in his literature classes had changed the way they saw themselves and the world through thoughtfully reading and then discussing together well-known modern novels, and he was convinced that anyone could have the same experience. Each student read the same story, but each one read it differently, mapping his or her own stories onto the stories assigned as reading. It was as if they themselves and their lives were in dialogue with the author and with the stories. This effect was then expanded through further dialogue in class, as the voices in the room enhanced and deepened the understanding of the stories and of the individual students themselves. Through this ongoing process of reading and discussion, the students began to appreciate the complex and multidimensional quality of their own lives and the lives of others. For the students, and for Waxler himself, the classroom became a place of ongoing journey, a quest to discover who those human beings were and who they might become.

Since its inception in 1991, the Changing Lives Through Literature program has expanded to several other states and to the United Kingdom, with significant results (see http://cltl.umassd.edu/home-html.cfm; https://en.wikipedia.org/wiki/changing_lives_through_literature). The CLTL website includes information on programs in several locations and suggestions as to how to set up a program as well as resources in the form of syllabi, reading lists, and instructional materials for reading and discussing specific works. The CLTL program seems to work because literature and the discussion of literature open people up to new ways of thinking and being: "Through literature, participants in CLTL … explore their identity, and the result is often their way out of crime" (http://cltl.umassd.edu/AboutPhilosophy.cfm). In "Why Literature? The Power of Stories," Waxler (1997) summarized the many ways in which literature was found, in the early days of the development of the program, to improve the lives of criminal offenders:

- Literature allows criminal offenders to feel personal experiences through their senses and encourages them to reflect on those experiences.

- Literature also contributes to the exercise of the moral imagination.
- Literature can teach criminal offenders that they are not alone.
- Literature helps offenders to understand that there are many ways of thinking about a person or an event.
- Literature compels criminal offenders to think about their motives and behavior in new ways.
- Literature can free criminals from the mind-forged manacles of their own consciousness by clarifying the experiences of their past and offering them opportunity to create a future.

(pp. 3–5)

In addition, as reviewed in the previous chapter, reading and discussing literature has the potential to make even hard-core offenders more open-minded, empathetic, and sympathetic to others, thereby offering significant potential to improve their prosocial attitudes and behaviors and to forge a more positive identity and direction for their lives going forward.

A number of studies of the program indicate that CLTL made a difference by cutting prisoners' recidivism rates dramatically. In 1998, for example, Roger Jarjoura and Susan Krumholz, criminal justice researchers, after carrying out a longitudinal study of the CLTL group and a comparison group of probationers who were not exposed to the CLTL program (Jarjoura & Krumholz, 1998), concluded that the recidivism rates of the CLTL participants were significantly lower than probationers who did not participate in the CLTL program. Those in CLTL had a surprisingly low recidivism rate of 19 percent, compared to the other group who had a rate of 45 percent. More recently, in a large study, Russell K. Schutt, Xiaogang Deng, and Taylor Stoehr looked at 673 CLTL participants and compared them to 1,460 other probationers selected at random, who formed a control group (Schutt, Deng, & Stoehr, 2013). As Schutt et al. (2013) concluded in their report, "Using Bibliotherapy to Enhance Probation and Reduce Recidivism," participation in the CLTL program made a significant difference, reducing both the number and the severity of criminal incidents in those who had participated. For the CLTL participants, there was a drop of 60 percent in post-program incidents – far exceeding that of the control group.

Not only the criminal offenders but also the judges and probation officers who have participated in the program have reaped the benefits of CLTL. They, too, often say that CLTL has made an important difference in their lives. Judges report that they think about the people coming before their bench in a different way than they did before; they have a more open-minded attitude. Probation officers praise the program for the way it creates a sense of empathy and community, and they credit the CLTL program for spurring many of the offenders to go back to school and to think in new, more generous and tolerant, ways about family and friends.

Waxler has brought a version of CLTL into halfway houses, and CLTL has been used as an experimental model aiming to get failing students back on track in alternative schools in New Bedford and Fall River, Massachusetts (Hall & Waxler, 2007, 2010). Teachers of literature and language arts have been introduced to the program in graduate Education courses (Hall & Waxler, 2010). Over the years, the CLTL program has proven to be an important testament to the power of literature to improve people and change their lives for the better (Trounstine & Waxler, 2005; Waxler, 1995, 2008; Waxler & Hall, 2011; Waxler & Trounstine, 1999). The program has been recognized and supported by grants from the National Endowment for the Humanities and the Massachusetts Foundation for the Humanities, and its achievements have been reported in feature articles in major newspapers such as *The New York Times* and *The Christian Science Monitor*, and in coverage by the *Today Show* and other television and radio shows in the United States and other countries.

Looking specifically at its use in schools, Hall and Waxler (2007) brought the CLTL program that had worked so well with prisoners to at-risk middle school students in the New Bedford Alternative School. Their goal was to create what they called "a new neighborhood" around reading and discussion of stories and poems, a safe space where those students could try out new ideas and experiment with new identities, far away from

> the hardscrabble streets ruled by the voices of gang leaders. By reading, thinking about, and discussing stories and poetry, [they] were given an opportunity to transport themselves through narrative texts and locate themselves in a new place, and to use their imagination and the engagement with language to reinvent themselves.
>
> *(Hall & Waxler, 2010, p. 92)*

The success of those efforts and the lessons learned, documented by Hall and Waxler (2007), led them to continue their work at another alternative school in the neighboring city of Fall River which was similar to that in New Bedford in that its students had been expelled from the schools they previously attended. Also like those from the New Bedford Alternative School, those attending Fall River came from troubled and low-income families, and had little hope or confidence in school and in themselves.

Hall and Waxler (2010) developed a program for this second school with participation by students at their university who were preparing to be teachers. First, the Education students read and discussed Robert Frost's poem, "The Road Not Taken," which focuses on themes of life's journey and choices, and then they helped to facilitate reading and discussion of this poem with the New Bedford school students. Next, the college student-teachers and the school students read and discussed together three stories selected for their relevance and interest to the students. The students engaged passionately in the discussions of the stories and saw how those stories mirrored aspects of their own lives. The story readings and discussions were important in building those at-risk students' confidence and in making them realize that they could enjoy learning. They were important also in helping future teachers to see that even the most at-risk students could be reached and might have much to share.

In these schools, the CLTL program both modeled and promoted new perspectives and a highly engaged and involved mode of learning in interaction with others. For both the school students and the future teachers, the process of reading and discussing literature made them think differently, and in so doing, perhaps also changed their lives going forward, in ways which, Hall and Waxler (2010, p. 99) reflect, might affect others in the educational system.

Our book can be seen as an outgrowth and expansion of the Changing Lives Through Literature program, as we attempt to persuade people of the value of literature through participatory experience with it and, further, through reviewing relevant evidence and carefully constructed argument that literature has the power to change lives. This is an argument which we link to our other main argument, that a literate culture offers an important alternative and corrective to the current dominant culture of "pop" and "bling." In this chapter, we give examples of the way literature might be read and discussed to help people reflect on their own and others' lives, with the potential for psychological and social change. The reading and discussion might take place in a reading group, a classroom or other institution (e.g., a prison or a hospital), or among family members. For reasons of space, the discussion of each story is necessarily summative, with a focus on the narrative content, but with attention paid as well to language.

Reading and Discussing "Greasy Lake" in a CLTL Group

Waxler always uses the short story "Greasy Lake," by T. Coraghessan Boyle (Boyle, 1985), in the first session of his CLTL classes, and he has commented on it in several places, including in the anthology *Changing Lives Through Literature*, co-edited with Jean Trounstine (Waxler & Trounstine, 1999); in *Finding a Voice: The Practice of Changing Lives Through Literature*, a book about CLTL co-authored with Trounstine (Trounstine & Waxler, 2005); and on the CLTL website at the University of Massachusetts Dartmouth (http://cltl.umassd.edu/resourcesin struct3d.cfm). The story is one that most readers seem to connect with, as it reminds them of an experience in their own lives, and it is one that works well in the classroom. We recommend it for use in middle and high school, the first and later years of college, and in graduate Education courses. In all of these contexts, it has been well-received.

"GREASY LAKE" BY T. CORAGHESSAN BOYLE

The title of the story and its epigraph are taken from Bruce Springsteen's song "Spirit in the Night," setting the context of what takes place and raising a question about what might be down the "dark side" of the road in the story to come. Three 19-year-olds are cruising the streets late one June evening, courting decadence and "badness" and looking for adventure. They seem to be typical middle-class American teenagers, bored at the beginning of summer vacation, driving the car owned by the narrator's mother, drinking and smoking, and not yet ready to go home. It is past midnight and they decide to see what's going on at the local hangout of Greasy Lake.

When they arrive at the lake, they spot a lone motorcycle and an occupied car that they think is their friend's. As a practical joke, they shine their bright lights into the car, imagining their buddy with a girl in the car. But out of the car jumps a "greaser," who rushes toward the three of them in the darkness and begins to attack them. The narrator instinctively grabs a tire iron and knocks the greaser unconscious. The greaser's girlfriend jumps out of the car, and the boys start attacking her, until another car pulls up, shining its lights through the darkness, and the boys flee. The narrator runs into the murky lake, his two friends into the adjacent woods. In the water, the narrator bumps into a corpse (apparently, the owner of the abandoned motorcycle) while on shore his mother's car is being attacked. Readers share the trauma of the narrator standing in the water and then his sense of relief when he hears the greaser he had hit with the tire iron cursing from the shore. Like the boys in the story, they can finally relax when everyone on the shore leaves, going their own way.

The three friends return to the shore as dawn breaks. After finding the narrator's lost keys, they are ready to go home, back to the comfort of their families. Another car pulls into Greasy Lake with two older girls who want to party, but these young men, who have had more than enough excitement for one night, are in no mood for more "bad-boy" behavior. Leaving the scene, they see in their rearview mirror the outstretched hands of the girls beckoning to them, as the three friends, together in the safety of the car, pull away from their nightmare adventure, having learned an important lesson about limits on the road to adulthood and the risks of the "dark side."

The characters in "Greasy Lake" seem to be ones that all readers can empathize with, recognizing aspects of themselves in those teenagers who courted trouble and then got more of it than they bargained for, and feeling the young people's experiences as ones they might have had themselves. The feelings of empathy and identification heighten readers' responses to the story and make them eager to reflect on it, to discuss it, and to carry it away with them to continue considering the questions that it raises. The questions raised by literary stories like "Greasy Lake" are always open-ended and challenging, and they help create a mood that allows for the kind of discussion which can lead to a shared sense of imaginative knowledge and rejuvenated possibilities. It is just that kind of mood generated by face-to-face discussion in the classroom, inspired by the reading of literature, which helps to create an experience that cannot be duplicated through a digital screen. Once started, the discussion never quite ends. It continues even when the participants leave the room and head down the corridor, across the parking lot, or in whatever direction they are going, often still talking about the experience and always taking the story away with them. Boyle's story of "Greasy Lake," like all stories read and enjoyed by human beings, is given new life in every reader, as it lives and breathes within each of them.

Reading and Discussing a Group of Thematically Connected Texts on Brothers

Previous work by Waxler and colleagues (Trounstine & Waxler, 2005; Waxler & Hall, 2011; Waxler & Trounstine, 1999) has demonstrated how reading and discussing literary stories in groups can lead students and other readers to take an interest in literature as a springboard to exploring and expressing themselves, their thoughts and feelings, through both internal and external dialogue. Through the combination of internal dialogue in individual reading and external dialogue in group discussion of the stories, common themes emerge that are of mutual interest but that also evoke individual responses and personal insights, as each person reads the story in a unique way reflecting personal responses and experiences. Discussing stories within a group creates a psychological and intertextual space between each story and each individual reader, as well as across and among the whole group of readers and stories. This is a space that opens readers to new dimensions of themselves and others, creating each one anew as it also creates a new and coherent community that shares experience and insight which everyone can acknowledge.

An increasing depth and breadth of discussion and insight through literary reading can be nurtured by having participants read and discuss a selected group of stories that can be connected in some ways. Often a group of stories is connected through the common themes or issues raised, offering opportunities for the group to consider how these recur in different circumstances. Sometimes a writer makes a connection to an older story through echoing some of its specific language, which can be a clue to readers of the writer's intent and the underlying meaning of the story waiting to be plumbed in reflection and discussion. Sometimes a more modern story connects to an older one by transposing the original story, or aspects of it, to a different time and place. Many writers use this technique to develop new works, thereby opening up myriad opportunities for comparison and contrast. All of these kinds of connection can be seen in the set of stories selected here to model the reading and discussion of literature in groups, a set comprising two very old stories as well as three modern ones. What they have in common is that they are all about the relationship and rivalry of two brothers. Besides illustrating the same thematic focus, the stories as a group show how literary culture is built on a very long tradition.

The Biblical Story of "Cain and Abel"

The story of "Cain and Abel," the sons of the Biblical Adam and Eve (Genesis 4), can be approached as a literary narrative in which issues related to siblings emerge as part of the family dynamic, issues that almost all humans are intimately acquainted with. In raising these issues, the story of "Cain and Abel" explores a central thematic concern of human life which recurs in many works of literature through the ages. Cain is the first human child to be born and then Abel, his younger brother, the first human being to be killed. It is a story that resonates with mythic possibilities: good and evil, life and death, human origins and endings. As such, it explores the limits of human identity, morality, and mortality – all within the context of family drama involving an older and a younger brother, the complexity and ambiguity of sibling rivalry and family ties, and the strong feelings and moral issues that arise in family relations. Some of the concerns in this story continue to be explored in other stories throughout the generations, including those we discuss later in this chapter.

"CAIN AND ABEL"

Cain works the soil, a hard-working and apparently strong farmer like his father. By contrast, Abel is a shepherd who tends his flock. When told to bring an offering to God, Cain brings the fruit of the soil, Abel a portion of meat from the firstborn of his flock. Cain's offering is rejected, while Abel's is looked on with favor. Cain seems to have somehow done wrong, but it is not clear what it is that he has done wrong, nor that he meant to do wrong. When his offering is rejected, he becomes "angry and downcast" and jealous of his brother, whom he kills – symbolizing the violence of the human race and the depth of sibling rivalry from the beginning of time.

When God asks him, "Where is your brother Abel?" Cain does not answer directly but replies with the question: "Am I my brother's keeper?" It is a powerful question that will echo down through the ages, deep within all of us. As a result of the killing, Cain is driven from his home soil and becomes a "restless wanderer," rootless, no longer welcome in his home, but with a mark on his forehead that allows him to live in the land of Nod, East of Eden. Cain has committed a dastardly act, and yet he is protected by God and is able to create a family of his own and become the builder of the first city. All this is accomplished, however, in the midst of endless corruption and violence, in a land soaked with blood. What kind of justice is this?

In looking at this Biblical story as a literary narrative, we note its moral complexity and the powerful feelings it can evoke in readers, who might sympathize with Cain, even though he has murdered his own brother, and feel protective of him, similar to the way God protects him. They might feel that Cain has not been treated well, triggering a sense of injustice that makes readers identify with him: they can understand his anger and even accept his murderous act, though there is much in the story that is not so easy to understand and can keep readers thinking and wondering what it all means. They might wonder why Cain was treated as he was or why Abel had to die. The story might also make readers wonder why so many Biblical stories about brothers privilege the younger brother (e.g., Isaac, Jacob, Joseph) rather than the older one. It might lead them to think about why people are often drawn to flawed and even bad characters in real life and in stories about mafia dons, robber barons, or Wild West outlaws. The "Cain and Abel" story opens up all kinds of questions and possibilities to explore and consider, questions and possibilities that will continue to be explored in stories created throughout the ages. Such stories as that of Cain and Abel evoke other stories and keep those who contemplate them on the journey of life, always questioning, always questing.

John Steinbeck's East of Eden *and Elia Kazan's Film Adaptation of the Book*

John Steinbeck's novel *East of Eden* (Steinbeck, 1952) transposes the stories of Adam and Eve, and Cain and Abel to 20th-century Salinas, California, its rich farmlands a sort of Garden of Eden. One of the classes that Denby (2016) observed read, discussed, and wrote on this classic, noting the ways in which the lives of its characters intersected their own. It might also be worthwhile to follow reading of the Steinbeck book by viewing and discussing the film by the same name directed by Elia Kazan (Kazan, 1955), which centers on the story of Adam Trask and his two sons, Cal and Aron.

EAST OF EDEN BY JOHN STEINBECK

East of Eden spans the lives first of two half-brothers, Charles and Adam Trask, and then of Adam and his wife and two twin sons, Caleb and Aron. The lives of both sets of brothers, Charles and Adam, and Caleb and Aron, intersect those of the Biblical Cain and Abel in many ways, and there are other parallels in Steinbeck's novel to Biblical stories. Thus, a reading and discussion of this book following the reading and discussion of the story of "Cain and Abel" can be stimulating, leading to all kinds of "detective work" to discover parallels in the stories while also exploring their characters and themes in depth, and how these relate to the readers themselves.

Steinbeck's novel centers on the themes of sons' love for their father and their own brotherly love, rivalry, and jealousy. As a reworking of the Biblical rivalry of brothers, Steinbeck's story creates the same kind of contrasting prototypes of two brothers, the "bad boy" Caleb and the "good boy" Aron, and, in the character of Caleb in particular, the same tragic figure and sympathetic protagonist of the younger brother, modeled on Cain. It also raises many of the same mythic-level themes, moral questions, and issues of justice. It can therefore be of considerable interest to consider this story in relation to the original "Cain and Abel" story as well as in relation to readers' own lives and experience.

Film adaptation by Elia Kazan

In the Kazan film, brother "Cal" is played by James Dean, an actor famous for his roles as a disaffected and misunderstood youth. Dean, a screen idol who tragically died young, became a cult hero. His presence in the film and his playing the role of Cal adds to the interest of this movie, as does the presence of other major actors of the time (Julie Harris, Richard Davalos, Raymond Massey, Jo Van Fleet, and Burl Ives), which is considered a cinema classic. In particular, it is worth discussing the ways in which the book and the film, which is only a part of the larger story developed by Steinbeck, differ.

Discussion comparing and contrasting the book versions and movie versions of stories like *East of Eden* can underscore the differences between books and films, and in general between print and screen versions of stories. Such discussion usually ends up with most of the group agreeing that the book version is superior, for reasons such as being more impactful, significant or important, or true to life. Those who have read the original books are often disappointed in the film versions of novels or, if they like the films, will nonetheless find the books to be more impactful in the long run. We believe this is because a book leaves it up to the reader to imagine scenes, calling on the reader to go deep into the unconscious to help create the story, whereas a film has already given the viewer the director's way of seeing and imagining the scenes. As Bergland (2014) remarks, "Even the most advanced special effects will always fall short of the visual power of your own imagination." Although a film may have more sensational and immediate impact, in this case and most others, the story of the book stays with a person in a way the story of the film does not. Rather, what stays with a person after the film is the images of the actors and the scenery: they are larger than life, in effect, overwhelming the story itself. Thus, while a film may have a greater immediate, short-term impact, it is usually the book that has the lasting, long-term impact. This is the peculiar and important nature of books that makes them so important to keep in our lives.

The Biblical Story of "The Prodigal Son"

The story of "The Prodigal Son" (Luke 15) can also be connected to the story of "Cain and Abel" and so is appropriately read next in this sequence of stories about brothers. For group reading and discussion, parallels can easily be drawn, and the two stories considered together can deepen readers' understanding of the complexity of sibling relationships and the weight of their responsibilities as members of families themselves.

"THE PRODIGAL SON"

In the story of "The Prodigal Son," the father, who will give his inheritance to his two sons (two-thirds to the older one, one-third to the younger), finds that his disobedient younger son (who apparently cannot wait for his father to die) leaves home immediately and goes to a "distant country" with his share of the wealth. The younger son squanders the wealth and becomes a lost son and lost brother, exiled and alienated from himself and his family. By contrast, the older brother "never disobeyed."

When the Prodigal Son returns home, planning to renounce his kinship and become a mere hired hand, the father runs toward him with a loving and welcoming embrace and immediately calls for a "fattened calf" offering (an echo of Abel's offering) for a feast and celebration. The father tells the older brother, "thy brother was dead, and is alive again." The older brother is self-righteous and refuses to attend the father's celebration for his younger brother, suggesting that he believes he is being unjustly treated for his loyalty and devotion. In his simple response of "You are always with me," the father seems to say that the older brother has been adequately compensated by constant connection to his father. As in the case of Cain and Abel, the reader may question the difference in how the two brothers are being treated and wonder about matters of love and fairness in families.

Human beings desire both mercy and justice, love and judgment, freedom and the law; however, as those who encounter this story acknowledge, it is hard to satisfy these contrary impulses, and people's existential condition remains complex and problematic. Like the story of "Cain and Abel," the story of "The Prodigal Son" illustrates a father's unconditional love for his son, even when he does evil, and in general how a father's actions towards two sons may not be fair, or may be perceived as not fair, and so lead to all kinds of other conflicts and consequences between siblings. Experiencing these stories of "Cain and Abel," *East of Eden*, and "The Prodigal Son," readers journey farther into the intriguing complexities of human life, and can gain a better sense of human motivations, making them more tolerant and more empathetic with others and the difficult struggles that all share. Through interaction with these stories, readers begin to acknowledge that there are no easy answers to the most important questions that life itself raises. The stories arouse in all those who absorb their meaning and the questions they raise a need to journey on, to pursue the paths that the questions point them towards.

James Baldwin's "Sonny's Blues"

Many modern writers have explored these same questions in their own works, drawing both consciously and unconsciously on these classic stories, which are embedded in our human heritage as well as in the wordings and narrative patterns that lie deep within our language and that have shaped our culture. They are a dimension of our human consciousness, open to endless exploration, symbolization, and intertextual referencing. Harlem-born writer James Baldwin, in "Sonny's Blues" (Baldwin, 1988/1957), first published in the now defunct *Partisan Review* and reprinted in the collection of Baldwin stories *Going to Meet the Man*, offers a significant example of a number of modern works which invoke these ancient stories in new contexts, and in so doing incorporate and extend a chain of ongoing intertextuality reaching back into prehistory.

"SONNY'S BLUES" BY JAMES BALDWIN

In "Sonny's Blues," the older brother, an unnamed narrator, tells the story of his complicated relationship with his younger brother, Sonny. The older brother is a math teacher and family man living a respectable middle-class life in Harlem. By contrast, the younger brother is a jazz musician struggling with heroin addiction and living on the margins of society.

Sonny has always seemed to live in a world apart within his own head, keeping his feelings bottled up inside. The older brother has never understood Sonny's passion for jazz nor the life this has led him to, playing piano in clubs and hanging out with people his brother fears are a bad influence. He is blind to the depth of his brother's life and experience, refusing to acknowledge who Sonny really is.

The older brother's narrative makes clear that he has always loved Sonny, though with the distance between them growing over the years. Now when Sonny gets arrested in a drug raid, the older brother is reluctant to accept the reality of his younger brother as a drug addict: "I couldn't find any room for it anywhere inside me. I had kept it outside me for a long time. I hadn't wanted to know" (p. 87). The older brother might remind us of Cain, who refuses to be his brother's keeper and has therefore essentially closed himself off from his brother. We might also be reminded of the older brother in "The Prodigal Son," the one loyal to the respectable, mainstream family values.

Like Sonny, their father was a musician. He loved Sonny (probably more than he loved his older son) but was hard on him because they were so much alike; we note again the favoring of the younger son. The father had witnessed the death of his own younger brother being hit by a car full of white men as they walked together on a dark road one Saturday night. In the mother's recounting of the incident to the older brother, the rest of their father's life was full of anger and fear. She tells him this story, she says, to make him realize that he needs to watch over his brother, and she makes him promise to do so. Yet for a long time the older brother does not keep the promise he made to his mother to be in effect his brother's keeper, and he takes no responsibility for Sonny.

Then when the older brother's baby daughter suddenly dies and he receives a letter from Sonny, who expresses his feelings of shame and sadness, the older brother's feelings for the younger brother and his troubles are aroused. After a long period of no contact, the older brother starts corresponding with Sonny, who is soon to return to New York, and he begins to find room for the suffering and vulnerability of his younger brother that he has long pushed to the back of his mind and feelings. It is as if his brother, who, like the younger brother in the "Prodigal Son," was once dead to him, "is alive again."

In the final scene of the story, the older brother sits in a nightclub, watching and listening to Sonny play, deep within his music. The older brother now can identify not only with the suffering of Sonny's own past, but with the suffering of his mother and father, of his little daughter and his wife – all of the suffering expressed in the blues, a music which Sonny has harnessed as his own voice, filled with the burning anguish of human existence. In Sonny's blues, his brother "understood, at last, that he could help us to be free if we would listen, and that he would never be free until we did" (p. 122).

When readers enter the depths of a literary narrative like this James Baldwin story, they are in dialogue with the story and with themselves. Such stories help readers expand their understanding of the capacious territory of their own consciousness, what makes them similar to and different from others, what makes them imperfect and human. They are not reading to acquire an abstract lesson or instruction; rather, they are reading to experience through the narrative language an opening into the interior of their own ambiguous makeup, the emotional and conceptual heart of their embodied identity and its relationship to the world they live in. Each reader is both Cain and Abel, Caleb and Aron, the older brother and the Prodigal Son, the unnamed narrator of "Sonny's Blues" and Sonny himself.

Tobias Wolff's "The Rich Brother"

As the next story in this sequence of readings and discussions, we turn to "The Rich Brother" by Tobias (Jonathan Ansell) Wolff (Wolff, 1985), which Waxler has previously used in the CLTL program (http://cltl.umassd.edu/resourcesin struct3s.cfm). This is another story that resonates with these earlier stories and further deepens readers' thinking about sibling rivalry, family ties, and the thematic issues of mercy and judgment, unconditional love, and the pain and vulnerability of our conflicted and imperfect existence.

"THE RICH BROTHER" BY TOBIAS WOLFF

At the beginning of the story of "The Rich Brother," Pete, the older brother, wealthy from real estate and with a family, seems at first to be the rich brother, successful by mainstream standards. In contrast, Donald, the younger brother, seems a failure by those same standards, living alone and single, always in debt, and existing at the "farm" (a cult of sorts) until asked to leave even that place. Pete comes to pick Donald up in his car after he has been thrown out of the farm. At that time, he gives Donald $100 to hold as they drive back to Pete's house. On the road, Pete and Donald pick up Webster, a man who appears to be a con artist. When Pete nods off, Donald gives Webster the $100 that Pete had originally given him, money which Webster claims he needs to invest in a gold mine. Pete is enraged when he finds out and throws Donald out of the car. But then Pete, alone in the car, begins to think about the remote chance that Donald's investment with Webster could pay off: "What a joke if there really was a blessing to be had, and the blessing didn't come to the one who deserved it, the one who did all the work, but to the other" (Wolff, 1985, pp. 218–219), Pete muses.

We might be led to question whether in fact Pete would deserve that hypothetical payoff, which is described as a "blessing." Perhaps Donald does deserve it, just like the Prodigal Son may. We might consider the ways in which the younger and materially poorer and less successful brother may deserve a blessing more than the older and materially rich and successful brother does, perhaps recalling the Biblical pronouncement that the meek are blessed and "shall inherit the earth." We can no longer judge with absolute certainty who the rich brother is.

When Pete abandons Donald on the road and heads home, he appears at first relieved of a burden, free from responsibility for his brother. But as he listens to the music from the radio, he is "already slowing down" (p. 221), thinking of turning back and imagining "his wife [standing] before him in the doorway of his home and ask[ing], Where is he? Where is your brother?" (p. 221) – questions invoking a natural connection and responsibility that have provoked us since Cain and Abel.

Thinking and talking about these last two modern stories in the context of the earlier stories enriches the journey of readers to know themselves and their place within the world and enriches them as empathic and moral beings. In showing how complicated human relationships are, how unpredictable and unfair life can be, and how easily people can end up in a bad place, these stories, individually and especially as a group, have an instructive purpose in reminding readers of social and political realities that raise questions of ethics and justice, of right and wrong. In so doing, these stories, like others, can be impactful in the way a factual description or logical argument may not be.

Stories can be especially impactful when they incorporate resonances of older and well-known stories. Earlier stories are carried down through the ages and imported into new literature because they raise fundamental issues of human life that are always with us and that can always engage us emotionally and intellectually. In addition, some of those older stories, such as of "Cain and Abel" and "The Prodigal Son," are deeply embedded within our narrative traditions, genres, and language, so that traces of them can be found deep within the literature of every age, and continuing into modern literature. The traces of earlier stories and their language are part of a writer's conscious and unconscious mental storehouse of ideas, images, and language, and exist as well in the depths of readers' experiential and linguistic unconscious – and so also in their retrievable long-term memory. Echoes of the themes, the structure, and language of those stories therefore resonate with all who share this literary heritage and so can spark our emotions, our imagination, and our interpretive processes.

By encountering this group of stories about brothers, readers can better understand that these brothers are like all of us, in need of each other and the stories that we have to tell each other. By reading and discussing them, people move more deeply into their own memory and linguistic unconscious, a rich environment that allows them to expand their own sense of self and sense of belonging with those in the world around them. The enjoyment which people gain from this deep exploration generates its own motivation to continue reading and learning from literature and to use the knowledge gained and the questions raised in their daily interactions. Thus does the reading of literature have impacts both broad and deep, changing the thinking and sensibilities of individual human beings and carrying on and developing our shared language-based culture.

References

Baldwin, James (1988/1957). Sonny's blues. In *Going to Meet the Man* (pp. 86–122). New York: Laurel/Dell Publishing. Originally published in *The Partisan Review*, Summer 1957, pp. 327–358. Retrieved on October 31, 2016 from http://hgar-srv3.bu.edu/col lections/partisan-review/search/detail?id=326024.

Bergland, Christopher (2014). Reading fiction improves brain connectivity and function. *Psychology Today* website. January 4, 2014. Retrieved on October 15, 2015 from www. psychologytoday.com/blog/the-athletes-way/201401/reading-fiction-improves-brain-con nectivity-and-function.

Boyle, T. Coraghessan (1985). Greasy Lake. In *Greasy Lake and other stories* (pp. 1–11). New York: Viking Penguin/Penguin Books.

Denby, David (2016). *Lit up: One reporter. Three schools. Twenty-four books that can change lives.* New York: Henry Holt.

Dickey, James (1972). *Deliverance*. Boston: Houghton Mifflin Harcourt.

Eliot, George (1856). The natural history of German life. *Westminster Review*. July 1856, pp. 51–56 and 71–72. Accessed in Nathan Sheppard (ed.), *The essays of*

George Eliot, Ch. V (pp. 141–177). Transcribed from the 1883 Funk and Wagnalls edition by David Price. Ebook, March 9, 2009. Retrieved on October 31, 2016 from www.gutenberg.org/files/28289/28289-h/28289-h.htm#page141.

Hall, Maureen P., & Waxler, Robert P. (2007). It worked for criminals: It will work for middle schoolers. *Journal of Urban Education: Focus on Enrichment, 4*(1), 122–132.

Hall, Maureen P., & Waxler, Robert P. (2010). Engaging future teachers to reflect on how reading and writing can change lives. *Writing & Pedagogy, 2*(1), 91–101. doi: 10.1558/wap.v2i1.91.

Jarjoura, Roger G., & Krumholz, Susan T. (1998). A program combining bibliography and positive role modeling as an alternative to incarceration. *Journal of Offender Rehabilitation, 28*, 127–139.

Kazan, Elia (Director) (1955). *East of Eden* (film). Hollywood, CA: Warner Brothers.

London, Jack (1904). *The sea wolf.* Serialized in *The Century Magazine.* January–November, 1904.

Schutt, Russell K., Deng, Xiaogang, & Stoehr, Taylor (2013). Using bibliotherapy to enhance probation and reduce recidivism. *Journal of Offender Rehabilitation, 52*, 181–197.

Steinbeck, John (1952). *East of Eden.* New York: Viking.

Trounstine, Jean, & Waxler, Robert P. (2005). *Finding a voice: The practice of changing lives through literature.* Ann Arbor: University of Michigan Press.

Waxler, Robert P. (1995). Journey down the river. In Ellen Slezak (ed.), *The book club book* (pp. 102–107). Chicago: Chicago Review Press.

Waxler, Robert P. (1997). Why literature? The power of stories. In Megan McLaughlin, Jean Trounstine, & Robert P. Waxler, *Success stories: Life skills through literature* (pp. 2–5). Washington, DC: Office of Correctional Education, U.S. Department of Education.

Waxler, Robert P. (2008). Changing lives through literature. *Publications of the Modern Language Association (PMLA), 123*(3), 678–682. doi: 10.1632/pmla.2008.123.3.678.

Waxler, Robert P. (2014). *The risk of reading: How literature helps us to understand ourselves and the world.* New York: Bloomsbury.

Waxler, Robert P., & Hall, Maureen P. (2011). *Transforming literacy: Changing lives through reading and writing.* Leiden and Boston: Brill.

Waxler, Robert P., & Trounstine, Jean (eds.). (1999). *Changing lives through literature.* Notre Dame, IN: Notre Dame Press.

Wolff, Tobias (1985). The rich brother. In *Back in the world* (pp. 197–221). Boston: Houghton Mifflin.

11

MAPPING AN ALTERNATIVE FUTURE

Twenty years ago when I became a high school teacher, I never imagined that I'd be exploring the question, why teach literature?

– *Janet Alsup,* A Case for Teaching Literature in the Secondary School: Why Fiction Matters in an Age of Scientific Literacy and Standardization *(Alsup, 2015, p. 1)*

Literature as Essential to Human Life and Education

In the passage opening Chapter 1 of this book, Hayakawa (1990/1939) points to the virtually infinite possibilities of great literature to provide new contexts for experience, not only for being in other places and times, which in itself can be highly stimulating and educative, but for living the lives of others vicariously through the words of an author, virtually *being* those characters and walking in their shoes. Such experiences of being The Other, of walking in another's shoes, are not only stimulating and educative: they fulfill the higher purposes of enriching human existence and opening the mind and emotions to different circumstances and ways of thinking and of doing things that can be life-changing. The kinds of experiences that can be gained from living and learning with these imaginative works, and the affective communication achieved through their finely crafted linguistic landscapes, belong in our lives and in the educational curriculum, where they should hold a place above that of experiences designed merely to inculcate facts or train utilitarian skills. Yet the curriculum that is currently in place in our schools does not give any special prominence to literature, nor does it make reference to such higher purposes.

In Part II of *The Republic of Imagination* (Nafisi, 2014, pp. 151–209), within a discussion of the novel *Babbitt*, Azar Nafisi attacks the Common Core curriculum and those political and business leaders who have had a major influence on the 21st-century educational system. It is a system heavily influenced by the electronic consciousness of the Digital Age – Bill Gates being one of its strongest advocates – and one dedicated to a belief that the success of education is best measured by how many jobs and how much money students can get from their degree. Nafisi mentions, as an example of this kind of thinking, a letter sent by Jefferson Beauregard Sessions, III, a U.S. senator from Alabama, to the then acting chair of the National Endowment for the Humanities (NEH), Carol Watson. Wanting to know why Watson was spending money on projects that he thought were worthless, Sessions, an influential legislator who became Attorney General in the Trump administration, categorized the projects and the cost of such apparent foolishness:

> "What is the meaning of life?" ($24,953)
> "Why are we interested in the past?" ($24,803)
> "What is the good life and how do I live it?" ($25,000)
>
> (Nafisi, 2014, p. 183)

Where have we arrived in our human history when questions like these, which are arguably the sorts of things that would normally be funded by a body set up to support humanities projects, are seen by policymakers as a waste of time and money? We might be reminded that Socrates died for the right to ask such questions because he knew that these kinds of questions are indications of a free and just society. He knew what was at stake. How have we forgotten this, and how can we get back to remembering it? One way is through the wisdom that can be found in great literature, in books. Yet these are not always or in all quarters treated in ways that recognize their special place in society or their value. Mohsin Hamid recently contrasted the way books are treated in France versus the way they are treated in the United States: "In France, books are treated as an 'essential good' like food and utilities, subject to low taxes" and limited price discounts, so that "it costs pretty much the same to buy a book everywhere in France, including online, and independent bookshops are holding their own against larger competitors" (Hamid, 2014). Hamid reflects that laws similar to those protecting books in France are virtually unimaginable in the United States.

How have books come to have a lesser place in the New World than the Old? We contend that the difference between the United States and France represented in their differing views of books – a commodity, like any other, to be competitively bought and sold versus something essential in need of price protection, furnishing nourishment for the mind, the heart, and the soul – is an indicator of the predominance of the life of the marketplace and the *pocketbook* rather than the *book* over all other aspects of life in the relatively young, affluent, and expansive American state. It is in other words an indicator of the extent to which corporate capitalism has come to dominate over all other values in what was once our revolutionary, breakaway democracy. While we may not be able to convince our leaders to pass laws protecting books as an "essential good," we are willing to try to convince educators and the general public that they are an essential good in the school system and the home and that they should remain an important part of child-rearing – the unofficial educational curriculum – and of the official educational curriculum. We propose that books, and the culture of books that gives a central place to literature and language, should be recognized as an important part of our cultural heritage and a superior resource for learning. Books, and the language and the imaginative worlds captured within literary works, are moreover a dynamic medium inspiring and supporting creativity, language development at an individual level and language evolution at a societal level, as well as the personal and social development of individual humans and the evolution of the human race.

Book Culture, Literature, and the Humanities as Counterweights to Digital Culture

As we have sought to show, the Internet is narrowing and focusing the information which people pay attention to and the kinds of activities which they engage in, in ways that may be seriously affecting their psychological nature, their brain structure, and their overall health. In so doing it is having great impacts on humanity and on the planet, some of which are looking to be extremely negative. The beginning of the "cure" for what ails us is, we believe, an increased emphasis on the human arts and, in particular, the reading and discussion of literature – poetry and what used to be called "Great Books." These are the gems of our language which encapsulate much of our human nature and civilization. They are the cumulative product of our linguistic evolution and hold a record of that evolution captured within their carefully crafted words and sentences, their stanzas and stories, and their great variety of genres and written forms.

Literature and the humanities have a critical role to play in teaching language, in modeling effective use of language for expressing ideas with power and imagination, and in maintaining and continuing to evolve language to its highest potential – beyond that of spontaneous speech or quick messaging. Literature and the humanities also have a critical role to play in teaching the lessons of history and the values of human culture, in providing models for living a life consistent with those lessons and values, and in maintaining and continuing to evolve human history and culture to its highest potential – beyond that of consumerism and popular culture. Literature and the humanities, what we have called the human arts, are essential for ensuring a broad and diverse, and an imaginative and exciting, educational experience – for creating education, that is, as what it should be: an environment encouraging students to explore new things and go in directions different from where they started. There is an important role for the human arts to provide social and communicative spaces where such adventuring and exploration can take place.

The social and communicative space that is created through interaction with mass media is entirely different from that created through interaction with the world of ideas as portrayed in books and human arts subjects. Both of these kinds of social and communicative space can be compared to the notion of the *agora* in ancient Greece, a place of public assembly and of exchange of goods and ideas among individuals: "Television and other forms of media have replaced the agora and provide a contemporary version of that simultaneously public/private space" (Webb, 2012, p. 47). Yet, in Webb's (2012) conception, the creative industries such as television are linked to the marketplace in terms of profitability and so create a public, agora-type space which has to appeal to a mass audience, one "that is reductive, that requires conformity to a central line of thinking" (p. 50). What we are calling the human arts, in contrast, are more naturally linked to the marketplace in terms of ideas, creating an agora "that is [a] simultaneously public/private space for social, intellectual and political encounters, for debate" (ibid.). Webb singles out the novel, in particular, as contributing in important ways to a democratic society, by creating a forum, or agora, where people are reading, thinking about, and discussing new ideas.

Beyond their value for keeping people in touch with the great diversity of ideas and perspectives in the world, books and the humanities have an important role of helping people sort through, evaluate, and interpret all the information that is out there. The humanities are needed to help people learn to navigate, to cull, and to curate the mass of information that is now available, help people learn how to select portions of it that they can make good use of for their own specific purposes. The humanities also have an important role in building people's character and the strength of mind and confidence to buck the trend and walk away from all of those blinking screens pressuring for everyone's attention – to be able to control their time and, sometimes, Just Say No: to the temptations offered by the great seas of free-floating information, their beckoning smartphones, and the vast conformist Hive and black-hole, time-and-energy-sink portal represented by the Internet.

Reading literary works, especially when combined with discussion of those works and the sorts of critical thinking that typify a human arts curriculum, are activities which help people to cut through what Shenk (1997) called the "data smog" of the current era and so discover the reality behind the "curtain" which Kundera (2006) reminds us is before our eyes, keeping us controlled and docile, and in the grip of the tycoons of media and hyper-capitalism. Such activity can then be seen as valuable for the kind of clear and independent thought that supports good citizenship and rational action in a free and democratic society. The human community, and young people in particular, need to pull themselves out of the great Hive of social media, the life-wasting activities of digital gaming and surfing the Net, and all of the meaningless "pop" and "bling" and dumbed-down activities in which they are currently engaging, so that they can re-establish human connection, reinvigorate the quest for human meaning, strengthen their values and sense of purpose, with the goal of making a better life for themselves and others, and a better world. We want to tell the young people of today – and their parents – to focus on making a good *life*, not only a good income. We want to encourage those young people to pursue literature and human arts, to allow their passions for these subjects to influence their direction in life and their career path. Following Pearlstein (2016), we remind the parents of "those passionate kids" to be glad they will not "make the mistake of confusing the meaning of life with maximizing lifetime income."

Mills (2014) calls on the generation of young adults to take responsibility for both resisting and fixing the problematic culture of pandering that they have inherited. Language and literature, intelligent and passionate discussion, story, and the self-reflection born of a culture of books and human arts can be a central means to that end. Our species needs literary narrative and poetry in order to battle against the conformity, the dumbing down, the amorality and immorality, the fragmentation, and the dehumanizing speed of the present age. As a thinking and feeling language-using species, we need to return to the reading and discussion of our print artworks, our literature, and we need those discussions to occur face-to-face, within interactive human spaces. We need to get to know each other from our faces, our voices, our copresence, not mediated through our machines across physical distance and via electronic, digital representations of reality as far less complex than it is – and than we are.

A Culture of Reading as a Counterculture

As reviewed earlier, what and how we read both involves and structures our human nature and our lives, as it both involves and structures a main part of our human experience and our brain, including our memory. What we read and how we read is a large determinant of the life of the mind and, on the level of a whole society, of our cultural life. Our literature, our books, are living things in ways our digital technologies can never be: "[B]ooks privilege language and story, narrative and the human voice. In contrast, digital devices privilege algorithms, formulas, and binary bits over language and story" (Waxler & Hall, 2011, p. 159).

Although visual perception is a very strong sense in humans, and it is natural that we are drawn to the flashing, colorful computer screen, we advocate for being attentive to language, respecting it for its ability to present perspectives as much as facts, to hint at truth while allowing for individual interpretation. Literary language is strong in these respects, offering the kind of complexity best suited to an exploration of the self and its relationship to the world. In this, literary language is opposed to the language of the media, of politics and advertising, which seeks to control and manipulate others by persuasive tactics such as selective withholding of information and "spin." Rather than power and control, literature encourages empathy and compassion. Literature moreover encourages thoughtfulness and interiority, privileging language and creativity, the human voice and the imagination. This orientation stands in sharp contrast to that of electronic media, which encourage visuality and exteriority, privileging the immediacy and accessibility of images and the attention-getting sensation of "pop" and "bling." The oversaturated use of electronic devices – iPods, smartphones, computers, and other screen-based media – fosters distraction and robs human beings of their own original voices and imaginative abilities. Books, especially reading and discussing good literature face-to-face, serve as a way to encourage people to slow down, to be mindful of themselves and others, and to find their place in the world. In the book culture, the journey that a person makes takes the person both *in deep* – that is, deep reading is a journey deep into the self – and *out far* – that is, on a simultaneous journey out into the world of other human beings, other places, and other times to which they become intimately connected through the reading process. Reading and discussing literature can be a part of building a culture of empathy (e.g., as promoted by the Center for Building a Culture of Empathy; http://cultureofempathy.com/).

Mainstream culture has now established a dominant set of values that are contrary to the older and more resilient humanistic values which we believe need to be reinstated and reinforced. These are the values of human culture which have endured through history and which will also help to ensure that our species – and indeed, the whole world in which humans live – endures into the future. To see this contrast clearly, we have laid out these values in pairs below.

CONTRAST OF VALUES

Current Mainstream Values	Enduring Human Values
efficiency & speed	*thoroughness & dedicated time*
short-term sensation & perpetual now	*history & long-term memory*
browsing & dispersed attention	*contemplation & focused attention*
cleverness & smartness	*knowledge & wisdom*
consumerism & amassing of wealth	*conservationism & the pursuit of happiness*
primacy of technology & machines	*primacy of humans & the natural world*
competition & achievement	*cooperation & empathy*
entertainment & popular culture	*enrichment & high culture*
visual images & flickering screens	*language & narrative*

Within this contrast of values, literature and book culture should now be considered as a significant type of countercultural activity – counter, in other words, to the contemporary mainstream culture represented by the values in the left-hand column. This current mainstream is a culture which moves us away from our traditional human identity – one of depth and coherence – to more of a digitally defined personhood – one of flatness and fragmentation.

At the beginning of this book, we suggested that reading significant literature can make a difference in people's lives. The kind of reading we had in mind, a high-quality experience of creative reading focused on high-quality products of creative writing – "deep reading" as it is often called – was developed over a long period of time, with the invention of printing contributing substantially to expansion of the book culture which promoted deep reading as a widespread practice. We also indicated at the beginning of the book that this kind of reading could create certain kinds of experiences that we consider particularly valuable. It is worth highlighting the experiences on that list again:

- dwelling psychologically in a peaceful place that contrasts with the restlessness of much of everyday life;
- reconnecting with our sensuous nature;
- arousing our emotions and so both exciting and calming us;
- engaging the mind and the imagination in ways that go beyond other media, through language that paints worlds in words;
- illustrating artful language which humans are drawn to and enjoy, but might otherwise not encounter;
- enhancing knowledge of and appreciation for fine language;
- adding to general knowledge and building vocabulary;
- improving our ability to interpret information, see deeply into its implications, and think for ourselves;
- enhancing self-knowledge and understanding and the development of individual identity;
- increasing openness to new ideas and experiences and thus enlarging creative potentials and the possibilities for change;
- appreciating the complexity of human beings and improving our ability to read and understand others;
- enhancing empathy towards others;
- offering a cultural bridge to the key themes of human existence;
- raising ethical questions without easy answers;
- providing models of inspiration and aspiration for human life; and
- giving us purpose and direction for constructing a road map and goals for our life's journey.

For us, this list represents a way to "the good life," a life that people all innately desire, a life of meaning and purpose as part of the human community. Humans' love of books derives, at least in part, from just this kind of desire. The wide distribution of books in the age of print opened the possibility for people to pursue and experience this kind of life as free and independent human beings. Over time, it also led to the consolidation of the humanities as a way to experience the meaning and ideals of a free and open society. Today both books and the humanities seem in jeopardy as society continues to move with great speed and lack of reflection in the "hyper" age – the age of hyper-media and hyper-capitalism, and their attendant hyper-activity, hyper-achievement, and hyper-profits.

As we lose the ability to concentrate in our super-fast, sensation-driven, and information-oversaturated world, not only language but also art may be at risk, given the time they take to conceive and express in their best and most creative manifestations. "*Works of art are feats of concentration*," Birkerts (2015, p. 21, original emphasis) says, fed by the imagination. We note that the same can be said about "works of language," those original linguistic creations that speakers and writers have taken the time to thoughtfully and carefully craft. In this hyper-age, we are therefore in danger of losing art itself, including literature, our art-in-words, and perhaps even the great gift of conversation. This present-day reality has prompted us to write this book, believing, as we do, that in and out of the classroom, the countercultural activities of non-hyper forms of living and the imaginative, linguistic, and artistic processes promoted by deep reading and discussion of literary works should be emphasized.

At the beginning of this book, we also made reference to the cognitive-nurturing and brain-building properties of literature through deep reading. There we suggested that these effects might be especially convincing to some people who might otherwise be skeptical about the value of literature and the culture of human arts structuring an educational curriculum based on Great Books and the exploration of life at an individual level. As we have reviewed in this book, the cognitive effects of deeply engaged and imaginative reading, of literature in particular, both balance and support a curriculum focused on STEM for building knowledge and intellectual power, while providing balance for technology-heavy and skills-centered curricula. Janet Alsup, in *A Case for Teaching Literature in the Secondary School: Why Fiction Matters in an Age of Scientific Literacy and Standardization* (Alsup, 2015), similarly advocates for the teaching of literature to rebalance the STEM-heavy standardized secondary curriculum of the U.S. Common Core State Standards (CCSS). The value and relevance of literature and human arts to building intellectual capacity and capability need to be seriously considered in light of the downside of the restricted and utilitarian focus of contemporary education and society's addiction to digital technology.

The documented effects of literary reading on empathy, sociability, and openness to new ideas also need to be seriously considered as a way to counter selfishness and close-mindedness as well as insularity and hostility to those who hold different views. There is nothing in the STEM curriculum that addresses these matters, whereas literary reading within a human arts curriculum offers a practical way to build humanity's social capacity and capability in the face of the limited vision of life that is provided in the utilitarian, science and technology focus of contemporary education. As an aspect of building social capacity and capability, the lack of attention to feeling or affect within a curriculum focused on practical ends and STEM needs to be countered by more emotion-saturated kinds of experience and students' reflections on these. As Vendler (2015) notes, "Within education, scientific training, which necessarily brackets emotion, needs to be complemented by the direct mediation – through the arts and their interpretations – of feeling, vicarious experience, and interpersonal imagination" (p. 24).

Thomas More, in *The Education of the Heart*, reflects on the value of educating not only the mind but the heart:

> Without an education, the heart presents itself as a cauldron of raw emotions, suspicious desires, and disconnected images. Dreams appear stupefying, longings inappropriate, and relationships confounding. Without an animating, educated heart, the intellect appears superior, and we give too much attention and value to it. Our institutions and ideas then lack the humanizing breath of the soul. Education of the proper kind brings into view the order and sense in matters of the heart that otherwise seem elusive, and position the heart to play a significant role in affairs of the mind.
>
> *(More, 1997, p. 5)*

Reading and contemplating great works of the written word can provide just such an education – educating the heart in ways that can help make sense of feelings, dreams, and sensory impressions originating below the level of consciousness, while also adding valuable perspective to conscious rational thought.

People's engagement with great written works can help them harness their feelings, their instincts, and their imagination, in concert with their logic and rational powers, to good purposes. As we might put it, the great works of literature help people to develop an "affective mind" that can influence and moderate the operation and decision-making of their "logical mind." The combined efforts of these two types of mind working together then helps to develop and refine further aspects or facets of mind – the "aesthetic mind," manifested in a keen sense of the quality of language, ideas, and experiences in different modalities; and the "ethical mind," manifested in a keen sense of fairness, justice, and morality. It can be concluded that the "education of the heart" through literature confers benefits that are worthy of significant curriculum time in the school system, to balance the primacy given to the education of the "logical mind." Another way of putting this is to say that literature helps develop an "educated subjectivity" to balance the "educated objectivity" that is the tradition and central aim of organized schooling.

If significant pedagogical weight is shifted in the direction of human arts, this would represent a significant change in an educational system which currently conceptualizes learning in terms of predictable uniform and practical outcomes involving applied skills and testable abstract-intellectual content or factual knowledge. An important effect of this rebalancing of the curriculum would be to reduce the current dominant emphasis on general knowledge and objective information while increasing the current restricted or negligible emphasis on individual knowledge and subjective experience. As a by-product of increasing the emphasis on individual knowledge and response, students might become more personally invested in their learning, as they are able to customize their learning to their own interests and abilities, and might enjoy school more. In the best solution of combining both domains – that of STEM and applied skills, on the one hand, with that of arts and humanities, or human arts, on the other – a base in general knowledge and practical skills would be enhanced by increased attention to aesthetic experience and subjective response. Adding human arts to STEM and applied skills allows for individual knowledge, abilities, and interests that can be expected to spur creativity and engaged, passionate and imaginative learning with innovative outcomes.

The Need to Refocus Education

What we are advocating is a central role in people's lives and in the education of children for book culture, and specifically the reading of literature offline, and the knowledge, behaviors, and values that a culture of literary reading embodies. The advice of experts is that young children should be read to – a lot – that they should be immersed at home and in school in language and story culture even as they are directed away from television and all digital screens; and that they should be taught the prosocial skills needed to get along with others and to do well in school – not only in their early years but also later in life. As we are reminded by the research of Jones et al. (2015) which followed kindergartners into adolescence and young adulthood:

> The growing body of literature that demonstrates the importance of non-cognitive skills in development should motivate policymakers and program developers to target efforts to improve these skills to young children. Much evidence has shown how effective intervention in preschool and the early elementary years can improve childhood noncognitive skills in a lasting way. Enhancing these skills can have an impact in multiple areas and therefore has potential for positively affecting individuals as well as community public health substantially.
>
> *(p. 2289)*

Reading literature enhances cognitive skills at the same time that it models and therefore teaches noncognitive skills connected to prosocial behavior. The advice for adolescents is to limit media use and incorporate a good dose of literature in order to support and enhance their vocabulary and general knowledge, their emotional and empathic responses, and their social skills while avoiding a host of physical and psychological problems, such as loneliness and social isolation, Internet addiction, and obesity. In this way, educators and parents will be giving children an important part of the essential foundation for becoming well-adjusted and successful adults.

Education bodies generally do not take sufficient note of the extent of reading as a socialization and enculturation process, much less as having potentially profound effects on the development of personality and empathy. Thus, for example, the report of the U.S. National Institute of Child Health and Human Development and National Reading Panel (2000) focused narrowly and traditionally on skills related to phonemic awareness and phonics, vocabulary development, reading fluency, and reading comprehension in their recommendations for the reading curriculum. Where is the focus on reading extensively and for pleasure, on personal engagement, individual response, and integration of knowledge? Where is imagination in this dry reading curriculum? And where is the exchange of ideas with others who read, think about, and talk about the same things? Where are the lofty goals of reading as developing the mind and nurturing the spirit, and as creating a public commons or agora that promotes analytical and critical, creative and hypothetical thinking at a societal level to support innovation and democratic ideals?

We advocate a whole-person educational experience that engages the imagination and is not about accumulation of facts and nuggetized information and competencies, not all science or math, technology or business, nor all skills-oriented, but rather an emotion-saturated experience of learning that builds passion and connection to other people, curiosity about all things, and active seeking after knowledge and understanding. The STEAM movement could be a good start, but we encourage the educational establishment to broaden the STEAM curriculum to mean Arts in our broader sense of human arts that includes language and literature, history and philosophy.[1]

By reading and engaging the imagination and emotions, educators will be maintaining an expansive and comprehensive focus, one which is attuned to the full complexity of the human experience and which will therefore be more realistic for learning than a strictly content-oriented or skills-based curriculum and will better prepare students for all of their studies and for their lives outside and beyond school. Marina Warner, in a book about the Arabian nights, underscores the critical role of imagination and "magical thinking" in human life and in all fields of study:

> The faculties of imagination – dream, projection, fantasy – are bound up with the faculties of reasoning and essential to making the leap beyond the known into the unknown. At one pole (myth), magic is associated with poetic truth, at another (the history of science) with inquiry and speculation. It was bound up with understanding physical forces in nature and led to technical ingenuity and discoveries. Magical thinking structures the processes of imagination, and imagining something can and sometimes must precede the fact or the act; it has shaped many features of Western civilisation. But its influence has been constantly disavowed since the Enlightenment and its action and effects consequently misunderstood.
>
> *(Warner, 2012, p. 23)*

Instead of the time schools are spending on inculcating and testing content and practical skills, what if educators focused instead on encouraging imaginative thinking and activity and how these can be directed to learning, discovery, and problem-solving?

If imagination and magical thinking connected to reason spur discovery, innovation, and new understandings, it can be maintained that literature has a key role in both developing and engaging imaginative and magical thinking. What if, instead of the Internet addiction that is afflicting so many in today's society, we aimed instead to give our young people a lifelong reading habit? It seems to us far better to be addicted to story, as Gottschall (2012, p. xiv) says our species is, or to fiction, as Burke (2011, p. 158) claims that readers of literature are, than to Facebook, texting, or video games. This reading addiction will lead them to exercise their imaginations, to go deep rather than shallow, to take their time rather than be consumed with excessive busyness and potentially harmful activity. Bertman (1998), who wrote about society at the end of the 20th century as a "hyperculture," is one of those who have stressed the need for society to slow down and reflect, while recognizing that this means subverting our natural tendencies to be drawn to external stimuli which present themselves to our senses: "To realize the full potential of our minds we will need to oppose our biological inheritance and our very neurologic design, overriding the seductive stimulation of the optic nerve in order to look within" (p. 39).

Towards the end of his book, Bertman (1998) urges us to "examine our lives so our journey has meaning. We need to decide what things are truly important and what things are not and then act upon our decision" (p. 204). In all of these ways, Bertman's reflections support a turn away from a largely digital culture and towards a culture of books and reading. This is not to say that we advocate for there being no influence of digital culture, a goal which is neither desirable nor possible at this point in time, but rather that we aim to keep it from dominating and shrinking the influence of other spheres of culture. Thus, educators, parents, and other concerned actors should continue to provide nurturing habitats where offline cultures can grow and flourish, seeking to ensure that digital culture does not overgrow or engulf all other cultural formations. In this postmodern era of electronic devices, engaging with language shaped into narrative and poetic forms creates just the kind of habitus that is needed to set against the power of the electronic mainstream. Reading and discussing with others poetry and stories in printed books preserves a fundamental connection to the past, to human history and accumulated culture, language skill, and literacy, a connection through memory which language embodies, and to the future, through the stirring of desire and imagination which language and literature excites.

We agree with the ideas of Ralph Peterson and Maryann Eeds, in *Grand Conversations: Literature Groups in Action* (Peterson & Eeds, 1990), and with those of Kathy Short and Kathryn M. Pierce, in *Talking about Books: Creating Literate Communities* (Short & Pierce, 1990), for creating contexts in which readers can interact with texts in ways that encourage deep thought and engagement with what they are reading about – the characters, the themes, and the life lessons that are woven into the plot and characterization – in conversation with others. We agree with Turkle (2012a, 2012b, 2015) that parents need to take actions to encourage more conversation among family members, such as creating dedicated, "sacred spaces" and "device-free zones" (Turkle, 2012b), and we believe that a significant portion of this conversation can be connected to the reading of books.[2] We also believe that engagement with and conversations surrounding texts can be beneficially linked to writing, such as Donald Graves proposed in *Writing: Teachers and Children at Work* (Graves, 1983) and such as was illustrated in the high school classes which Denby (2016) reports on in his book describing inspiring practices for teaching Great Books with adolescents.

Alternatives within Digital Culture

Gottschall (2012) sees a future for stories that may or may not involve literary fiction:

> We were creatures of story before we had novels, and we will be creatures of story if sawed-off attention spans or technological advances ever render the novel obsolete. Story evolves. Like a biological organism, it continuously adapts itself to the demands of its environment.
>
> *(p. 180)*

Gottschall predicts that traditional fiction will not die but that "storytelling will evolve in new directions over the next fifty years" (p. 190). He expects that interactive fiction, in the form of live-action role-playing games (RPGs) carried out with very large numbers (up to millions) of others will proliferate in cyberspace. He points to the example of World of Warcraft (WoW), which is continually being evolved by all its players, as a model for the fiction of the future: "Most great art is created by individuals, but WoW is the product of hundreds of creative people weaving the power of story art together with visual and sound art" (p. 194). In his view, those who spend a lot of time in the virtual world can gain a sense of community and competence (p. 196). This suggests a role for creative storytelling in online environments as having potential value in education and society.

Yet inhabiting such online story worlds can easily become a form of escapism. Moreover, being a form of gaming and being connected to everything else in the ultra-connected, always-online, digital culture that we have been warning about, interactive fiction can have some of the same downsides which Block (2005) describes as Internet addiction and Aiken (2016) describes as psychologically abnormal, criminal, and otherwise seriously negative cyber effects. Participation in online story worlds seems at times to promote highly creative behavior that is at the same time highly risky. This is especially worrying in young people, given their lack of impulse control, which can lead to dangerous activities and rash acts.

It can be noted that offline activity involving storytelling connected to literature has proven value, with none of the hazards.

As Gottschall (2012) points out:

> Humans evolved to crave story. This craving has, on the whole, been a good thing for us. Stories give us pleasure and instruction. They simulate worlds so we can live better in this one. They help bind us into communities and define us as cultures. Stories have been a great boon to our species.
>
> *(p. 197)*

Gottschall (2012) then speculates that too much story may not be good for us, referencing his personal communication with Brian Boyd to the effect that overconsumption of "junk story" could result in a "mental diabetes epidemic": "The real threat isn't that story will fade out of human life in the future; it's that story will take it over completely" (p. 198). We share this concern about "junk story" taking over human life completely, and we go farther in sharing our fear of the whole digital realm taking over human life and culture. This is why good stories, in the form of literature, are so important to preserve and to continue passing down to our children. Once you experience the real thing, those junk stories fail to satisfy the need for story, which goes beyond a mere craving to being a deeply engraved part of human nature.

Use of digital texts and gaming may however help students whose experiences, preferences, and brain circuitry have been shaped by interaction in digital environments maintain their concentration, imagination, and focus on language to an extent. Digital games that involve story lines and characters adapted from Tolkien, Rowling, and other fantasy fiction might lead school-age children into reading books, and educators might consider ways to use them for this purpose. Today's students might enjoy and learn from working collaboratively to create texts, simulations, and games that centrally involve language and story. We are also potentially supportive of online applications that help older children learn to read critically (Wolf & Barzillai, 2009), and we are potentially open to the use of learning apps with school-age children. However, we remain skeptical of those designed for preschool children, even those interactive ones which Quenqua (2014, p. 27) reports help children learn words. The experience with the Baby Einstein program should serve as a warning that just because it seems, on the face of it, to be a good learning app does not mean it is. In fact, as reported in *Time* magazine (Park, 2007), infants who used what appeared to be a highly engaging video program to learn vocabulary actually learned less than young children not exposed to the program.

Not only is more research needed to decide the effectiveness of such applications of screen technology to teaching and learning, but there is also a need for consideration of the trade-offs involved, what is gained and what is lost by adopting electronic media for educational purposes – as for all purposes. Wolf and

Barzillai (2009, pp. 34–35) comment on the positive potentials of digital text for literacy and its countering negative effects, as interest in a piece of literature "can drive a discovery process" carried out online that leads to various kinds of connected information at the same time as it might lead a learner to become more passive and less critical. It is up to educators to help ensure that students get the most out of their online experience related to literature so that it is not only enjoyable but expands the breadth, diversity, and depth of experience and thinking. As Aiken (2016) reminds us: "Technology is not good or bad in its own right. It is neutral and simply mediates behavior – which means it can be used well or poorly by humankind" (p. 13).

Towards a Reading Society

As we have reviewed, reading literature has profound effects in the form of:

- intense personal pleasure
- personal growth
- understanding and insight
- increased openness to new experiences
- enhanced social expertise in the form of empathy and understanding of others
- language development
- brain activation and connectivity, and the complex exercise of memory and imagination

These specific benefits in the way of personal fulfillment and self-actualization, increased cognitive fitness, and increased social fitness argue strongly for the inclusion of literary reading in human life and the educational experience of children. In addition, Slouka (2009) observes the "'deep' civic function of the humanities" (p. 38), specifically noting the value of reading to shape people to become "individuals just distinct enough from one another in our orientation toward 'the truth' or 'the good' to be difficult to control" (ibid.). Thus, literary reading has a role in promoting independent thinking and democracy.

As Nussbaum (2010) points out in *Not for Profit: Why Democracy Needs the Humanities*, there is a long and progressive tradition which supports just such thinking. That tradition is rooted in the belief that the goal of life is to know the self and the other, and to create a compassionate community of concerned human beings who seek wisdom over quickness and cleverness, who patiently and critically delve into the depths of human thinking and feeling, and who expect and demand more from students than the surface skills that are needed to perform adequately as an employee. Such a tradition favors the dignity of individuals over the utility of commodities or the spectacle of media. It is a tradition grounded in the belief that human beings desire to learn and, when given the chance, want to create meaning for themselves and for those around them, living the Socratic dictum of *gnowthi seauton*, to "know the self," and, through deep reflection on the self, to also know the other. Human beings want to be part of something larger than themselves; they want to belong, to be part of a human community.

Unfortunately, that tradition is rarely celebrated these days. Rather, we see a world which privileges speed over contemplation, employable skills over wisdom, the visual surface over the depth of human understanding and feeling, and the attentional moment over deep reflection. The power of literature to change lives can make a significant difference to the human experience, provided, of course, that people still dream about knowing themselves and belonging to a community – in other words, provided people are still committed to developing as social beings who express complex feelings, thoughts, and imaginative possibilities, questing alone and together for an intelligent, purposeful, and meaning-filled world. The experience of literary reading, the interactive and interdependent discussion of literature with other people, and the public recognition of the role of literature and reading in human life and culture, remain the best hope we have to preserve the complexity of human life and the uniqueness of each human being, and to promote a fully informed, maximally intelligent and maximally human, truly connected community.

A culture of reading and literature may even be required for strengthening or correcting the cognitive circuitry of today's students. Thankfully, research shows that reading at any age can alter the anatomy of the brain and increase its inter-connectivity, as, for example, in an investigation comparing the brains of adults who had recently learned to read with others who had yet to begin a literacy program (Carreiras et al., 2009).[3] Denby (2016, p. 232) speaks of the possible need to "replant" the deep reading circuits or to plant them for the first time in teenagers addicted to Facebook or texting or gaming. We would add that replanting or planting those circuits may require pruning or building bypasses around the circuits that have been developed through all that online activity. Other circuits that may need replanting or fertilization through reading and discussion of literature are those for empathy, which may be weakened because of diminished face-to-face contact.

Why the Future Needs More Than Technology, Science, and Business

As has always been the case, new technologies tend to turn the human experience in a new direction – to change it in ways that are not simply describable as an expansion of human life. Indeed, as we discussed earlier, each new technology can be seen to narrow experience in the sense that it constructs and focuses it in certain ways and not others, based on its properties. Digital technology, in both obvious and not-so-obvious ways, tends to mechanize and to digitalize the world and our experience in it. The world, thus technologized, is de facto also dehumanized and in an important sense contracted as well.

A central part of our discussion in this book is based on the idea that an unattended consequence of digital technology has been to narrow the mainstream view of what is important in life and hence in education as well. The speed and power of digital technology reinforces and privileges the activities and values associated with quantification and measurement, the how-to skills, the practical and the utilitarian. What people used to think of as *wisdom* may no longer seem relevant – it may even seem like an archaic word known only from old books or from grandparents, an old idea that people do not talk about or think applies in the Information Age. As the notion of wisdom disappears under the onslaught of information, so is even *knowledge*, as a concept, absorbed into *information* within a technologized and digitalized worldview.

With wisdom out of the picture and knowledge revisioned as information, what cannot be presented as data becomes secondary, if not irrelevant or even meaningless. In such an environment, educators and their students are judged by outcomes-assessment measures and standardized tests, which do not pretend to have anything to do with wisdom and which of necessity reduce and thereby distort complex knowledge by requiring that it be broken into easily measurable informational quanta (Pennington, 2011b). The cries of humanities professors that all they do and aim to do in their classes cannot be captured in such measures fall on the deaf ears of the administrators, politicians, and test developers who are running the show. Those professors are criticized as out of touch with the modern world – teaching old "legacy content" by old-legacy, digital-immigrant methods rather than the future-oriented content of all things digital and technological[4] – and ready to be relegated to the dustbin of history, thus ignorable. Their credibility and relevance questioned, their influence is thereby reduced, leading to a weakening of their voice in decision-making and a loss of their share of the curriculum. The success of literature and arts courses – like all others – is measured by how many students get well-paying jobs, and legislators fund state colleges by how many students they can pack into each class.

To us, it is somewhat ironic that advocates for science and mathematics claim that those subjects need even more support and emphasis in the curriculum than they already have. What needs to be considered instead are the consequences of not allowing humanities professors to have a strong voice and of not having an emphasis on human arts courses equal to the emphasis on STEM, business, and practical courses of all kinds. The values associated with electronic and mass-media technologies have contributed to this state of affairs in education and life. They de-emphasize the activities of the humanities, such as reading and discussion of literature and philosophy, classifying those activities as old-fashioned and comparatively useless or irrelevant – becoming, like wisdom, for all intents and purposes, ancient history – a relic of the past. As Wieseltier (2015) observes, in our technologized world, "there is no greater disgrace than to be a thing of the past" (p. 14). This de-emphasis on literature and humanities is not simply inevitable, nor is it progress in any unarguable sense. The current situation is neither necessary nor sufficient for education or for life. It is in fact a worrying situation with negative consequences such as the rampant consumerism that has produced an increasingly large divide between rich and poor and that has fueled planetary degradation at an alarmingly fast rate (Klein, 2014; Kolbert, 2014). In order to begin to address these problems, which have been accelerated in the digitally interfaced and electronically interconnected world, human society needs to reconnect with the traditions that encourage people to understand and appreciate the beauty, goodness, and truth of an alternative world available to all. Education can offer the means for providing the foundation and the spark for revival and reinforcement of this alternative world.

An essential action towards providing the foundation and spark for revivifying this alternative world is to reinstate in the curriculum the central importance of language, especially the richly textured language which writers who are recognized to be the masters of their craft have shaped into all of the genres of literary form. When we think about language from this perspective, we are not so much thinking about language as a practical means to a utilitarian end that can be measured but rather as a way to experience the depth and fullness of human life. Yet we must also point out that much research suggests the power of story and of aesthetic reading experiences to affect people in profound ways, both psychological and social, which have in fact been measured. A focus on literary language complements the focus on oral language and conversation which seems critical for the development of empathy and reflectivity, including self-reflectivity, as Turkle (2012a, 2012b, 2015) notes.

We acknowledge that such a curricular approach has lost favor these days, that it might even be considered sentimental, part of an outmoded humanistic tradition or "legacy curriculum"; but we are unapologetic about our stance here. For us, such an approach offers the best chance people have to open possibilities to know and understand themselves as individuals and their relationship to others, to enhance compassion and tolerance, and so to support fair treatment and equal rights for all. This is the foundation on which can be built not only a full, happy and successful human life, but also a unified global effort to save the planet. This is not a sentimental dream from the past without merit or value today; it is, as the policymakers like to say, an evidence-based recommendation. For literature can indeed change people's lives, through changing their perceptions and beliefs, their ways of thinking and of acting. We have seen it happen over and over again; and now there is an increasing body of research, as reviewed in this book, to back up our own observations.

Making the Big Change

In today's world, people need space and time in schools and in public places where they shut off their electronic gadgets, where they quietly read works of great literature, and where they discuss that literature, face-to-face, with other human beings. Libraries and bookstores can logically take the lead in this, by setting up No Wi-Fi zones that include quiet spaces where people can concentrate on reading books and other spaces where groups can discuss what they are reading. We find it an encouraging sign that some owners of bookstores (e.g., in London; Banks, 2016) are removing their Wi-Fi connections and coffee counters and going back to the concept of a bookstore as a place to browse books and talk about them with like-minded people. Schools can also play a role by implementing CLTL programs drawing on the guidelines and materials provided on the program's website and perhaps also on the story sequence provided in our Chapter 10. And, as the CLTL prison initiative has shown, literature-focused groups can be organized in other settings where people can reap significant benefits from the focused attention and the mind- and behavior-altering effects of concentrated reading and shared discussion of literature.

Since the founding of the CLTL program, other initiatives have been developed to tap into the power of reading and discussing literature to build relationship and shared experience that can lead to changed attitudes and behaviors. The non-profit organization Books@Work, which first piloted its program in 2008 (Petrilla, 2016), has a purpose similar to that of CLTL, aiming to both engage minds and transform communities through reading and discussion of a shared selection of good books. As described on its website: "Books@Work brings professor-led literature seminars to workplaces and community settings to build confidence, critical thinking, communication, collaboration, and creativity. Through shared narratives, Books@Work builds human capacity to imagine, innovate and connect, strengthening cultures of trust, respect and inclusion" (www.booksatwork.org/).

The Books@Work program, which has a focus on helping build morale and unity among people who work together, has been implemented in businesses as well as in community centers and schools. Testimonials on the website document the profound effects of reading and discussing literature together in terms of deep thought and expression of feelings, and how this helps to create better relationships, as those in the reading group share personal experience and find common ground, while also raising the level of organizational enthusiasm and satisfaction and encouraging new ideas. Research is currently underway to study the effects of the program, which the founder, Ann Kowal Smith, sees as going beyond the workplace to improve people's ability to navigate in the home and the community (Petrilla, 2016). We are heartened to learn of this grand social goal, which may seem idealistic but which we know from the CLTL program and from our own experiences with students can result from reading and sharing around literature.

People need to have the time to read without feeling rushed. As one of his recommendations for combatting the negative effects of hyperculture, Bertman (1998) had called on people to consider "that 'slow' is not necessarily bad, nor 'fast' necessarily good" (p. 194). In connection with their discussion of the reading of literature, Koopman and Hakemulder (2015) emphasize the need for "slow thinking," which Daniel Kahneman, in *Thinking, Fast and Slow*, has stressed is a necessary complement to "fast thinking" (Kahneman, 2011), and for "stillness." In their view, "stillness is an empty space or time that is created as a result of reading processes: the slowing down of readers' perceptions of the fictional world, caused by defamiliarization" (Koopman & Hakemulder, 2015, p. 79, Abstract) in the reading of literature and fictional narratives in particular.

We might all take a cue from the Wellington, New Zealand, Slow Reading Club (Whalen, 2014), whose members meet once a week in a café to settle into its comfy chairs, their smartphones turned off, and read quietly for an hour. A Slow Reading movement has begun, and it seems to have legs: it has a website offering guidance (http://slowreadingco.com/2014/09/ten-tips-for-slow-reading/), its own Facebook page, and groups springing up around the world, including many places in the United States. It is but one of the ways in which people are choosing to slow down from the pace of a life lived always in the fast lane, and to shift to a life emphasizing quality over quantity of time. Honoré (2004) is one of those making the case for less fast and more slow: "Fast is busy, controlling, aggressive, hurried, analytical, stressed, superficial, impatient, active, quantity-over-quality. Slow is the opposite: calm, careful, receptive, still, intuitive, unhurried, patient, reflective, quality-over-quantity. It is about making real and meaningful connections – with people, culture, work, food, everything" (pp. 14–15).

There are now many kinds of initiatives that fall under the heading of the Slow Movement, which, according to its website, encompasses

> a wide range of efforts taking place around the world that seek to connect us more meaningfully with others, with place, and with ourselves. It emerged as an effort to counteract the fast–paced, commodity–focused, unbalanced, and impersonal nature of much of modern human culture.
>
> *(www.create-the-good-life.com/slow_movement.html)*

The Slow Movement has spurred such initiatives as Slow Food, Slow Travel, Slow Exercise, and Slow Homes, and dovetails with our push for people to live a better life, The Good Life, by getting unplugged, reading literature offline and contemplating and discussing its ideas, and in general taking time to smell the roses. There is even a Slow Money initiative that encourages people to use their money "toward the things that really matter and that support the well-being of yourself, others, and the planet" (www.create-the-good-life.com/slow_movement.html). Taking a cue from the Slow Movement, people can begin to experience, or to re-experience, what it means to be fully human – a feeling which can provide the foundation for wanting to lead a much fuller and more meaningful life than can be lived at a lightning pace, or online, or focused on making money, or competing with everyone else.

We take note of the significance ascribed to the Slow Movement by Honoré (2004), who is one of those who warned about the damaging effects of capitalism operating at hyper-speed and who supports the need for a "lifestyle revolution"

(p. 17) to change the whole style of how humans consume resources and live in interaction with each other – much more slowly and therefore more mindfully, and with a much more intimate connection to all of the resources and people touched by any kind of human activity. Honoré (2004) reflects:

> By treating people and the environment as valuable assets, rather than as disposable inputs, a Slow alternative could make the economy work for us, rather than vice versa. ... In our hedonistic age, the Slow movement has a marketing ace up its sleeve: it peddles pleasure. The central tenet of the Slow philosophy is taking the time to do things properly, and thereby enjoy them more. Whatever its effect on the economic balance sheet, the Slow philosophy delivers the things that really make us happy: good health, a thriving environment, strong communities and relationships, freedom from perpetual hurry.
>
> *(pp. 278–279)*

Reading literature is one of these inherently pleasurable activities, something that is embedded in our long history and culture as linguistic beings, as a mode of organizing experience and of expressing and imagining our human world in ways that link us to our past, our present, and our possible future, and to our fellow human beings.

In being one of the activities that requires slowness, reading literature has an obvious part to play in the lifestyle revolution captured by the Slow Movement. In being an activity that promotes contemplation, reading literature motivates reflection, which is the starting point for change. But the value of reading literature goes beyond the slow and concentrated manner in which it is done, as it is the language and the content of literature which is crucial to the effects it has. Reading literature is a superior vehicle for building knowledge of language as well as general knowledge, thus giving it a valuable role in supporting communication and achievement in any field, and in expressing and disseminating innovation. In linking to previously acquired language and knowledge, literature keeps our human history and linguistic heritage alive, even as it builds new language and new knowledge, and helps people imagine worlds different from the one they live in. Literature therefore has a role to play in maintaining the vitality of language and advancing human knowledge and creative thinking. In addition, the language and content of literature makes people both feel and think deeply, building empathy and opening up the mind and personality to changes that can also change behavior. Reading literature therefore has a role to play in changing the self and in changing society, through improving human relations – a critical step in making the world better for all rather than exploiting it for the few.

In promoting the latter sorts of changes and improvements, reading literature contributes importantly to a kind of human revolution that is not sufficiently captured by referring to it in terms of *lifestyle*. Perhaps we can refer to this as not a revolution in lifestyle but rather a revolution in human life itself, meaning a change in something deep within human nature that will help draw people away from hyper-speed, online and onscreen culture, and hyper-capitalism. We are talking about life change that will make a Slow and more sustainable world more attractive and more likely to take hold on a wide scale. We believe that this revolution in human life depends on ensuring the strong influence of the cultural values and activities engendered by the human arts to balance those of capitalism, spectacle, and Me Culture – the "pop-and-bling" lifestyle – and to move people away from *self-aggrandizement* as their primary goal and into *self-fulfillment*, in all the ways in which a human being can feel fulfilled. These include not only exceling at something but also being honest, kind, and fair to others – the old moral or "eulogy" virtues. These traditional virtues together amount to "doing the right thing" as defined not just on the self but on all people, not just on the immediate circumstances but on the larger context, up to and including the entire history of the planet. In keeping these traditional virtues front and center, we are shifting the focus from the "outer" life of consumption and those pursuits that attract immediate attention and can be shown off or listed as skills or achievements on a person's résumé to the "inner" life of satisfaction of deep human needs for intellectual and emotional connection. A fully realized human life depends on satisfaction of these deep needs as a basis for self-actualization.

Living Life in a New Way

What we are advocating is a return to a life defined as a journey, with a past, a present, and a future, a continual quest to know, to understand, and to connect – all on a deep level. A life of questing is one that is attentive to language (more than to images), to the imagination (more than to data), to the wisdom of books (rather than to the spectacle of screens), and to thoughtful, complex discourse (rather than bits and bites – or bytes – of fragmented information). It is a way of establishing a counter-culture to serve as a contrary movement and counterflow to the dominant mainstream that is almost overwhelming the human cultural base, our heritage, built up through the ages in which we developed our language and our stories. Reading literature can help ensure that we do not lose the depth of our language or our human history, while also bringing us back to the depths of our own selves. In the view of Dehaene (2009): "In the midst of many cultural treasures, reading is by far the finest gem – it embodies a second inheritance system that we are duty-bound to transmit to coming generations" (p. 324). In countering the forces now flooding our human cultural base and heritage, we will also be countering those same forces which are threatening our civilization, the foundation for all our societal institutions that have ensured our continuing existence, which we are even more duty-bound to transmit to coming generations.

Throughout this book, we have sought to show you the great power and relevance of reading literature, to remind you of its capacity to engage and stimulate, and of its relevance to you and to everyone. In so doing, we hope we have inspired you to go to back to the literary works we have discussed – the poems, the stories, and the Great Books – those wonderful products of individual imagination growing out of human intelligence and passion, aesthetically designed and expressed in exquisite language, which offer endless surprise and discovery. We encourage you to savor them yourself, in private as well as in conversation with others. We also hope we have inspired and guided you to link those experiences to your own life journey, enriching your enjoyment as well as your understanding of the human experience – and, if you're lucky, being transported to other places and times, away from the glare of screen media and the press of consumption values and the perpetual present.

Our greatest hope is that we have inspired and convinced you that the reading of literature and the culture of books should have a much stronger position in human life and experience than they do at present, having been edged out by the STEM curriculum and by the all-pervasive forces of electronic and mass media, hyper-capitalism, and the warp speed of Now. The weight of these forces is so heavy that it may not be possible to balance them by making a counterweight of equal mass. Rather, tipping the scales back may only be possible by recalibrating the culture away from mega-scale activities and values and back to the scale of human beings and other natural species, as the Slow Movement advocates and as we have argued that a focus on the human arts and literature in education and everyday life can help to promote. We believe that restoring a balance to the physical ecology so that it can sustain life depends on such a recalibration of the scale-points used to measure value, which means first creating a healthier and more nourishing and sustaining cultural ecology, one that supports the interior needs of human beings, as thoughtful and imaginative creatures, and can both inspire and enable us to tackle the problems confronting the world.

This is precisely the kind of culture that is offered in a future with books, the literate alternative to a life of illusion lived too fast, attending to "bells and whistles" instead of deep meaning and purposes in life, pursuing information rather than knowledge, wealth and fame rather than truth and beauty, and immediate rather than deep satisfaction. Surely a focus on deep meaning and purpose in life, and the pursuit of knowledge, truth and beauty, and deep satisfaction stand as much higher and more worthwhile goals for life than "pop" and "bling," which not only lead to an unfulfilling and superficial existence but also waste rather than conserve and build resources for the future. In both of these ways a "pop-and-bling" lifestyle leads down a negative path of maintaining the status quo and thereby providing neither the motivation nor the means to change the world. The powers behind Big Business and Big Media fueling this illusory and "hyper" way of living continually escalate people's expectations and desires even as they also escalate the sense that *they* (ambiguously referring to people's expectations, the Big Media and corporate powers, and *their* expectations) are not being satisfied. If you slow down and reflect for a moment on the paradox inherent in this kind of existence and its dynamic of leaving people always unsatisfied, you may start to feel a sense of unfulfillment and active *dis*satisfaction in life.

A sense of dissatisfaction with this kind of life is increased by being aware of the other life that is possible in a world of books and human arts, of how inherently satisfying such a life is and how much is to be gained by living in that other way. This is essentially the project which we set for ourselves in writing this book and trying to convince you as readers of the need for that alternative culture. We hope that we have both reminded you of and raised your awareness of that other life, by contrasting it with mainstream culture, arguing its value, and bringing you into it for a time, through examples of literature: its greatness, its power, and its importance to human language, culture, and life itself. To the extent that we have succeeded in drawing you and others into the culture of literature, to that extent have we also won potential converts to the program which we believe is the essential starting point for turning around our current culture. If we have succeeded, we have contributed to creating the mind-set and the will to ensure that the future world will be a better one, built on the foundation of our literate heritage and alternative: a future with books.

Concluding Remarks to This Book

We wish to end this journey we have taken you through by drawing on something that Denby (2016) says near the beginning of his book: "Together and alone, we need literature as the California valleys need rain" (p. xvii). We think this is a very apt metaphor, as life is dry indeed without the nurturing refreshment which literature brings to the human mind and spirit. The metaphor captures the thirst for literature and the need for literature to sprinkle inspiration and sprout ideas, and to sustain the richness and fertility of the ground from whence all our ideas spring and blossom forth, human culture and language. Our 21st-century culture is polluted and shallow, like a once-rich ocean that is rapidly being overrun by waste water and that is losing its sources of sustenance. This is an environment where cultural resources are declining, as language is reduced, the arts become fringe activities, and values focused on altruism and community are lost in the face of those focused on immediate satisfaction and show.

The once great ocean of human culture has receded to the point where it now threatens to become a barren wasteland, a cultural desert. The shrinking of the human world to a sensation-obsessed, screen-obsessed, and money-obsessed culture, as we have argued, has created conditions that threaten the same fate of desertification for the planet as a whole. We need literature and human arts to help reverse both of these kinds of desertification, to replenish and replant the current parched and scraggly mainstream culture and bring it back to full life, through providing the resources of language, arts, and values that can increase our species' fitness for tackling the urgent job of making the physical ecology healthy again.

Our grand proposal is to give a culture of books a central place in education and everyday life, as a way to reverse human cultural wastage and aridity and as both a possible and a necessary strategy for ensuring that the future will be one not of drought and scarcity, but one inundated with great works – both the literary kind and those which flow from the knowledge and insights that can be gained from literature, together with the passion and sensitivity which literature encourages. We need a liquid not a dry environment, both metaphorically and literally, for life on this planet to flourish.

In the present culturally and physically dry conditions, literature offers oases where people can tarry for rest and rejuvenation, tell their stories, and hear the stories of others. It is our hope that we will get past this dry spell and see many more of those oases springing up, and eventually vast literary pools where people can exercise their imaginations, keep their mental muscles supple and strong, and give their hearts a good workout, too. At our very depths, we need a life saturated with art and with language, fed by literary streams which continually supply and replenish the wellsprings of human imagination, memory, and life itself.

> The waters of the past converge in memory's long present,
> Washing over the shimmering reflection of a life's distilled fluid essence.
> – M.C. Pennington, "Pool Culture" (Pennington, 2011a, p. 252)

Notes

1 An example of an integrated curriculum can be found in a forthcoming primary teacher reference book developed in Hawaii by Miki Maeshiro, Meleanna Meyer, and Anna Sumida that offers lessons for teaching science and local language and culture through reading, writing, and "arting" (drawing and painting) activities which are focused on the stories and the ecology of the children's home environment and which reinforce attitudes of caring for others and the environment (Maeshiro, Meyer, & Sumida, in press).

2 We note that Jeff Bezos, who has four children, is reportedly going to start "a family book club" (The 2016 New Establishment, 2016, p. 124), and we sincerely hope that this very influential figure of the online world and global capitalism can be a force leading families back to reading and discussing books with children.

3 Participants were Colombian guerillas reintegrating into mainstream society who learned to read for the first time as adults (late-literates) and a carefully matched comparison group of illiterates. As compared to those who had not experienced reading, the late-literates had more of the brain's connecting gray matter as well as its facilitating white matter and more connections between certain areas of the left and right hemispheres.

4 Prensky's (2011/2001, p. 8) contrast of "Legacy" versus "Future" content not-so-subtly implies the inferiority of humanities as contrasted with STEM.

References

Aiken, Mary (2016). *The cyber effect: A pioneering cyberpsychologist explains how human behavior changes online.* New York: Spiegel & Grau.

Alsup, Janet (2015). *A case for teaching literature in the secondary school: Why fiction matters in an age of scientific literacy and standardization*. New York: Routledge.

Banks, Grace (2016). Books, yes. Just don't look for a latte. *The New York Times*. August 14, 2016, p. 11.

Bertman, Stephen (1998). *Hyperculture: The human cost of speed*. Westport, CT: Praeger.

Birkerts, Sven (2015). *Changing the subject: Art and attention in the Internet age*. Minneapolis, MN: Graywolf Press.

Block, Jerald J. (2005). Issues for DSM-V: Internet addiction. *American Journal of Psychiatry*, 165–307. doi:10.1176/appi.ajp.2007.07101556.

Burke, Michael (2011). *Literary reading, cognition and emotion: An exploration of the oceanic mind*. London: Routledge.

Carreiras, Manuel, Seghier, Mohamed L., Baquero, Silvia, Estévez, Adelina, Lozano, Alfonso, Devlin, Joseph T., & Price, Cathy J. (2009). An anatomical signature for literacy. *Nature*, *461*, 983–986. doi:10.1038/nature08461.

Dehaene, Stanislas (2009). *Reading in the brain: The science and evolution of a human invention*. New York: Viking.

Denby, David (2016). *Lit up: One reporter. Three schools. Twenty-four books that can change lives*. New York: Henry Holt.

Gottschall, Jonathan (2012). *The storytelling animal: How stories make us human*. Boston, New York: Houghton Mifflin Harcourt.

Graves, Donald (1983). *Writing: Teachers and children at work*. Portsmouth, NH: Heinemann.

Hamid, Mohsin (2014). Bookends. *The New York Times*, Book Review. November 16, 2014, p. 31.

Hayakawa, S. I. (1990/1939). Language in thought and action (5th edition). New York: Harcourt Brace & Company.

Honoré, Carl (2004). *In praise of slowness: How a worldwide movement is challenging the cult of speed*. New York: HarperCollins.

Jones, Damon E., Greenberg, Mark, & Crowley, Max (2015). Early social-emotional functioning and public health: The relationship between kindergarten social competence and future wellness. *American Journal of Public Health*, *105*(11), 2283–2290. doi:10.2105/AJPH.2015.302630.

Kahneman, Daniel (2011). *Thinking, fast and slow*. New York: Farrar, Strauss & Giroux.

Klein, Naomi (2014). *This changes everything: Capitalism vs. the climate*. New York: Simon & Schuster.

Kolbert, Elizabeth (2014). *The sixth extinction*. New York: Henry Holt & Company.

Koopman, Eva Maria, & Hakemulder, Frank (2015). Effects of literature on empathy and self-reflection: A theoretical-empirical framework. *Journal of Literary Theory 9*(1), 79–111. Abstract available at www.jltonline.de/index.php/articles/article/view/759/1779.

Kundera, Milan (2006). *The curtain: An essay in seven parts* (trans. Laura Asher). London: Faber and Faber.

Maeshiro, Miki, Meyer, Meleanna, & Sumida, Anna (in press). *Arting & writing as transformation: An integrated approach to culturally and ecologically responsive pedagogy*. Sheffield, U.K. and Bristol, CT: Equinox.

Mills, M. Anthony (with Mills, Phil). (2014). The Harry Potter Paradox. *Real Clear Religion* website. January 24, 2014. Retrieved on August 9, 2016 from www.realclearreligion.org/articles/2014/01/24/the_harry_potter_paradox.html.

More, Thomas (1997). *The education of the heart: Readings and sources for care of the soul, soul mates, and the re-enchantment of everyday life*. New York: HarperCollins.

Nafisi, Azar (2014). *The republic of imagination: America in three books*. New York: Penguin.

National Institute of Child Health and Human Development and National Reading Panel (2000). *Teaching children to read: An evidence-based assessment of the scientific research literature on reading and its implications for reading instruction*. NIH Publication No. 00–4769. Washington, DC: U.S. Government Printing Office. Also available at www.nichd.nih. gov/publications/pubs/nrp/Pages/smallbook.aspx.

Nussbaum, Martha C. (2010). *Not for profit: Why democracy needs the humanities*. Princeton, NJ: Princeton University Press.

Park, Alice (2007). Baby Einsteins: Not so smart after all. *Time* website. August 6, 2007. Retrieved from http://content.time.com/time/health/article/0,8599,1650352,00.html.

Pearlstein, Steven (2016). Meet the parents who won't let their children study literature. *The Washington Post* website, Post Everything. September 2, 2016. Retrieved on September 3, 2016 from www.washingtonpost.com/posteverything/wp/2016/09/02/meet-the-parents-who-wont-let-their-children-study-literature/?utm_term=.0807b8d51c09.

Pennington, M. C. (2011a). Pool culture. *Southern Humanities Review*, *45*(3), 250–252. Available at http://www.southernhumanitiesreview.com/the-2010s.html.

Pennington, Martha C. (2011b). Teaching writing: Managing the tension between freedom and control. *Writing & Pedagogy*, *3*(1), 1–16. doi:10.1558.wap.v3i1.1.

Peterson, Ralph, & Eeds, Maryann (1990). *Grand conversations: Literature groups in action*. Broadway, NY: Scholastic, Inc.

Petrilla, Molly (2016). Reading Room: Better living through books. *Bryn Mawr Alumnae Bulletin*, Summer 2016. Bryn Mawr, PA: Bryn Mawr College, p. 44.

Prensky, Marc (2011/2001). Digital natives, digital immigrants. In Mark Bauerlein (ed.), *The digital divide: Arguments for and against Facebook, Google, texting, and the age of social networking* (pp. 3–11). New York: Jeremy P. Tarcher/Penguin. Originally appeared in *On the Horizon*, *9* (October 2001), 1–6.

Quenqua, Douglas (2014). Is e-reading to your toddler story time, or simply screen time? *The New York Times*. October 12, 2014, pp. 1, 27.

Shenk, David (1997). *Data smog: Surviving the information glut*. New York: HarperCollins.

Short, Kathy, & Pierce, Kathryn M. (1990). *Talking about books: Creating literate communities*. Portsmouth, NH: Heinemann.

Slouka, Mark (2009). Dehumanized: When math and science rule the school. *Harper's Magazine*, September, 32–40.

The 2016 New Establishment (2016). *Vanity Fair*, November 20, 2016, pp. 124–143.

Turkle, Sherry (2012a). *Alone together: Why we expect more from technology and less from each other*. New York: Basic Books.

Turkle, Sherry (2012b). The flight from conversation. *The New York Times*, Sunday Review. April 22, 2012, p. 1.

Turkle, Sherry (2015). *Reclaiming conversation: The power of talk*. New York: Penguin Press.

Vendler, Helen (2015). *The ocean, the bird, and the scholar: Essays on poets and poetry*. Cambridge, MA: Harvard University Press.

Warner, Marina (2012). *Stranger magic: Charmed states and the Arabian nights*. Cambridge, MA: The Belknap Press/Harvard University.

Waxler, Robert P., & Hall, Maureen P. (2011). *Transforming literacy: Changing lives through reading and writing*. Leiden and Boston: Brill.

Webb, Jen (2012). Creativity and the marketplace. In Dominque Hecq (ed.), *The creativity market: Creative writing in the 21st century* (pp. 40–53). Bristol, Buffalo, Toronto: Multilingual Matters.

Whalen, Jean (2014). Read slowly to benefit your brain and cut stress. *Wall Street Journal* online. September 15, 2014, revised September 16, 2014. Retrieved on August 9, 2016 from www.wsj.com/articles/read-slowly-to-benefit-your-brain-and-cut-stress-1410823086.

Wieseltier, Leon (2015). Among the disrupted. *The New York Times*, Book Review. January 18, 2015, pp. 1, 14–15.

Wolf, Maryanne, & Barzillai, Mirit (2009). The importance of deep reading. *Educational Leadership*, *66*(6), 32–37. Available at www.ascd.org/publications/educational-leadership/mar09/vol66/num06/The-Importance-of-Deep-Reading.aspx.

INDEX